"Provocative."—CourtTV.com

"In covering the Durst case for nearly two years
I've found there has been one constant—
that what appears to be the truth,
what has been told to be the truth, is not."

—From the author's preface

A Deadly Secret
The Strange Disappearance of Kathie Durst

From award-winning investigative reporter
Matt Birkbeck—
the first journalist to have access to
the NYPD files on the Durst case.

Also based on interviews with family, friends,
and acquaintances of the Dursts'
and others involved with the case.

...phs

A DEADLY SECRET

The Strange Disappearance of Kathie Durst

MATT BIRKBECK

BERKLEY BOOKS, NEW YORK

A DEADLY SECRET

A Berkley Book / published by arrangement with
the author

PRINTING HISTORY
Berkley hardcover edition / September 2002
Berkley mass market edition / September 2003

ISBN: 0-425-19207-5

BERKLEY®
Berkley Books are published by The Berkley Publishing Group,
a division of Penguin Group (USA) Inc.,
375 Hudson Street, New York, New York 10014.
BERKLEY and the "B" design
are trademarks belonging to Penguin Group (USA) Inc.

PRINTED IN THE UNITED STATES OF AMERICA

10 9 8 7 6 5 4 3 2

For Donna, Matthew, and Christopher
With love

This book is dedicated to
Donald W. Birkbeck

PREFACE

IN November 2000, my bureau chief at *People* magazine asked me to cover the story about the renewed police investigation into the disappearance of Kathie Durst.

Since 1997 I have reported on dozens of stories for *People* as a freelance correspondent, but none as bizarre, and tragic, as the Durst case.

Kathie Durst, twenty-nine, was married to Robert Durst, thirty-eight, the heir to a New York real estate fortune, now estimated to be worth $2 billion. Kathie was last seen January 31, 1982, her disappearance front-page news. The New York City police investigated Kathie's disappearance, but Robert, who reported his wife missing, later hired a criminal attorney and refused to cooperate. His family, notably his powerful father, Seymour, also refused to cooperate.

Charges were never filed, and Kathie's body was never found.

LIKE Kathie, the case disappeared. Seventeen years later, in 1999, the New York State Police reopened the investigation after receiving an innocuous tip.

In November 2000, as I was reporting on the story for *People*, interviews with the friends and family of Kathie Durst, and with the NYPD, suggested that Robert Durst had indeed killed his pretty wife, who was just months shy of graduating from medical school.

The *People* story was published on December 4, 2000. Three weeks later, on Christmas Eve, a woman named Susan Berman was found shot to death in her Los Angeles home.

Berman, the daughter of a well-known Las Vegas mobster, was considered one of Robert Durst's best friends and was long rumored to have known what happened to Kathie. Several of Kathie's friends suggested I interview Berman. Regrettably, calls were made but a fast approaching deadline prevented it from happening.

Berman's death sent shock waves from coast to coast. The Durst story again became front-page news, and subsequently the subject of numerous print and television news reports.

———

IN September 2001, the case took yet another bizarre turn when a human torso washed up on a shore in Galveston, Texas.

The victim was Morris Black, seventy-one, a drifter. He was dismembered, his arms and legs found floating in garbage bags near the torso. His head was not recovered. Little more than a week later, Galveston police arrested Robert Durst and charged him with Black's murder.

Durst had quietly rented a $300-a-month apartment in Galveston nearly a year earlier after learning about the new investigation into the disappearance of his long-lost wife. In yet another bizarre twist, Durst arrived in Galveston in drag, masquerading as a woman.

Police searched Durst's blood-soaked apartment and his car and found two guns, a .22 and a nine-millimeter, the same type of gun used to kill Susan Berman.

Durst posted bail but later slipped out of Texas, skipping a hearing and becoming a fugitive and one of America's most-wanted men.

He was found six weeks later in Bath, Pennsylvania, arrested first for stealing a chicken salad sandwich from a local supermarket, his true identity later revealed to an alert Pennsylvania cop.

In January 2002, Durst was extradited to Texas. His trial for the murder of Morris Black is scheduled for 2003.

———

IN covering the Durst case for nearly two years I've found there has been one constant—that what appears to be the truth, what has been told to be the truth, is not.

The story that you are about to read is the result of hours upon hours of research, along with painstakingly long interviews with the friends, family, and acquaintances of the Dursts' and others who are involved in the case.

The 1982 investigation into Kathie's disappearance, as it unfolds in *A Deadly Secret*, was taken from interviews and first-person accounts of those involved, along with access to the actual NYPD files. No other journalist has had access to those files, until now.

The same methodology, along with a good dose of investigative reporting, was used to pull together the shocking events that have transpired since the investigation was reopened in November 1999.

All the names in the book are real, except for one, where I agreed to withhold an identity. (It is marked by an asterisk*.) The events in the book are real, or as close to real as humanly possible, based on interviews and first-person accounts of the participants.

ACKNOWLEDGMENTS

I would like to thank Maria Eftimiades, the New York bureau chief at *People* magazine, Helen George, a journalist and associate professor at Northampton Community College, Tannersville, Pennsylvania, and Paul Moses, a former reporter and editor at *Newsday* and associate professor of journalism at Brooklyn College, for their invaluable help and guidance with this project.

PROLOGUE

A cold wind blew easily through the thick oak trees that protected the palatial home on Hampton Road, pressing down the almost bare branches and forcing them back and forth in rhythmic fashion, blowing off the few remaining leaves, which were swept out into the open air.

Some of the leaves were hurled to the ground while others were caught in the draft and forced upward, landing on the roof of the picturesque two-story home and at the bare feet of a woman, who was standing alone in the cool, nighttime air, high above the concrete driveway, wearing only a nightgown and robe.

Below her, in the driveway, was Scarsdale police Sergeant Vincent Jural, who arrived at the house around 8:30 P.M., the wailing sounds of a fire engine not too far behind in the distance.

Jural spent several minutes trying to convince the woman to sit down, since the dark brown, ceramic roof was pitched sharply, making it almost impossible for someone to stand on it without losing her balance. But there she stood, her toes pointed downward, her weight supported by the balls of her feet, performing a kind of balancing act as she looked up toward the starry fall sky, oblivious to the elements.

Standing nervously behind Jural were three men. Just a half hour earlier they had been sitting in the living room, discussing the woman's condition, a radio turned on in the background, a newscaster reporting that United Nations forces were battling the Chinese in Korea.

With cigar and cigarette smoke slowly rising toward the ceiling, their quiet discussion about depression and paranoia had been interrupted by a loud scream. It came from a little boy, only seven, who had ventured into his mother's bedroom to see if she was comfortable. Instead he found the bed empty, and he raced through the upper floors, frantically searching from room to room, then running down the stairs.

He found his mother.

"Mommy! Mommy!" he said, panting. "Mommy's on the roof!"

"On the roof? Where?" said the boy's father, jumping up from his seat.

"In the back. Over the garage. Hurry up," he said. "We have to get her."

The three men followed the boy, who ran toward the back of the home, out through the kitchen, and onto the driveway.

"Look, up there," the boy said, pointing.

The men could see her, standing above a second-floor bedroom window and far above the driveway, which was sloped downward, half a floor below the ground level.

"Bernice, Bernice, are you all right?" shouted one of the men. "You have to get down from there. Do you hear me? Walk over to the window and come back inside."

The woman slowly turned her head and looked down toward the men, focusing on her husband, but she did not reply. She stood there, staring intensely, before taking her eyes off him and redirecting her blank gaze out beyond the trees.

"Somebody call the police," said the husband.

The call went out at 8:18 P.M., and the husband, wearing a pained expression on his face, greeted Jural upon his arrival.

"She's in the back, on the roof," he said.

As the two men took hurried steps, Jural asked why the woman was up on the roof in thirty-five-degree November weather.

The explanation was brief: his wife had suffered what appeared to be an asthma attack earlier in the day. The doctor gave her some prescription medication, which helped her fall asleep.

The man said he was in the living room talking with his father-in-law and the doctor, thinking his wife was still asleep, when they heard his oldest son scream.

Jural was now in the back of the house looking up at the woman, knowing he had to get her off the roof.

"Ma'am. Can you just sit tight while I come up there to help you back into the house?"

"No, I'm not ready to come in," she said.

"Are you okay?"

The woman didn't answer.

The fire truck finally pulled up to the front of the house, and Jural yelled out for someone to tell the firemen to bring a long ladder.

The firemen unhooked an extension ladder and two of them, each carrying one end, headed down the driveway, the truck's flashing red lights attracting several neighbors like moths to a porch light. They swarmed, gawking, from the side of the house between the swaying oak trees.

The lead fireman, Tom Langan, reached the back of the driveway, looked up, and could see that the woman was in trouble.

"Hey, Tommy," said Jural. "We need to get that ladder up there and get her down. She's not going to move herself."

"What's going on?"

"I don't know. Her husband and father were telling

me that she had some kind of asthma attack and was on medication. They thought she was sleeping, but one of the kids noticed she wasn't in her room and found her up on the roof. I don't know what her condition is. She seems distant."

Langan looked up and called out, telling the woman he was going to prop his extension ladder against the house, in front of the garage, and would pull the rope, raising the extension just high enough to reach over the gutters.

"What's her name?"

"I think it's Bernice," said Jural.

"Ma'am, please don't move. I'm coming up to get you," said Langan, who locked the ladder in place and began his ascent.

"No, I'm all right," she said. "I'm really all right."

"Bernice, I want you to stay put. Don't move. I'm going to climb up there and you can come down with me, okay?" said Langan.

The woman peered over the gutter as Langan slowly made his way toward the roof, putting one foot on a step, then placing the other foot on the same step.

She looked down onto the driveway, where her husband and father were standing. Her eyes remained fixed on her husband. There were no words, no facial expressions, just a blank stare.

The husband looked back, but said nothing.

As Langan neared the roof, he could see that the woman had moved forward and was now teetering on the edge, her robe whipped by the cold wind.

"Ma'am, you can't move," said Langan nervously, extending his arm out. "You have to stay still. Let me come up there and we'll come down together."

Her father cried out from the driveway, "Bernice, don't move, don't move!"

Langan checked his feet to secure his footing, then looked up, only to see the woman falling over the edge, headfirst, as if she were diving into a swimming pool.

Langan heard the screams coming from neighbors

who were standing among the trees as he reached out
with his left hand, hoping to grab onto a part of her robe,
or maybe a limb. He touched the robe, but it slipped out
of his hand. The woman fell to the cold, hard concrete
pavement below with a sickening thud.

Langan raced down the ladder while Jural and the
three men ran over to the woman, who lay still.

"Bernice, Bernice!" shouted her husband.

Behind him was his seven-year-old son, his oldest
boy, teary eyes open wide, his mouth trembling.

"Mommy!" he cried. "Mommy!"

1

THE low hills surrounding the eleven-acre horse farm in Bedford, New York, made for perfect jogging trails for New York State Police investigator Joe Becerra, who enjoyed running along the narrow paths that traversed the acreage surrounding the farm.

At least once a day, usually in the early morning, Becerra would leave his rented one-bedroom cottage with his two black rottweilers, Bullet and Roxy, in tow, and run. Becerra always felt better when he was running, his feet hitting the ground in a rhythmic pace, his five-foot nine-inch frame tight and trim.

It was late November 1999, and a misty haze enveloped the northern New York City suburbs, soaking the landscape. Becerra, who ran his usual four miles on the muddy trails, never once had to call out to his dogs to keep up, and worked up a good sweat in the unusually warm, late-fall-morning air. Becerra was drenched, beads of sweat and rain falling from his brow. At the end of the run, which took him in a full circle back to his cottage, he stood bent over, breathing heavily, his palms down on his knees.

The dogs were right with him, their paws, lower legs, and underbellies muddied. They barked and reached up to Becerra on their hind legs.

Becerra pushed them off, then wiped the mud from his sweatpants.

"C'mon, you guys. You're filthy," he said, still taking deep breaths.

The dogs continued to bark.

"Okay, I know," he said.

Becerra loved his dogs. They were his best friends, as they should have been.

Becerra had found Bullet on the side of I-684 when he was just five weeks old. He sat there in a cardboard box, part of a litter discarded by someone who thought, for some reason, a highway was a good place to get rid of five puppies.

Roxy's story was even better. He had become part of Becerra's family as a result of a murder investigation. Roxy's former master had shot his wife, who was lying dead on the floor with Roxy barking away when Becerra arrived. Becerra followed the dog to the pound. He was an orphan, and Becerra asked the dog warden how long he'd have to wait until he could adopt him. Becerra had left the pound that night with Roxy in tow.

Now the dogs were thirsty, and Becerra obliged, filling up a five-gallon pail with a garden hose, which had running water only because the last few days had been warmer than usual.

He left the two dogs outside and walked into the cottage. It was quaint—a living room, bedroom, bathroom, and small eat-in kitchen. The furniture was gifts from friends and family. A sofa from a brother, a small kitchen table from an old schoolmate. Becerra had found his new home six months earlier after living like a nomad, some nights out of his car.

Becerra liked living on this farm, even though the foul smell of manure often drifted over from the distant barns that housed the horses. It was quiet and private, which was fine for Becerra and his two dogs. He was a single guy now, and the solitude was welcome.

Becerra left his wet, dirty sneakers by the front door and walked into the kitchen, pulling off his blue New York State Police sweatshirt and grabbing a towel from a closet.

He threw the sweatshirt into a corner by the bathroom, rubbed his head and face with the towel, and walked over to the kitchen sink, turning on the faucet and filling a glass with cold water, which he finished off with one gulp, placing the glass down on the counter next to several unopened envelopes.

It was yesterday's mail, which Becerra didn't have time to look at, having arrived home after midnight thanks to a mound of paperwork following a late-night arrest. By the time he'd gotten home, he could barely get his clothes off before collapsing into a deep sleep.

As he looked at the letters, he noticed one was from a law firm and shook his head. It was from the attorney representing his estranged wife.

He was in the midst of a divorce, five years of marriage ended with some harsh words. He got the two dogs. She got the raised ranch. Luckily, they didn't have any children, though Becerra thought he got the wrong end of the deal, except for the dogs, which he'd had now for eight years, even before he met his soon to be ex-wife.

Becerra put the envelope down and headed for the shower. He'd read it later.

After washing up and feeding his dogs, and with the clock nearing 8 A.M. Becerra pulled his green, 1994 BMW 540 out of the driveway for the ten-minute drive to the Somers barracks, where he worked as an investigator with Troop K of the New York State Police.

Becerra was one of the few troopers who loved his job. He'd earned the unwanted nickname of "Hollywood" for his good looks and sharp clothes. And it didn't help that Becerra always seemed to find his way into the local newspapers or the Channel 12 cable-TV news. He wasn't a media hound, though he probably didn't mind the attention. The name stuck because Becerra looked like he'd jumped out of the pages of *GQ*. His suits were neatly pressed and his jet-black hair was always perfectly coiffed and slicked back. He'd inherited his ruggedly handsome, dark features, including his dark brown eyes, from his Spanish mother and his Spanish-Italian father. He smiled easily, his teeth pearly white. Of medium height, he stood straight, with his shoulders back, giving the appearance of a taller person. While some troopers resented his smooth appearance, he was, on the whole, well liked. He was the kind of guy who was still friendly with high school classmates from Archbishop Stepinac, even after twenty years.

As he drove into the parking lot in front of the barracks, his thoughts drifted to the envelope he'd left behind at home. He should have opened it, he thought. Now he'd have to go through the whole day wondering what was inside. Another demand? He'd already lost their four-bedroom home. And it couldn't be more money.

Damn, he was thirty-five years old, making $65,000 a year, which doesn't go far in Westchester County, living in an $800-a-month cottage. Money? He didn't have any money, but his wife knew that, which was one of the reasons why things had ended like they did. Money and a career chasing bad guys, which hadn't been part of Becerra's original plan.

He was majoring in education at the State University of New York at Cortland with designs on becoming a teacher when a Beta Phi Epsilon frat brother, a six-foot seven-inch behemoth named Big Al, dared him to take the state police exam.

Big Al talked about nothing else but being a state trooper. It was his life's dream.

"Shut the fuck up," was all Becerra would say to him. Being a cop was the furthest thing from his mind.

But when it was announced in early 1984 that the state trooper test was scheduled to be given at the Syracuse War Memorial Coliseum, Big Al knew he was going to take it, and he was going to convince his friend Becerra to come along.

"Cop? Are you kidding?" he asked Big Al, who in turn suggested that Becerra was either too dumb or too stupid to pass the test.

Big Al's taunts didn't bother Becerra, at first. But he just wouldn't stop talking about it. So to shut up his friend, hopefully forever, Becerra decided to take the test, and passed with flying colors.

Six months later Becerra was admitted to the state trooper academy and graduated in 1985. His youthful looks soon earned him an undercover assignment posing as a student at a high school in a suburb north of New York City.

For four months, he attended class and gathered information on drug dealing at the school, where the kids were mostly white and from wealthy families.

The experience helped Becerra develop a taste for investigative work, and after seven years in uniform, mostly handing out speeding tickets on the New York State Thruway, he was promoted to investigator with the Bureau of Criminal Investigations in 1992.

He enjoyed working as an investigator. Actually he loved it. He could wear a suit and tie and was working everything from burglaries to homicide investigations.

One piece of information led to another piece, and another, until finally, there was a suspect and an arrest. It was like putting together a puzzle.

The biggest puzzle of his career to date had been his work as an investigator working with the multi-agency team that probed the explosion and crash of TWA Flight 800 off the coast of Long Island in July 1996.

Becerra was one of hundreds of police officers from throughout the New York area called in to help interview witnesses and collect thousands of the 747 airplane parts that had settled on the bottom of the ocean. Becerra spent three months on the case, processing and tagging evidence. Though he had only four years experience as a detective, he never really bought into the final explanation that the plane just exploded in midair. There were too many witnesses who saw a light streaking up to the sky moments before the plane crashed into the sea. Planes just don't "blow up" in midair, reasoned Becerra. And the FBI guys, always so tight-lipped, like they had rocks jammed up their asses, even with other investigative teams. What was up with that? he'd thought. The official explanation—a fuel-tank explosion—never made any sense to him.

But he was always the good soldier, a guy who followed the instructions of his superiors, and kept his opinions to himself. After three months on Long Island working Flight 800, Becerra returned to Westchester County.

And here he was, three years later, in the midst of a divorce, only six years from retirement, if he chose, though Becerra had grown to love the job so much, he thought he'd stay there forever.

Becerra walked into the barracks, where the uniformed troopers occupied the left side of the single-floor brick building, while the Bureau of Criminal Investigations occupied the right side. The investigators shared a large, square office, each with his own desk. Becerra sat in the front of the office, with a window view of the entrance and parking lot.

He offered a "good morning" to Henry Luttman, a thirty-five-year veteran who was engrossed in his newspaper and replied with only a nod as Becerra walked to his desk.

"Henry, I didn't get out of here until midnight."

Luttman nodded again, sipping his morning coffee.

Becerra wasn't going to get anywhere with his superior, at least not until he finished off the sports section. He took off his jacket, a dark blue tweed, and settled into his chair, turning on his computer terminal.

He was reaching over to check his voice mail for messages when his phone rang.

"BCI, Becerra," he answered.

"Hello, is this Joe?"

"Yes, it is. Who is this?"

"Um, Joe. It's Tim Martin."

Jesus, Becerra thought to himself.

Tim Martin was a lowlife he'd arrested for indecent exposure, ending a two-year investigation in which Martin, as it turned out, had been exposing himself to women of all ages in towns surrounding his home in Ridgefield, Connecticut. This guy was so screwed up, he even masturbated in front of a group of elderly women after crossing into New York.

Connecticut police finally picked Martin up on a warrant for failing to appear at a hearing in Westport after he was arrested there for flashing several high school girls.

Becerra got his hands on him, and after his arrest Martin had pleaded guilty and was sentenced to probation.

"What's the matter, Timmy? You in trouble again?"

"No, I'm not in trouble. Actually I'm calling because I respect the fact that you chased after me for two years, and I want to give you something."

"And what's that?" said Becerra, holding the phone between his left shoulder and ear and organizing several files on his desk.

"I have some information on an old case, something that might interest you."

"Go ahead, Tim, I'm listening."

"Have you ever heard of Kathie Durst?"

The name didn't register with Becerra.

"No," said Becerra. "Who is she?"

"She was married to Bobby Durst, a rich guy whose family is worth millions. They had a home in South Salem. He killed her in 1982. Only he was never arrested."

"You know this guy killed his wife?"

"Yeah."

"How do you know?"

There was silence on the other end of the phone.

"Tim? How do you know?"

"I can't tell you over the phone."

In his fourteen years on the job Becerra had never heard of a Kathie Durst. He didn't trust Martin, a guy he thought should have been dropped in a jail cell and forgotten. On the other hand, Becerra knew from experience that tips often came from the scuzziest of characters. Maybe he could call Martin's legal-aid attorney in White Plains and set up a meeting.

"I'll tell you what. I'll call John Ryan, we'll get together at his office, and you can tell me the story in person. That sound okay?"

"That's fine with me," said Martin. "I respect you, Joe."

"Yeah, right," said Becerra. "Are you back out on the street? You're not—"

"No, I'm staying out of trouble," said Martin, cutting him off.

Not likely, thought Becerra as he hung up the phone. Martin had spent most of his adult life being chased by the police, having been busted for a variety of burglaries and other petty crimes over the years before graduating to exposing himself.

Becerra thought for a moment, then looked over to Luttman, who was still reading his paper.

Becerra liked Luttman, an easygoing veteran who had been with the state police since the 1960s. Luttman was a relic, and he was approachable. If Becerra ever had a question about a case, Luttman had no problem trying to answer it. He wasn't a hard-ass like so many of his superiors had been.

Becerra walked over to Luttman's desk.

"Henry, did you ever hear of a woman named Kathie Durst?"

Luttman quickly took his eyes off the paper.

"Kathie Durst? Yeah. That's an old one. Early 1980s. Maybe 1982. Married to a rich guy and disappeared. Probably dead. Why are you asking?"

"I just got a call from someone who said he had information, that she was killed by her husband."

"Who's the source?"

"Timmy Martin."

"Timmy Martin?" said Luttman, letting out a laugh. "Didn't you put him away?"

"He got probation."

Luttman folded his newspaper, took a last sip of coffee, and stood up.

"Give me a couple of minutes," he said, walking away.

Becerra went back to his desk, called John Ryan, told him about the conversation with Tim Martin, and scheduled a meeting with Martin at Ryan's White Plains office.

Five minutes later Luttman returned with a folder in his hand.

"Here you go, the Durst file," he said, dropping the file on Becerra's desk. "Have a party."

The file was thin and the first report was dated February 5, 1982. Two troopers had been sent to the Durst home on Hoyt Street in South Salem, which was about three miles from Route 35, a busy thoroughfare.

The troopers were called to the house after receiving a missing-persons report the night before from a woman named Gilberte Najamy. She claimed her friend Kathie Durst hadn't been seen since January 31. Becerra noted that Kathie was spelled with an *ie* instead of a *y*. Her full name was Kathleen, and she had been twenty-nine years old at the time of her disappearance. Her husband was Robert Durst, thirty-eight, who worked for the Durst Organization, a firm with vast real estate holdings in Manhattan.

There were several interviews in the file, nothing revealing, mainly accusations from Gilberte Najamy that there were problems with the Durst marriage.

Becerra looked over to Luttman, who was back at his desk.

"Is this it, Henry?" said Becerra, holding the file up in the air.

"Yeah, that's all we have. Call down to New York.

It was their case. They did the bulk of the work, if I recall correctly."

New York's case? Becerra looked at the file again. The interviews said she had left her home in South Salem and was last spotted in Manhattan.

Becerra picked up the phone, called down to NYPD headquarters at One Police Plaza in Manhattan, and asked if they could fish out whatever files the NYPD had on the Kathie Durst case.

He was told that since the file was seventeen years old, it was in the archives and would take a few days to retrieve.

After Becerra hung up the phone, Luttman walked over and sat on the edge of his desk.

"Whaddaya got?"

"I don't know," said Becerra, scribbling with his pen on a piece of paper. "But I think I want to find out."

2

TIMMY Martin sat in a small waiting area in John Ryan's legal-aid office in White Plains, his deep blue eyes staring down at his feet. Martin wasn't much to look at: his thinness was the kind you suspected by sight was the result of an enduring drug habit. Of medium height, he had cracks and crevices around his eyes that made him look much older than he was. His cheeks were drawn in toward his mouth, his brown hair pointed in different directions, and a pale complexion gave him a sickly appearance.

It was early December, a week after Martin first called Becerra, who was still waiting for the NYPD file on Kathie Durst. The information in the state police file was intriguing, but didn't reveal much. The two troopers who had visited the house back in 1982 saw Mr. Durst, but didn't see anything out of the ordinary. The interviews with some of Kathie Durst's friends and neighbors, if taken at face value, revealed a woman who seemed to be having some difficulties in life, particularly with her marriage. She was scared of her husband, but Becerra couldn't find anything definitive in the file that screamed out that she was murdered or that her husband had anything to do with her disappearance. Maybe she didn't disappear. Perhaps she just decided to jettison one life and pick up another somewhere else.

Seventeen years was a long time, and no one but Martin had even mentioned this case. But Becerra was the curious type, and he wanted to hear what Martin had to say.

Ryan, an easygoing fellow with a middle-aged lawyer's physique—round in the middle and in the face—explained that Martin was out on probation, but wanted the time cut down from six months to one.

Becerra wasn't buying it, knowing that probation was the only thing keeping Martin from opening his pants in public again. Another bust, and Becerra knew that Martin would do some jail time.

"See what he has to say and we'll talk some more," said Ryan.

Becerra agreed, and Martin was led into the office. He shook Ryan's hand first, then looked toward Becerra, who was standing with arms folded across his chest.

"Hello, Joe," said Martin, sheepishly looking at the floor.

"How ya doing, Timmy? Staying out of trouble, I hope."

Martin nodded, but didn't reply. Ryan told him to sit down. Becerra remained standing.

"So, Timmy, what do you have for me?"

Martin tried to make eye contact with Becerra, but he just couldn't lift his gaze off the floor.

"Well, like I told you on the phone, I know who killed Kathie Durst," he said.

"Keep talking. You got me here, so I'm listening," said Becerra.

Martin told Becerra that his older brother, Alan, had once been married to a woman named Janet Finke, who owned a maid service. One of her clients was the Dursts. Finke regularly cleaned their cottage in South Salem.

Tim Martin explained that after Kathie Durst disappeared in January 1982, talk centered on her husband, Bobby.

"Janet told us that Bob killed her and buried her," said Martin.

Becerra listened, but didn't believe what he was hearing.

"Why would he kill his wife?"

"Because he was nuts. Janet used to say he had a really bad temper. She also said his wife was threatening him. Janet used to talk to Bobby. I think he liked her. She was very pretty. Janet hung around with Kathie, too, said Kathie was going to be a doctor but she was failing school. She was doing too much blow and was hanging out with a lesbian who kept trying to get her to divorce her husband."

"Come again?" said Becerra. "The maid was friendly with the Dursts and said the wife was threatening her husband and was friendly with a lesbian who liked her? Are you kidding me?"

"No, no. That's what Janet said. We all knew what happened," said Martin.

"Do you know how he killed her?"

"No."

"Do you know where he buried her?"

Martin shook his head.

"But Janet told us that she was in the house a couple of days after Kathie disappeared and it didn't look right. She was cleaning that house for years and knew it well. She said some of the furniture was out of place, like it had been moved," said Martin.

Becerra, unmoved by the story, looked at Martin, who was again staring at the floor.

"So you're telling me you think this guy killed his wife because of a story you heard from a woman who was once married to your brother? You don't know this for a fact, and you don't know where he buried her," said Becerra.

Martin just shrugged his shoulders.

Becerra asked Martin if he knew where Janet Finke lived. He said somewhere in Connecticut, that she had divorced his brother and married some other guy.

"It that it, that all you got for me?"

"Well, I thought that was something," said Martin. "I wanted to give it to you because—"

"Because you respect me. Okay, right," said Becerra, stopping Martin in midsentence. "Why don't you take off while I talk to your attorney here. And Tim, I don't want to hear that you're in trouble again."

Martin stood up and reached across the floor, extending his thin, bony hand to Becerra, who offered his hand in return.

After Martin left the room, Ryan turned to Becerra and asked him what he thought.

"Not much. That's a crazy story. But let me take some time to look into this and I'll get back to you," said Becerra. "Besides, I'd rather have him on probation. One more slipup, and he'll be flashing in prison."

———

ON the drive back to the Somers barracks Becerra stopped for lunch—a Caesar salad with chicken and a diet Coke. Timmy Martin's story didn't give him much to think about, and he wasn't about to ask his superiors for permission to commit himself to a seventeen-year-old cold case based on a tip from a guy who'd been busted for flashing.

As he neared the barracks his cell phone rang, and he recognized the number. It was his attorney, probably with some news about his divorce. He asked Becerra if he had received a letter from his estranged wife's law firm. Becerra lied, telling him no but remembering the envelope he'd seen earlier in the day.

The conversation ended as Becerra pulled up to the barracks. The letter was nothing, just some perfunctory legal drivel he had to sign. He sat there for a few minutes, thinking about the divorce. He came from a big family, the fourth of six children, some of them married with kids. That's how it was supposed to be for me, he thought.

As he slowly got out of the car, thoughts of the Kathie Durst story were replaced by a wave of depression that numbed his thoughts, almost knocking him back into the driver's seat.

He walked into the barracks, past Luttman, who was talking on the phone but pointing with his left hand to Becerra's desk.

It was the Kathie Durst file, courtesy of the New York City Police Department.

"Came in this morning," said Luttman, holding the phone to his chest. "How'd it go with Martin?"

Becerra shook his head and stared down at the file. It had to be about four-inches thick.

Luttman hung up the phone and walked over to Becerra, whom he considered a protégé. Luttman had always liked Becerra. He thought he was a real gumshoe, a guy with a curious nose for the truth. Investigators came and went, but Luttman knew Becerra had talent.

Luttman also knew that the divorce had weighed down on Becerra.

"What ya gonna do with that?" said Luttman, looking at the file.

"I don't know. I guess I'm going to have to read it. All of it."

"Good luck, buddy boy. That's a whopper of a file. You know where I am if you need me."

Luttman walked back to his desk while Becerra opened the file, if only to have a glance at what was in store for him. There were dozens of interviews, police reports, requests for search warrants, medical records.

Nobody skimped here, thought Becerra, looking at the fastidious notes, most written by a Detective Michael Struk.

Becerra closed the file, put a rubber band around it, and tucked it under his right arm.

He walked out of the office, whispering to Luttman that he was taking the file home to read. It was late on a Friday afternoon, and Becerra had the weekend to absorb the report. Besides, he had nothing else to do. It wasn't like he had a family outing to go to.

Becerra stopped on the way home for some Italian takeout, lasagna and a ginger ale. When he arrived home, he was greeted warmly, as usual, by Bullet and Roxy, who weren't just happy to see him but wanted their dinner, too.

Becerra changed into sweats, fed his dogs, and finished off his lasagna.

Then he settled in on his couch and opened the Kathie Durst file.

3

THE detectives' squad room on the second floor of Twentieth Precinct in Manhattan was empty, save for one lone detective, Michael Struk, who was sitting at his desk, a cheap cigar tucked in the corner of his mouth, the smoke curling up slowly around his nose.

Struk was an hour into his 4-P.M.-to-1-A.M. shift and was staring at a picture of his five young children as a steaming cup of freshly brewed black coffee teased his taste buds. The coffee smelled good, but, as usual, it tasted like paint thinner.

It had been a month since Struk had seen his kids, and he was hurting. He missed everything about them, even the confusion that came from having such a large family. The screaming, the yelling, the toys all over the house, the mad dinners, the breakfasts. It wasn't easy raising five kids.

Not being with them, not hearing their voices, was much harder.

Struk was working a "stay-over," otherwise known in detective circles as a flip. He'd work nine hours, early into the morning, and then come back at 8 A.M. for another tour. It was often grueling and was known throughout the ranks as a marriage killer. Struk's had been no exception. The only thing left between him and his wife after eighteen years of marriage was the five children he was staring at and his signature on the divorce decree.

Struk put the photo in the top drawer in his desk. His eyes were moist. The room was empty, but he knew someone could walk in at any moment. The last thing he wanted anyone to see was Mike Struk crying.

He stood up and took a handkerchief out of his pocket, rubbed the last few tears from his eyes, cleared his throat, took a deep breath, and looked out the window onto West Eighty-second Street.

This was the Two-0, Columbus Avenue and Central Park to the east, Amsterdam Avenue and Broadway to the west. Actors, celebrities, captains of industry, all lived here. With its trendy bars, restaurants, and ultra-fashionable clubs, this was fertile ground for any cop—married or unmarried—a playground within a playground, professionally and socially.

In front of the precinct, police cars lined up, front ends parked facing the building, while several uniformed officers mingled.

Struk went back to his desk and finished off his ten-cent cigar, crushing it into an ashtray. He looked at his watch; it was only 5 P.M.

Struk wished his timepiece counted off years.

He had been on the job since 1965 and was but three years from retirement. He was as experienced as they came: Brooklyn-born and bred with the kind of street smarts that carried him through his seventeen years on the job and countless drug, porno, and murder busts. But seventeen years was a long time on the front lines. It was now 1982 and he was fatigued from engaging the enemy.

He hadn't always been this tired. When he joined the force right out of the army, he was tall and handsome and looked like a poster boy for the NYPD.

He walked a beat in Brooklyn, accumulating collars and earning a promotion to plainclothes with the First

Division, which patrolled the breadbasket of lower Manhattan, from Wall Street to Thirty-fourth Street, and boundaries that stretched from the East River to the Hudson River.

Struk didn't waste any time fitting right in. He worked nights, taking part in raids on the West Side meat markets, which were owned by the mob and served as fronts for a number of profitable gay clubs.

And he didn't complain when he was asked to dress in drag and tag along with another cop. There they were, two undercover cops in a third-floor loft, holding pinkies, drinking beers, and watching guys fuck on the bar, or scanning the long line of men waiting to enter a closet, where a guy sat hidden inside, dressed as a penguin, giving round-the-clock blow jobs.

The real targets weren't the clientele, even though Struk wanted to lock them all up for masquerading as men. It was the ownership, which was any one of New York's crime families. This was the early 1970s. Big business. Hundreds would walk through the door paying a three-dollar cover charge, and then get hit for one to two dollars for a can of beer, or more for a mixed drink.

Tens of thousands of dollars passed through clubs like this and others throughout the city every night. It was a cash business, and every time the NYPD shut them down, the mystery owners would eventually find a new place to start up again, get the word out, and be back in business.

Struk worked vice for three years, a long stretch for any cop, before he was transferred to the Thirteenth Division narcotics task force back in Brooklyn. It was a good move. He was going to work with some tough, fearless, maybe even crazed cops. But Struk had bought a house in Middletown, in upstate New York, and his young family saw little of him as it was. So he put in for a hardship transfer and landed farther north, in the Bronx, with another narcotics unit in the Eighth District.

The commute was easier, but it didn't matter. He was hardly home, first spending time on the street making low-level drug buys, then graduating to the twenty-to-thirty-kilo investigations complete with wiretaps.

Struk did his job well, and he was rewarded in 1975 with a promotion to detective working in the Fourth Homicide Zone, which encompassed three police precincts and covered the "gold coast" of Manhattan, from Fifty-ninth Street in the south up to Eighty-sixth Street on the West Side, and Fifty-ninth Street up to Ninety-sixth Street on the East Side, from river to river, including Central Park.

Headquartered in the Two-0, this was the crème de la crème of detective assignments, and Struk was living a detective's dream. He had the heart of the city during the day, and he'd go home to his wife and five children at night. At least he tried to go home.

By 1980, the NYPD eliminated its specialty units, including the Fourth Homicide Zone, but Struk managed to stay at the Twentieth Precinct, as only one of two experienced detectives working in what he described as a *Barney Miller* squad—soft detectives with no real, hard experience.

Struk volunteered to stay at the Two-0 even though some of the better detectives were sent to the Manhattan task force, which, under the new system, would assist local precincts when they needed additional manpower. Struk would now catch murder cases within the Twentieth Precinct, and on July 2, 1980, he caught the case of his career, what the press dubbed the "Murder at the Met."

When Struk arrived on the scene at the Metropolitan Opera House that morning, the body of Helen Hagnus Mintiks, thirty-one, lay naked and broken, having been tossed down an airshaft from the third floor of the famed building. She had been performing the night before with the Berlin Orchestra. Around 10 P.M. she left her station in the orchestra pit. She never returned, her $20,000 violin left on her seat.

Early the next morning, around 5 A.M., Mintiks was found dead, bound and gagged.

The Met was hallowed ground, and the murder of a world-class violinist from British Columbia was front-page news, even in the staid *New York Times*.

Struk knew this case was big when Manhattan Chief of Detectives Richard Nicastro arrived on the scene. Top brass like Nicastro wouldn't have come if it had been just some mom-and-pop murder.

Surrounded by a media circus, with reporters poking and probing every which way, Struk had needed less than a month to find the killer, Greg Crimmins, a twenty-two-year-old Met stagehand who later confessed that he boarded the elevator with Mintiks during her break. He was smoking a joint and drinking a beer and made a clumsy sexual advance toward Mintiks, who responded with a slap to his face.

His beer muscles took over. He pulled out a hammer from his belt, grabbed her, and forced her to a lower level that housed some of the Met's large, magnificent sets. There he tried to rape her on a stairwell. Mintiks was having her period, but Crimmins told her to take out her tampon. Mintiks did, but Crimmins couldn't get erect. Too much beer and too much pot. So he pulled her up to her feet and took her to the roof, three floors above street level. Bound, gagged, and naked, she still tried to make a run for it, jumping over a large water pipe. Crimmins chased her down, leaving his palm print on the pipe.

He grabbed her around the waist, brought her to the edge of the roof, and threw her off, later confessing to Struk after learning that his palm print matched the one left on the pipe.

It was by far Struk's biggest arrest, and for several weeks he was something of a celebrity, the detective who solved the Murder at the Met. He expected a promotion, at the very least a bump up from his third-grade status.

But the police brass did not react kindly when they learned not only that Struk had cooperated with a writer who wrote a book on the Met murder case, but that portions of the book were to be serialized in a porno mag. Struk was forced to cancel a national book tour, his "fifteen minutes" of fame lasting but a few months.

And here he was, two years later, February 5, 1982, sitting at his desk with the rank of detective, third grade, smoking cigars he bought at a bodega, drinking bad, black coffee, and longing for his family, when a short man and his dog walked into the second-floor squad room.

The man stood at the wood gate that served as an entrance to the area that contained detectives' desks, which were lined up along the cinder-block wall of the rectangular squad room. The beige color of the wall only added to what was a depressingly dour environment.

Struk glanced up from his desk, and was less than pleased with what he saw.

He wanted to say, *Who let you the fuck in here with a dog? This is my office, my domain, and you dare bring a dog in here?*

Instead, Struk got up, pulling his tall, lanky frame into view, and slowly walked over to the man.

"Can I help you?"

"Yes, I'd like to report my wife missing."

Struk waved his hand for the man to follow him, and he did, with the dog following right behind him.

Struk sat down at his desk, the third of six, and the man followed suit, sitting in a chair on the side of the desk. He didn't look like much. Probably some pissant rich guy, thought Struk. His hair was short, and he only stood about five-feet, eight-inches tall. Struk was much taller—six three. The man pulled out a magazine from under his arm. It was a *New York* magazine from May 1980 and on the cover was a photo of five men standing underneath a headline, THE MEN WHO OWN NEW YORK. Struk recognized Donald Trump and that other guy, Harry Helmsley, but no one else.

"What can I do for you?"

"My name is Robert Durst, and I believe my wife may be missing."

Durst spoke slowly, and deliberately. He initially made eye contact with Struk, but then turned away, keeping his head facing down toward the desk.

"What's her name?" said Struk.

"Her name is Kathie, or Kathleen."

"Why do you think she's missing?"

Durst explained that he and his wife had last spoken five days earlier, on Sunday night. They spent the weekend in South Salem, where they had a cottage. He said he drove his wife to the Katonah, New York, train station around 9 P.M., where she boarded a train for a trip back into the city, to their apartment on Riverside Drive and West Seventy-seventh Street. They had spoken later that night.

"Where's South Salem?"

"It's up in northern Westchester County, near the Connecticut border. We have a small home next to a lake—Lake Truesdale. We go there on weekends and during the summer."

Struk followed Durst's answers, writing notes on a yellow pad.

He paused to pull out a cigar from his shirt pocket, then resumed the questioning.

Durst said he had spoken to his wife after she arrived in Manhattan, around 11:15 P.M.

"What did you talk about?"

"Nothing really. Just small talk. We had an argument before she left and she wanted to get back. So I drove her to the train station."

"What time was that?"

"Uh, she got on the nine-seventeen train, up in Katonah."

"And you spoke to her on the phone when she got back to your apartment?"

"Yes."

"You said you had an argument?"

"Nothing major. She had been gone during the day and we were supposed to go out for dinner."

"And you haven't heard from her since you spoke to her Sunday night?"

"No. But that's not unusual," said Durst. "She attends medical school, the Albert Einstein School in the Bronx, and she's often studying. So we can go days without seeing each other."

"So why do you think she's missing?"

Durst said he spoke to some of his wife's friends, who hadn't seen her since Sunday. He didn't seem overly concerned, thought Struk. He was cool, unemotional. He could have been sitting in a diner ordering a tuna sandwich.

"I guess I'm a little concerned. I made a report with the New York State Police and I thought I should file one here."

As Durst spoke, Struk sensed something about him, that aura, that New York look that shouted wealth. It wasn't his clothes or any jewelry. He looked more like a vagabond, one of those guys who hangs out on the corner begging for quarters. It was just his attitude. This was the West Side of Manhattan, and Struk knew that attitude well. This wasn't a street guy, that's for sure, thought Struk.

"How's your marriage?"

"It's okay, I guess. No major problems."

"What's your occupation?"

"I'm in real estate. My family owns commercial and residential buildings in the city," said Durst, who was now making direct eye contact with Struk. "My father is Seymour Durst."

I knew it, a rich punk, thought Struk, who had no idea who Seymour Durst was.

Struk then looked down at the *New York* magazine.

THE MEN WHO OWN NEW YORK stared out at him. Struk wanted to ask him if one of these guys on the cover was his father, but he hesitated. He knew if that should prove to be the case, he'd probably take the magazine and stick it up this punk's ass. Struk hated these money guys and the way they flaunted their wealth and their power, claiming they were prominent.

Here, on the West Side, everyone was prominent.

"Mr. Durst, how old is your wife? And can you give me a description?"

"She's twenty-nine. Sandy hair, hazel eyes. About five-feet, five-inches tall, one hundred and twenty pounds," said Durst.

Durst told Struk that he and his wife had been married for nine years and had two apartments, the penthouse on Riverside Drive and a smaller apartment at 12 East Eighty-sixth Street near Fifth Avenue. As far as Durst knew, there hadn't been any ransom demands.

"And you say there aren't any marital problems?"

"No, not really," said Durst. "She just has a problem drinking. She was seeing a therapist for a while but stopped."

He handed Struk a photo of Kathie. She was very pretty, he thought. Long, straight hair, a nice full smile.

Struk took down Durst's home and business phone numbers and the number to the medical school. He also asked for phone numbers to speak with Kathie's relatives.

"I don't have those," said Durst. "Her maiden name is McCormack. Her mother, Ann, lives in New Hyde Park, Long Island. Her brother, Jim, lives in Queens."

Durst signed a single missing-persons form, then got up from his chair.

"Okay, Mr. Durst. I'll be in touch. There's a criterion that has to be met for this to become an official missing-persons investigation, and I don't think we've met that yet. I'll make a few calls and get back to you. Of course, should you hear from or see your wife please give us a call," said Struk.

The two men shook hands and Durst quietly left the building, his dog, a Norwegian elkhound, following at his heels.

Struk knew plenty of guys like Durst who walked meekly into the precinct all the time claiming their wives were missing. He also knew, in most cases, the women had either shacked up with another guy or had had enough of their beloved and jumped a bus.

After seventeen years on the force, Struk would know if someone was missing.

He reviewed his notes and filled out an initial report, or a "scratch," which was really nothing more than a blank sheet of paper with a name and address and phone number.

This wasn't a missing-persons case, he reasoned, but he'd make a few phone calls, at least make some effort to see where this woman was.

After all, the work would keep him busy, and keep his mind off of his family.

———

THE walk back to Riverside Drive and Seventy-seventh Street took less than fifteen minutes, and Robert Durst walked past the doorman and boarded the elevator.

As the doors closed, another tenant entering the building called out to hold the elevator, but Durst offered a quick glance to the elevator operator, who knew to ignore the plea.

He arrived at the door of his sixteenth-floor penthouse apartment. Once inside, he opened a bag of dry dog food and filled the bowl, placing it on the kitchen floor.

He calmly walked into the living room, sat on his sofa, and picked up the phone, dialing a familiar number.

"Hi, it's Robert. There's something I have to tell you. I just came back from the police station."

———

THE paint chips hanging from the ceiling caught Mike Struk's attention as he sat with his head back. The squad room, which had been empty the last two hours, was now coming to life. Two detectives led a handcuffed teen wearing a green parka and black Jefferson Starship T-shirt into the room. One detective stayed with the teen, the other, Eddie Regan, walked over to his desk, which was behind where Struk sat.

"Wake up," said Regan. "You working or you sleeping?"

"No, I'm just thinking," said Struk, who lifted his head up and pulled his chair closer to his desk. "What did you bring in?"

"Remember that break-in last week at the music store on Eighty-ninth? We found the kid, sixteen. Got him hanging out in Central Park. Anything going on here?"

"Just some guy, came in with his fucking dog to file a missing persons on his wife. Can you believe these people? He brings a dog here? Anyway he tells me he thinks his wife is missing, I take down the details, he leaves, and I make a few calls. Turns out the guy didn't tell me everything, and I'm sitting here figuring who to call next."

Struk picked up a yellow legal pad and pointed to his notes from an interview he completed minutes earlier with Dr. Jean Cook, the dean of the Albert Einstein Medical School in the Bronx.

Struk had circled several words, including "failing" and "marital difficulties" and "stressed."

"The guy comes in here with the dog and tells me everything is all right with the world, that his marriage is okay, and his wife may have a little drinking problem. This dean tells me a different story. Says she was supposed to repeat a class on Monday but called in sick and hasn't been heard from since."

"When did the husband last see her?"

"On Sunday."

"That's five days. He waits five days to report her missing? What's his name?"

"Durst. Robert Durst. Says his father is some big real estate guy."

"Shit, he is. You know who his father is? Seymour Durst."

"He said that, said his father's name was Seymour."

"Did he also tell you that his family owns half of Manhattan?" said Regan, walking away from Struk to attend to the teen, who was taken downstairs to the holding pen.

As Regan left the room, and with the police radio squawking in the background, Struk decided he would call Larry Cohen, a suggestion made by Dr. Cook.

Cohen was a medical student at Einstein whom Cook knew to be friendly with Kathie.

When he picked up the phone and learned he was talking to a New York City detective, Cohen seemed disturbed, not with Struk but because he hadn't spoken to or seen Kathie in over a week.

Cohen was also perturbed when he learned that it had been her husband who reported her missing.

"Why is that bothering you?" said Struk.

"Because he was beating her. He scared the hell out of her."

"He was hitting her?"

"Yeah, a lot, from what I could tell."

"You ever see any marks on her?"

"No, but she'd call me late at night, sometimes crying, telling me she was slapped or punched. She was pretty scared of him."

"Did she ever say she was planning to leave him?"

"She was talking about divorce. But she's scheduled to graduate this summer, so I told her to sit tight, finish school, then take care of her marriage."

Struk wanted to ask Cohen if he was involved with Kathie. Cohen wasn't married, and Struk was old school. In his world, men and women didn't confide in each other unless they were sleeping together. The words were there, rolled on the end of his tongue, ready to spit out.

But he didn't ask the question. He hung up and circled Cohen's name on his pad, then wrote "boyfriend?"

Before breaking for dinner, Struk decided to make two more calls—to Ann McCormack, Kathie's mother, and the New York State Police.

Ann McCormack was a widow, she said, her husband passing from cancer in 1966. Kathie was the youngest of five children; having moved into Manhattan when she was only nineteen, renting an apartment in a building owned by the Durst Organization.

She met Robert Durst one morning while paying her rent. They'd had but two dates when she decided to move with him to Vermont, where he was going to run a health-food store.

Ann said at the time she wasn't pleased with her daughter's decision, reminding her that Catholics marry, they don't cohabitate.

She told Struk she wasn't fond of her son-in-law. He rarely socialized with Kathie's family and, despite his wealth, lived on the cheap. He drove old cars, wore old clothes, and hovered over Kathie's spending, watching every penny.

"That's why she's in medical school," said Ann. "She needs her own career. She needs her own money."

Ann hadn't spoken to her daughter in a week or so, but said she had been in good spirits.

"Did your daughter have any problems with her marriage?" said Struk.

"We all have problems with our marriages sometime or another," said Ann.

"Yes, we do," said Struk, who thanked Ann for her time and said he'd be in touch.

He then made his second call, to the New York State Police, and spoke to a Sergeant William Kidney.

Kidney knew all about Kathie Durst, thanks to her friend Gilberte Najamy, who had called Thursday night insisting on filing a missing-persons report.

"I told her we could only take a report from a family member, but this woman wouldn't take no for an answer. So I sent two troopers to the South Salem home Friday morning."

Kidney said Robert Durst answered the door and invited the troopers inside. Although they didn't search the house, they later reported nothing out of the ordinary.

Kidney said one of the troopers asked Durst when

he'd last spoken to his wife. Sunday night, after she returned to New York, he replied.

When Durst was told the call could be traced, he said he spoke to his wife from a pay phone off of Route 35, which was three miles away.

"Why would he walk that far to make a phone call?" said Struk. "It was raining that night."

"And snowing up here," said Kidney. "The Najamy woman said some other friend, a Michael Burns, told her that Kathie had taken off, that she'd had enough."

"Enough of what?" said Struk.

"Don't know. He told Najamy to leave Kathie Durst alone, that she didn't know Kathie as well as he did. What do you make of that?"

"Sound's like he's doing her," said Struk. "And it sounds like she took off."

"That's what it sounds like to me," said Kidney.

———

STRUK went to the Dublin House on West Seventy-ninth Street around 10 P.M., the corned beef always a good choice. Struk sat alone, saying little to the waitress. He left her a three-dollar tip for a seven-dollar meal.

Upon his return from dinner, the squad room was still devoid of any activity. Regan was back at his desk filling out paperwork for his arrest.

Struk said nothing, hung up his black trench coat, sat down, and began typing his report, using only his two forefingers.

An hour later he called missing persons and gave them Kathie Durst's name, address, and phone number.

On his notepad, he scribbled "Wife took off . . . or possible suicide" before signing out at exactly 1 A.M.

4

THE steam rose slowly from the manhole covers that line the middle of West Eighty-second Street, the cold morning air biting Mike Struk's face as he walked up the front stairs of the Twentieth Precinct.

It was 8 A.M. and he was back in the office, greeted with the smell of fried eggs. It was Regan. Like Struk, he'd been working a stay-over, only he'd decided to spend the night on a bunk in the back of the squad room. Regan was cooking breakfast on a hot plate. Along with the bed and hot plate there was a small TV and a refrigerator.

Regan motioned to the eggs. "Want some?"

Struk shook his head, held up a brown paper bag, placed his coat in his locker, and sat at his desk, opening the bag and pulling out a fresh coffee and hard bagel.

The morning winter sun was bright, casting long shadows that filtered over one side of the squad room through the broken window blinds and illuminating the half-inch of dust that lined the sills.

Two other detectives walked in just after 8 A.M. and Struk pointed to his watch.

"I told you guys you have to get home by five A.M.

when you work a stay-over, not stay out all night and stumble into work," he said, smiling widely.

The two detectives didn't appreciate the humor. They needed coffee, and a lot of it.

Struk was in better shape. He'd been in bed by 2 A.M. and up exactly five hours later. He could function on limited sleep. If he had been out drinking until dawn like his two cohorts, he'd be sitting at his desk, eyes closed, praying no one would bother him and the next nine hours would somehow whiz by.

Struk had come to work with the Durst case on his mind. He tried to reason why a young woman, married to a millionaire, six months away from being a doctor, suddenly takes off. It didn't make much sense. Struk was sure Durst had lied to him when he said their marriage was fine. But what self-respecting man would acknowledge that there were problems in his marriage? Struk himself wasn't exactly standing out in the middle of Broadway announcing to the world, or even his close friends, that his marriage was over.

And if Durst was hitting his wife, as was suggested, was there a reason? Durst spoke softly, gently. He didn't appear to be the violent type. Maybe she was sleeping with another man, maybe this guy Burns, or Larry Cohen, and Durst had found out about it.

Struk realized the real problem he had with the story: Why would Kathie Durst leave a husband who was a member of a wealthy family? Struk could glean from the conversations of the previous night that Durst had money, and lots of it. He even put together the bit with the magazine, the picture of the five guys and the brazen title that spoke of ultimate power.

Durst was trying to tell Struk who he was and what family he came from.

"Tread lightly here, boy" was the unstated message.

The squad commander, Lieutenant Robert Gibbons, had Saturday duty, and was sitting in his office toward the back of the room reading Struk's initial Durst report.

Unlike most supervisors, Gibbons was well liked by those under his command. In fact, the word throughout the precinct was that Gibbons had taken a step back when he made lieutenant. Everyone thought he was a hell of a detective.

Struk finished off his bagel and walked over to Gibbons's office.

"Not much happened last night, eh?" said Gibbons, who was now scanning the Friday-night log.

Struk told Gibbons about the visit from Durst, the missing-persons report, the interviews.

"I think she took off," he said. "The only thing that's bothering me is why leave the golden goose? This guy has money."

Gibbons looked at the name again on the report. Robert Durst. The last name sounded familiar.

"His father's name is Seymour," said Struk. "This little puke actually showed me a magazine with his father on it. Says he's one of the most powerful men in the city."

Gibbons nodded. "I know this guy. They own a lot of property in the city. Some very big buildings."

Gibbons signed the report. He saw that Struk had only phoned in the bare essentials to missing persons; her name, address, age, and physical characteristics.

"She's not missing, at least not yet, from what I can tell," said Struk.

"I agree," said Gibbons. "You going to stay on it?"

"Yeah, I want to make a few more calls. She wasn't born with a silver spoon in her mouth. Blue collar, from Long Island. They were married for nine years. You don't just leave this kind of money. Fucking rich people. You think they have it easy, but in reality they're more fucked up than we are."

Struk spent the morning at his desk, talking to New York State Police trooper John Harney, one of the two troopers who'd entered the Dursts' South Salem home on Friday, to Gilberte Najamy, and to Jim McCormack, Kathie's older brother.

Harney repeated what Sergeant Kidney had said, a friend of Mrs. Durst's phoned in a missing-persons report, and he visited the house Friday morning. But following the conversation, Struk turned to his notes from the night before. Something had occurred to him, and there it was, midway through his report. Robert Durst said *he* had called the state police.

Struk made a note of that discrepancy and called Gilberte Najamy, who seemed surprised, and relieved, when she answered the phone and learned she was talking to a New York City detective.

"Something is wrong, something is really wrong," she blurted. "I've been trying to call Kathie all week and I can't find her. She was supposed to meet me Monday night and she never showed. Oh, God. Oh, God, what did I do?"

"Excuse me?" said Struk, who was baffled by Gilberte's ramblings. "Why don't we start from the beginning. You are her, what, a friend?"

"I'm Kathie's best friend," said Gilberte. "She was at my house last Sunday. I'm a caterer and I have my Christmas party at the end of the month; it's mostly family. We planned to meet for dinner the next evening, Monday, at six-thirty at the Lion's Head Restaurant in Greenwich Village. But she didn't show up."

Struk asked about the Sunday party, and Gilberte said it was a small affair. She explained that Kathie had called earlier that day and asked if she could come over. She was in South Salem with Bobby, and they were arguing. She needed to get out of there. It was a forty-five-minute drive from South Salem to Newtown, Connecticut, where Gilberte lived, and Kathie arrived early in the afternoon.

"Bobby?" said Struk.

"Yes, Bobby. Everyone calls him that," said Gilberte. "The minute Kathie arrived at my house, Bobby called, demanding that Kathie return home."

Struk asked if Kathie had had any alcohol, and Gilberte said just a few glasses of wine.

"Any drugs?" asked Struk.

"No. It was a family party," said Gilberte.

Bobby called several more times through the afternoon, and by 7 P.M. Kathie'd had enough, calling him back and telling him she was leaving. Gilberte said she expected to see her the next night at the Lion's Head. The dinner at the dark and cozy restaurant would be a celebration of sorts for Gilberte, who'd closed a deal to cater the postshow party for Johnny Carson's new NBC special.

Kathie's sister, Mary Hughes, was an account executive with the Mahoney & Wasserman public relations firm and in charge of the party. Hughes and Gilberte had met for lunch that Monday afternoon and Gilberte couldn't wait to break the news to Kathie. She told Struk that she had sat at the bar near the Lion's Head front door, ordered a Bloody Mary, and waited for her friend, making small talk with the bartender and a couple of patrons waiting for a table. The restaurant, which was shaped like a railroad car, was crowded. The dining area was toward the back.

By 7 P.M. Kathie had yet to arrive. Gilberte said she grabbed some change and walked over to the pay phone tucked away near the rest rooms between the bar and the dining area. She called the penthouse on Riverside Drive, but there was no answer. She called Kathie's apartment on East Eighty-sixth Street, but again no answer. Both times she left a message.

Gilberte said Kathie had never stood her up before. And if she couldn't make a dinner or planned meeting, she always called. But Kathie had been an emotional wreck these last few months. And with the added burden of finishing medical school, Gilberte figured her friend wasn't herself, especially after Kathie told her that Bobby wasn't going to pay the rest of her tuition.

Sunday had been especially bad. Kathie was really out of sorts, complaining about Bobby. That's all she talked about, her problems with Bobby. He had already cut her off financially, leaving her with no money. Gilberte said Kathie had to borrow money from friends.

"I understand his family has millions," said Struk.

"Tell me about it," said Gilberte. "I had to cash a check for Kathie for one hundred fifty dollars on Sunday."

Kathie was also upset over an incident that had occurred a year before when Bobby kicked a friend of hers, Peter Schwartz, in the face because he thought the guy was having an affair with Kathie.

"Was he?"

"No, he was just a friend, a photographer. We had a small party at the East Eighty-sixth Street apartment, then we all went out dancing at Xenon. Kathie and Peter stayed behind. Bobby got pissed, so he went back to the apartment and bashed him in the face. Broke his jaw."

Gilberte said Schwartz pressed assault charges and filed a civil suit against Bobby, but the charges were later dropped and Schwartz settled the litigation.

"Kathie couldn't believe Peter did that, settled with Bobby. She was so hot about that. Said the Dursts always win," said Gilberte.

By Wednesday, Gilberte said several other friends, including Kathy Traystman and Eleanor Schwank, left messages with Gilberte wondering where Kathie was. No one, it seemed, had heard from Kathie since Sunday. Did she have an exam no one knew about? Was she with another man? Was she just looking for some quiet time alone? None of the friends had any answers.

She had to be somewhere, they agreed.

On Thursday, around 3 P.M., Gilberte said she called Kathie's number at the South Salem home. No one answered, so she left another message, telling Kathie that her friends were a little concerned since no one had seen her since Sunday. Five minutes later Gilberte said her phone rang.

It was Bobby.

"He said he hadn't seen Kathie all week."

"Did you believe him?"

"Yeah, I did. There were times they'd go days without seeing each other. But there were never instances where days would go by and Kathie wouldn't talk to one of her friends."

Gilberte paused for a moment.

"Listen, Detective. Bobby called her Sunday night at my house and Kathie turned to me and said she had to go. I walked her out onto my front porch and she gave me a warning. It was something she said to all of her friends."

"What was that?"

"She said if anything ever happened to her, suspect foul play. Suspect Bobby."

Struk could hear Gilberte weeping. The story didn't make much sense to him. If Kathie Durst was that scared of her husband, he reasoned, why in the world had she been spending the weekend with him?

"Oh, one more thing," said Struk. "Do you know a Michael Burns?"

"Not really. I mean, I know of him, but I don't really know him."

"The state police tell me he's the guy that told you to leave Kathie alone, that she's had enough. Is that true?"

"Yeah, he did. But I didn't know what he was talking about. I don't think Kathie really knew him that long. Listen, I have to run, I have an appointment. You have my number. You can call me anytime."

———

JIM McCormack sounded groggy, explaining he had been up half the night with his newborn daughter. His wife, Sharon, had given birth two weeks earlier. It was their first child.

The call from Mike Struk was greeted with surprise. Jim said he had heard from Bobby Thursday night.

"He asked me if anyone knew where Kathie was, which was pretty unusual."

"Why is that?"

"Bobby never called me. Ever."

Jim said the conversation with Bobby lasted maybe two minutes, if that.

"He didn't sound especially concerned. I know he and my sister were having problems."

"What kind of problems?"

"A year ago, Christmas, they were at my mom's house on Long Island and Bobby wanted to leave. He never liked socializing with my family, and when he did it was only for a special event. Kathie was enjoying herself and wanted to stay. Bobby went outside, started his car, then came in and said they were leaving. Kathie said no. So Bobby walked behind where Kathie was sitting and pulled her off the sofa by the hair. He had chunks of hair in his hand," said Jim.

"What did you do?"

"I know what I wanted to do, and that was grab him by the neck. But Kathie said she was all right and that they were going to leave."

"Any other incidents?"

"Not really. I mean, Kathie didn't really confide in me. My wife just had the baby, so we're preoccupied with our stuff. My sister Mary would know more. She and Kathie talked all the time."

———

IT was noon, midway through his shift, and Struk was busy typing up his second report on the Durst case.

He had decided that Kathie Durst had run off, only he didn't know with whom. As he finished up his report, Gibbons called out.

"You have a phone call. It's Robert Durst."

Struk picked up the phone with the thought that Durst's wife had returned home.

"Mr. Durst? Detective Struk."

"Detective, there's something I think I should have told you last night."

"And what was that?"

"My wife has a friend, a man. His name is Michael Burns."

"Who's he?" said Struk, pretending he never heard the name.

"A cocaine dealer," said Bobby. "I know he and Kathie have become friendly over the past few months."*

"Is your wife using cocaine, Mr. Durst?"

"Yes. About two, maybe three grams a week."

"Why didn't you tell me this last night?"

"I was hoping that she'd have come home by now, and I could save her the embarrassment. As it is, I'm beginning to worry."

"Well, I'm glad you told me. Is there anything else?"

"Yes. I believe my wife is having an affair with this man."

"You told me there weren't any problems in your marriage, Mr. Durst."

"I know. Again, this is extremely personal, as you can imagine. I was thinking about this last night after I returned home and thought you should know."

Bobby told Struk he believed Burns lived in Mount Vernon, north of the city.

"Okay, Mr. Durst. I'm still making calls. When I hear something I'll let you know."

Gibbons walked over as Struk hung up the phone, curious about the conversation.

"He thinks his wife is having an affair with some lowlife, a Michael Burns. Says he's a coke dealer," said Struk. "He also says she's snorting a couple of grams of coke a week."

Gibbons walked back to his office. Struk turned to his report and typed "marital runaway."

*Michael Burns denied dealing drugs or having an affair with Kathie Durst, see p. 67.

FIVE uniformed members of the New York Police Department's elite Emergency Service Unit combed 37 Riverside Drive, checking every common area inside the sixteen-floor building. The elevators, elevator shafts, basement, backyard area, roof, stairwells, and water tower were meticulously searched.

It was Monday afternoon, February 8, and five detectives from the Twentieth Precinct, including Mike Struk, had joined the search, doubling the police presence at the building. Some of the residents gathered in the lobby, wondering why nearly a dozen police officers were poking and probing throughout their home.

One woman stood wearing her sable fur while an elderly man tried to control his four dachshunds, which were bouncing wildly.

One ESU truck, painted in the familiar blue and white of the NYPD, sat in front of the building, along with one patrol car and two unmarked cars driven by the detectives.

Struk didn't want to attract attention to the search for Kathie Durst, but his conversation just a few hours earlier with Lieutenant Gibbons had set all this activity at Riverside Drive in motion.

Struk had left the Twentieth Precinct Saturday afternoon all but convinced that Kathie had fled and was sunning herself somewhere with a lover, probably enjoying unfamiliar surroundings and indulging in wine and cocaine. He didn't think highly of Kathie, believing her to be an out-of-control wife who drank excessively, snorted coke, and slept around. Struk would have closed the book on the case if it hadn't been for one lingering thought—a doubt he tried to erase, but that just wouldn't go away. Women left their husbands every day. But his experience was telling him that a woman like Kathie Durst, blue-collar background and all, didn't just up and leave a guy like Robert Durst, given his wealth and standing. She was in medical school, for Christ's sake, only a few months away from graduation. What was she thinking?

Struk's thoughts centered on Bobby. Gibbons thought it was odd that Bobby would wait five days to report his wife missing. And Bobby said *he* called the New York State Police to report his wife missing when it was one of Kathie's friends who made the call. In reality, Bobby was surprised to see the state police show up at his door Friday morning.

As the squad room came to life that morning after the slow weekend—with phones ringing incessantly, detectives talking, the noise from other parts of the busy precinct rumbling through the floors—Struk and Gibbons talked at length about the case.

Struk observed that Bobby displayed little emotion or genuine concern about his missing wife.

"He just doesn't seem to care," he said.

Both agreed that Struk should make a few more calls and perhaps even pay a visit to 37 Riverside Drive. If anything, they could get this settled and move on to other things.

THE penthouse was on the sixteenth floor, with the Hudson River just across from the Henry Hudson Parkway. Struk showed his badge to the doorman, who called upstairs to Bobby, announcing he had a visitor.

Once inside, Struk noted that the rooms were of medium size and that the apartment was somewhat bare and unkempt, with the furniture nondescript.

If he hadn't known it already, Struk would never have guessed that the penthouse was the home of a man of Bobby's means. Kathie Durst might have been a bright woman, a medical student, but she wasn't much of a homemaker, thought Struk. The place needed a good cleaning.

There was one attraction, the balcony, which offered spectacular views of the Hudson River.

Bobby quietly followed as Struk entered each room, searching for any signs of a struggle, or blood, or anything that might suggest something was amiss.

The tour lasted ten minutes. Struk hadn't expected to find anything. After all, if something did happen here, Struk reasoned, would Bobby Durst let a detective nose around?

When the two men settled down in the living room, Bobby seemed more relaxed. At six-feet, three-inches tall, Struk towered over Bobby, but sitting, they were close to being eye to eye. Bobby's Norwegian elkhound, whom he'd named Igor, settled down at his feet. Bobby offered Struk something to drink, which he declined. Struk was more interested in hearing where Bobby had been the past week.

Bobby answered each question, slowly and deliberately, a slight twitch noticeable on the corner of his mouth.

"We had an argument that Sunday night. Kathie came home from Gilberte Najamy's in a foul mood. She walked in and started yelling and screaming. She appeared to be drunk. She opened a bottle of red wine and poured full glasses, yelled some more, then said she was driving back to the city. I told her she was in no condition to drive, so I drove her to the Katonah train station, where she caught a nine-seventeen P.M. train back to Manhattan."

"What were you arguing about?"

"Issues, with us. Things concerning our relationship. She always argued with me whenever she hung around with Gilberte Najamy."

"And you spoke to her later that night?"

"Yes, I was walking my dog, so I called her from a pay phone near Route 35."

"That's pretty far from your house, isn't it?" said Struk, remembering the conversation with Trooper Harney, who'd wondered out loud why Durst would make a call from so far away.

"Yeah, a couple of miles, but I was walking my dog and we ended up there, so I made a quick call to see if she was all right."

The conversation shifted to Bobby's week, where he was and what he did. The answers came quickly: a couple of business trips, one in Connecticut on Tuesday to scout properties. Nothing really special.

"I'm usually very busy during the week," said Bobby, who didn't look very busy this Monday morning, wearing sweats and sneakers.

Struk flipped to a fresh page in his small notebook, easily following Bobby's responses, which were delivered in a slow drawl.

Bobby reiterated his suspicions about Michael Burns, whom he believed to be a drug dealer engaged in an affair with his wife.

"Is that just a feeling you have, that he's having an affair with your wife, or do you know this for a fact?"

"It's more a feeling. He's always with her. I thought it was for the cocaine, but now I'm not so sure."

"Any idea how they met?"

"Gilberte Najamy. He knew Gilberte and she introduced him to Kathie. When Burns wasn't around, Kathie would get her drugs through Gilberte."

"Gilberte Najamy?"

"Yeah, she's like a drugstore," said Bobby. "She is a

very bad influence on my wife. She's also been trying to break us up. I don't know why. I mean, I heard she liked women, though I don't think she'd be silly enough to think she'd ever get Kathie into bed with her. Have you met her? She looks manly. Always wears these awful combat boots. I think Kathie just hangs out with her for the drugs. When they're together, Kathie's always coming back here, picking a fight."

Struk noted Bobby's comments on Najamy, folded his notebook, and slipped it into an inside pocket in his black trench coat. As he got up to leave, he had one more question for Bobby.

"Did you ever hit or beat your wife?"

Bobby handled the questions easily. "No, I'd never hit Kathie."

He walked Struk to the door, assuring him of his continued cooperation, maintaining he only wanted to see that his wife was safe.

Struk boarded the elevator and told the operator to take him to the ground floor. The operator closed the door and the elevator descended down. Struk reached into his pocket and pulled out his notebook, scribbling some quick notes, including Bobby's denial that he ever hit Kathie. He then took out his badge and showed it to the elevator operator.

"Say, buddy, do you know Kathie Durst?"

The operator nodded yes.

"Were you working last Sunday night?

The operator paused for a moment, then said he worked until 6 A.M.

"Did you see Mrs. Durst?"

"Um, yeah, I did. I did see Mrs. Durst. Last Sunday night, yeah, right, I took her up to her apartment."

Struk took out his pad again. "What's your name?"

"Eddie, Eddie Lopez."

"And you saw Mrs. Durst last Sunday night? On January thirty-first?"

"Yes, about eleven P.M."

"Was she with anybody?"

"No. Mrs. Durst was alone. But I did take a man up to her penthouse about an hour or two later."

"Can you describe him?"

"White guy, I don't know, maybe thirty-five years old. Good dresser, dark pants, leather jacket. He had a very thick neck and, I remember, marks on his face, like little craters."

"You're sure he went to Mrs. Durst's apartment?"

"Yeah," said Lopez. "I see her open the door."

"Ever see this guy before?"

"No."

Struk returned to the station house around noon and told Gibbons they had an eyewitness, an elevator operator, who saw Kathie and even brought a visitor to her apartment.

Struk had quizzed another building employee, a doorman named Phillip Marrero, who said he thought he saw Kathie Durst leave the building Monday morning and get into a cab. When asked if he was sure it was Kathie Durst, Marrero said he saw her from behind, but was almost certain it was her.

The two sightings were enough for Gibbons and Struk to agree that the building should be thoroughly searched. Gibbons made the call to the Emergency Service Unit and directed Struk and four other detectives from his squad to go to 37 Riverside Drive at 2 P.M.

As Struk headed for his desk to check his messages before leaving for the search, he turned around to Gibbons, a quizzical look on his face.

"Hey, Lou, one more thing. Durst says he never hit his wife."

"What guy would admit to smacking his wife around?" said Gibbons. "If that was my wife running around like that, I'd be pretty pissed off."

Struk agreed, returned to his desk, and decided to make several more calls before leaving for Riverside Drive.

The state police had nothing new to report, and an admissions officer at Einstein, Noreen Kerrigan, said Kathie was thinking of traveling to North Dakota for a clinical study. If anything, it was to get away from her husband, said Kerrigan.

Struk placed another call to Dr. David Kaufman, the course director at Montefiore Hospital in the Bronx, where Kathie went for several classes. Kaufman repeated the same story everyone else had, that Kathie's marriage was shaky and she appeared to be incredibly stressed over the last year. So bad was the stress, said Kaufman, that Kathie wasn't just doing poorly, she was on the verge of flunking out. She'd failed a urology clerkship the previous summer and was less than thrilled when informed she had to repeat the course.

In fact, said Kaufman, Kathie had missed far too many classes and clinics. And she'd offered the most absurd reasons as excuses: things like her car breaking down, sometimes for two or three days at a time. Once for a whole week.

The coke-fiend doctor is missing classes, thought Struk, and called Dr. Al Cooperman, a dean at Einstein, who had interesting news: he was the dean whom Kathie called early Monday morning to say she wasn't going to make it into school, complaining of headaches and diarrhea.

"Are you sure that was Kathie Durst?" said Struk.

"I believe so. Who else would make a call like that?" said Cooperman.

Struk hung up the phone and headed back over to the penthouse.

———

THE search at 37 Riverside Drive lasted about two hours. Two detectives took the elevator to the top floor, then walked down the stairwells, stopping on every floor to check the halls. The basement, where the generator and boiler and building supplies were located, was thoroughly combed, every corner, crack, and crevice.

The roof was searched from end to end, and a single detective checked inside the water tower. The backyard, which was between two large buildings, was clean.

When the police left around 4 P.M., Struk was pleased that they got out of there with little notice. He wasn't concerned so much about the neighbors, but he was leery of the press. The wife of a man like Bobby Durst reported missing? That would make the front page of any newspaper, particularly in New York, where tabloids like the *Daily News* and *Post* existed for stories like this. And Struk had firsthand familiarity with front-page news, having solved the Murder at the Met.

But there were no reporters at the scene. The escape was clean, as was the search, which came up empty.

By the time Struk returned to the Twentieth Precinct, he was tired. Thoughts that Bobby Durst perhaps knew more about his wife's disappearance than he was letting on still nagged at him, but he was less concerned about Bobby Durst than about this "mystery man" who'd visited Bobby's wife late Sunday night.

———

TUESDAY morning, February 9, began like any other morning for Mike Struk, who pushed himself out of bed around 6:30 A.M., showered, and had a quick cup of coffee and half a corn muffin.

The radio was tuned to one of the all-news radio stations, but he wasn't paying attention, and missed the report about the wife of a real estate tycoon who was missing and the large reward being offered for information.

As he dressed, buttoning a wrinkled white shirt and a two-piece suit pulled from the racks of JCPenney, his phone rang, but he was busy tying a knot in his tie and let it ring.

He arrived at the Twentieth Precinct just before 8 A.M., and once inside, he walked up the stairs to the detectives' squad room. A couple of uniformed officers were heading down and said something to Struk about the *Daily News,* but Struk wasn't paying attention. He just nodded and opened the door to the squad room, where he noticed Lieutenant Gibbons on the phone in his office, frantically pointing toward Struk to come inside.

Gibbons pushed copies of the *New York Daily News* and *New York Post* toward Struk, who picked up the papers and saw their front pages.

WIFE MISSING: IOOG REWARD was on the cover of the *News*.

There, in black and white, was a large picture of a smiling Kathie Durst next to a subhead that read *Real Estate Tycoon's Son Asks for Search.*

The *Post* headlined blared IOOG TO FIND MISSING BEAUTY.

"Jesus Christ," Struk mumbled, as he flipped the page to read the full story, which detailed the search for Kathie the day before at 37 Riverside Drive.

It was all there, in both papers, the ESU units, Twentieth Precinct detectives, and a quote from Gibbons to the effect that Kathie had been missing for more than a week.

There was a new wrinkle: Bobby Durst was offering a $100,000 reward for information.

"How the hell did they get this?" said Struk.

Gibbons was still on the phone, and moved his head quickly from side to side, telling Struk not to say a word.

"Okay, Cap," said Gibbons as he hung up.

"So?" said Struk.

"So, that was the captain. He got a call from Nicastro, and they want to know who's doing what, when, and how," said Gibbons.

Of course Nicastro, the chief of detectives, would stick his beak into a high profile case like this, just like he'd done with the Met Murder, thought Struk.

But this case was even more important: the daughter-in-law of one of the city's largest landlords, Seymour Durst, was missing.

"You know, they called me last night. The reporters. I don't know how they got the story," said Gibbons. "I told the captain that you were on it, and they said you're to have unlimited support."

"That's good," said Struk. "I'm gonna need it. Let's call in the task force."

6

THE headquarters of the Durst Organization was located at 1133 Avenue of the Americas, and on Tuesday morning, February 9, Seymour Durst sat behind his desk ignoring phone calls from an impressive list of individuals who read the morning papers, offering to provide assistance in the search for his daughter-in-law.

Seymour even received a call from Mayor Koch's office. With a wave of the hand a secretary walked out of his office and said to thank the mayor for his concern, but explained that Seymour was on the phone with his son, helping him through this difficult time.

Seymour spoke to no one that morning, and was content to let his oldest son set the course of family involvement. If Robert needed his father, or any other family member, he'd simply have to ask.

The Dursts were notoriously private. It was how Seymour was raised, and it was how he raised his four children.

Family business remained within the family.

That's how the Durst Organization, and the Dursts themselves, operated since Seymour's father, Joseph, had founded the company in 1915.

Joseph Durst arrived in the United States at the turn of the century riding the exodus of European Jews. He had three dollars attached to the lapel of his coat. Joseph purchased his first property in 1915 on Thirty-fourth Street. By 1922, he had incorporated his business, and after World War II he had his three sons—Seymour, Royal, and David—by his side, buying and selling properties. The sons added their vision to the growing company, realizing that the postwar years would stimulate the need for more office space. In the 1950s Seymour emerged as the leader of the Durst Organization, quietly buying up properties at key sites throughout the city, mostly in Midtown along Third Avenue, changing the focus of the family business from buying and managing properties to building skyscrapers. David ran the construction end of the business, while Royal was in charge of management.

Seymour was exceptionally clever at piecing together smaller property purchases to create parcels large enough for erecting skyscrapers. If there was a butcher's store that he felt he needed to buy to own a whole block, he'd walk into the store himself—dressed down—and ask how much the owner would want in order to sell. If the price was right he'd buy it. The last thing he wanted was to give the owner the impression of wealth. He'd also buy up crucial properties just to keep other developers from improving them.

By 1982, the Durst Organization was worth an estimated $500 million, owners of forty commercial buildings and forty-six residential apartment buildings. Some of their major holdings included the Lorillard building, the Random House building, the Conover-Mast building, and the Harcourt Brace Jovanovich building, all in Midtown.

The Durst Organization was now one of the top five real-estate-development companies in the city, and Seymour was one of the city's kings.

In May 1980, *New York* magazine pictured the diminutive Seymour on its cover, sharing space with other powerful developers like Harry Helmsley and Donald

Trump under the headline THE MEN WHO OWN NEW YORK.

The story suggested their real estate holdings made these men the most important people in New York, and they were treated as such, sought after for their apartments, office spaces, and generous campaign contributions.

Their political contacts reached the highest levels of government, and it gave them enormous power, which was needed in their sometimes never-ending battles over regulations, zoning laws, taxes, and building codes.

They employed an entire subculture of former city and state officials to do their bidding, gaining influence wherever they could, influence that was required as the New York skyline changed with each passing decade and each multimillion-dollar deal.

Along with his business prowess, Seymour was known as an expert on New York City, having amassed an impressive collection of some ten thousand books, pictures, and maps, all of which centered on the city he truly loved. He called the collection the Old York Library.

Each Saturday morning he could be seen leaving his town house for a visit with a dealer to examine some new artifact or photograph or book. He was a little man with a big checkbook, and he was willing to buy most anything.

His four-story town house was literally covered, every inch of every wall, with his collection. Students of New York City history were simply fascinated with what was universally considered the best collection of books on the city.

Seymour was considered brilliant, yet was known for several peculiar habits, one of which was buying space, or small advertisements, on the bottom of the front page of the *New York Times,* touting, among other things, the virtues of Robert Moses, the master builder who was also responsible for much of the regions' road network. "Resurrect one Moses—or the other" read one ad. He'd write letters to newspapers and local public officials, expressing his disdain for Section Eight requirements, which he believed would lower property values, and for new laws that hampered construction.

Despite his prominence, Seymour's career was not without his controversies. In 1972 the Durst Organization was identified as one of several large developers that owned buildings in the Times Square area, which leased space to massage parlors, peep shows, and brothels. Four years later Seymour was asked to step down from a committee charged with cleaning up Times Square after it was learned that the Luxor Baths, a notorious massage parlor, operated in a Durst-owned building.

Durst sold the building to the Luxor Baths' owners, resigned from the committee, and dropped out of the public eye.

Seymour also endured great tragedy. On his own, he raised four children—Robert, Douglas, Wendy, and Tom—after his wife, Bernice, fell from the roof of their Scarsdale, New York, home in 1950. Seymour would always describe it as a tragic accident. His wife was taking medication to curb her asthma, became disoriented, climbed onto the roof, and fell to her death.

Seymour never remarried, instead devoting his life to building his business and raising his children, two of whom, Robert and Douglas, were now working for him.

Both sons managed Durst properties. Robert was given the task of overseeing residential buildings and commercial properties, including several hotels earmarked for future development. It was a midlevel job within the organization. He collected rents and attended to the daily management of the properties.

Of Seymour's four children Robert was the most troubled. As a child, he had witnessed the death of his mother and had later developed an intense rage, expressed particularly toward his father, whom he blamed for her death. Robert was sent for psychiatric counseling, which appeared to quiet his anger.

Their relationship remained somewhat cool, though Robert joined his father in the Durst Organization in 1973, at the age of thirty, after he married Kathleen McCormack.

Like his father, Robert was a private man. He said little in public and, aside from his difficulties following his mother's death, had never been cause for concern for his father.

Until now.

With the Durst name plastered all over the newspapers, Seymour made it clear to all that this was Robert's problem.

He would handle it.

7

THE phones in the detectives' squad room at the Twentieth Precinct were ringing out a never-ending cascade of noise, nearly all of the calls coming from a frenzied media, which had firmly latched onto the Kathie Durst story. It was on every newsstand, morning TV news show, and all-news radio station in the New York area.

Civilian employees answered the phones while Gibbons sat on the edge of a desk in the middle of the room, having called a meeting to review the case with Struk and a half-dozen other detectives, including John Kelly, Eddie Regan, and Sergeant Tom Brady.

Gibbons said the papers reported only part of the story, that eyewitnesses had spotted Kathie Durst in Manhattan, and that she had called in sick to school on Monday.

"As we know, if you read the papers today, Mrs. Durst is the daughter-in-law of Mr. Seymour Durst, a very influential New Yorker. Of course, that doesn't mean shit to us, but it does to our bosses. Mrs. Durst was last seen Monday morning in Manhattan hailing a cab. She's a medical student at the Albert Einstein

School in the Bronx. Struk has all the details. Let's jump on this quickly, and please, don't talk to any reporters. Refer them to me. Okay, meeting's over."

A couple of the other detectives, Kelly and Regan, pulled Struk aside, asking about Bobby Durst, wondering why he'd waited five days before reporting his wife missing.

"Put it this way, they weren't Ozzie and Harriet," said Struk.

The squad room cleared out quickly as six detectives headed outside, some to the Riverside Drive area to check local bars and restaurants, others to the apartment at East Eighty-sixth Street. Struk stayed behind to work the phones and await the task-force detectives, who were due in around the same time Struk received a call from Kathie's brother, Jim McCormack.

Struk remembered the conversation he'd had on Saturday with Jim, the big brother who was preoccupied with a new baby and didn't seem overly concerned that his sister might have been in trouble.

But now, with Kathie's picture on the front pages of the papers, he was worried.

His sister Mary had woken him up that morning. She was sobbing uncontrollably, spitting mostly unrecognizable words, except for the dozen or so times she mentioned Bobby's name.

Jim was less concerned with Mary and his other sisters, Carol and Virginia, than he was with his mother, whom he called after hanging up with Mary.

Ann was sitting at her small kitchen table sipping a cup of tea and staring out the window when the phone rang. She was calm, the news stories having less effect on her than they had on her children.

"You know I spoke to the detective over the weekend, Jim," she told her son.

"I know, Mom. I think, with the stories in the paper, it's hitting everyone pretty hard."

"We need to have faith, Jim. Let's have faith that she went somewhere to clear her mind. Medical school is very difficult. Let's have faith she'll soon come back, with a big, happy smile."

"Mom, it wasn't medical school that was bothering her. It was her husband. You know that. If she ran, it was because of him. And when she comes back, she's going to have to leave him. Understand?"

Ann didn't respond. Divorce wasn't an option in her mind. Married couples always stuck it out, even if only one of the spouses was Catholic.

Jim left it alone and promised his mother he'd call her later in the day, or earlier if there was any news.

Two hours later he was on the phone with Mike Struk and he had a story to tell, something he'd failed to tell Struk when they first spoke on Saturday.

"Detective, my sister gave me a folder to mail several months ago. Inside, there were documents, Bobby's tax returns and other financial statements," said Jim. "She wanted me to send them to her lawyer. She said Bobby had falsified his income tax statements and she was going to use this to get her settlement."

"What settlement?"

"Her divorce settlement. She hired an attorney and was planning to file for divorce."

"You're telling me that your sister was filing for a divorce?"

"Yeah, she gave me a folder and told me to send it with Purolator Courier. It went to her first lawyer, but nothing came of it. Kathie said the lawyer was bought off by Bobby, so she hired another attorney."

"Who was the first attorney?"

"I don't remember."

"Who was the second attorney?"

"Her name is Dale Ragus."

"When did your sister serve Bobby with papers?"

"She didn't," said Jim. "She was planning to, but never did. She should have. That guy has some problems."

"What kind of problems?"

"Aside from the violence? He's loaded, right? Has

more money than God, yet he has this thing for shop-lifting. He just takes stuff. Remember that last transit strike? Kathie told me Bobby would go down to the lobby of their building and take the tenants' bicycles. He'd just take them downtown to work and leave them there. I think it's all that pot he smokes."

"How much?"

"At least several joints a day. He's addicted to the stuff."

———

THAT same morning, some thirty miles to the northeast of Manhattan in Fairfield County, Connecticut, Eleanor Schwank was desperately trying to get her two children through breakfast and off to school when she received a call from Gilberte Najamy, who was beside herself.

"Did you see the paper? Did you see the paper?" screamed Gilberte.

"No," said Eleanor.

"Go get the *Daily News*! She's on the front page! Bobby is offering a one-hundred-thousand-dollar reward!"

"What? Who's in the paper?"

"It's Kathie, it's Kathie!"

Eleanor asked Gilberte to read the story.

"It says that Bobby went to the police on Friday and that she was last seen in Manhattan on Monday, February first. An elevator guy saw her after she called in sick to her school."

"Where, what elevator guy saw her?"

"Riverside Drive, the penthouse. He took her up."

"And Bobby went to the police? Where?"

"The Twentieth Precinct, Detective Michael Struk is investigating. They're saying it's a missing-persons case. It says Bobby's offering a one-hundred-thousand-dollar reward to find her!"

"No, no, no!" said Eleanor, who then hung up the phone, ran out of her house with her two children, dropped them off at school, then stopped by a grocery store for copies of the *News* and *Post*. She raced home and called Gilberte.

Eleanor, like Gilberte, had met Kathie Durst while studying nursing at Western Connecticut State College in Danbury. Eleanor was ten years older than her friends and married, with two small children. Over the past week Eleanor, Gilberte, and two other friends, Kathy Traystman and Ellen Strauss, had spoken every day on the phone, hoping for some news of Kathie.

Now Eleanor held the papers out in front of her.

"How did they get these photos of Kathie?"

"I got them," said Gilberte, who told Eleanor she had traveled into Manhattan on Monday with pictures of Kathie and visited the *News* and the *Post,* hoping they might publish her photograph somewhere in the paper.

Gilberte said she had no idea Kathie's smiling face would be on page one.

Eleanor was equally surprised, not that the photos were on page one but that Gilberte had gone into New York the day before without telling her.

Gilberte had other secrets about her friend Kathie Durst; some she knew she could never reveal to Eleanor, others she was ready to disclose.

"Eleanor, I went to the house."

"What house?"

"South Salem. I broke in Sunday night. I threw a rock through the side door, broke the window, and let myself in."

"No, you didn't do that. Please don't tell me you did that."

Gilberte described, in detail, how she had gone to the stone cottage with her sister, Fadwa, arriving around 7 P.M. She rang the bell, but no one answered. She returned to the car and sat there for forty-five minutes. She wanted to get into the house, and told her sister she was going to break in. Fadwa tried to talk Gilberte out of it, but Gilberte was like a woman possessed. She got out of the car and walked through the snow and around to the side door. It was dark, the only faint light coming from several homes on the other side of Lake Truesdale.

Gilberte pushed away some snow from the ground and picked up a rock. She looked around, then flung the rock through the door window. She reached in and turned the lock, opened the door, and let herself in.

"Are you crazy?" said Eleanor.

"Eleanor, you have to hear this," said Gilberte, who continued her story. She had been inside the house many times before and knew the layout well. It was small, to some people claustrophobically so, maybe 1,200 square feet in total. The kitchen, dining room, living room, and bedroom on the main floor, another bedroom and mud-room downstairs, which offered access to the backyard and pier.

While Gilberte was in the mudroom she looked inside the washing machine and dryer. They were empty. She checked the hamper, hoping to find Kathie's sweatpants and sweatshirt, the clothes she'd worn to her party on Sunday.

The clothes weren't there.

Gilberte then walked upstairs and through the bed-room, living room, and kitchen. Everything seemed to be in order. Najamy was looking for something, any sign of a struggle, maybe even blood. But the house was crisp and clean. As Gilberte tiptoed around the kitchen, she noticed there was mail inside a plastic garbage can next to the sink. She reached over and picked it up. Her eyes opened wide. It was Kathie's mail. And it was unopened.

"Why would Bobby throw out her mail?"

"I don't know. But I found something, a small sheet of paper. It was an itinerary of some kind, in Bobby's scribbled handwriting. It listed days and times, from Monday to Wednesday. And I found a receipt for boots Bobby bought on February third."

"Why would he write up an itinerary?" said Eleanor.

Gilberte didn't have any answers. More important to her was the condition of the house.

"Eleanor, I think there's something very wrong. The

house was clean. Too clean, pristine. It looked like someone even scrubbed the floors."

Kathie wasn't much of a housekeeper, that much was certain, often leaving clothes lying around or dishes in the sink.

"What about the housekeeper? What's her name? Janet. Janet Finke."

"I don't know. But I've never seen the house like this," said Gilberte. "There's more, Eleanor. I spoke with Bobby this morning. He said the reward was really ten thousand dollars. Somehow the papers screwed it up. He also said he was devastated."

"Cheap bastard. That's all she's worth to him?" said Eleanor. "And he's not the least bit 'devastated.' I don't believe it."

"He thinks she had some kind of breakdown."

"No, Gilberte. He killed her. I know he did."

————

MICHAEL Burns sat inside the small, mirrored room, tapping his forefinger on the thick wooden table under the watchful eye of Mike Struk.

Burns had been summoned to the Twentieth Precinct by Struk, who called Burns at his Mount Vernon home the day before. Burns knew the request to talk about Kathie Durst was more like a command, so he obliged.

Before the meeting Struk had run a background check that showed Burns had no criminal record. As he sat there tapping his finger on the table, Burns looked around the room while Struk pretended to be reading through a file. He wanted Burns to be nervous. The first few questions were perfunctory, such as age and occupation. Burns said he was thirty-two years old and unemployed.

"So, tell me how you met Mrs. Durst."

"At a party, at the Dursts' penthouse, last summer."

"Who invited you to the party?"

"I don't remember."

"You became friendly with Mrs. Durst?"

"Yeah. She seemed lonely. We went out for dinner a couple of times."

"Did you ever spend the night with her?"

"You mean did I fuck her? No. I spent a couple of nights there, but that was because I was too drunk to go home. We were just friends."

"Did you ever supply Mrs. Durst with cocaine?"

Burns crunched his lips together, turned his head, and rolled his eyes.

"Detective, don't waste my time. You called me down here, so just ask me your questions. Did we ever have sex? No. Do I deal drugs? No. Did Kathie do drugs? Yes. She used a lot of cocaine, maybe two, three grams a week. Where she got it, I don't know. Did she have a fucked-up marriage? Yes. Bobby Durst is an asshole. He was beating the shit out of her. She kept talking about leaving him, but she never did. She had the other apartment on Eighty-sixth Street. She'd use that sometimes. But she stayed with him, even after she found out about his affair."

"And what affair was that?" said Struk.

"Prudence Farrow. She's the sister of that actress, Mia Farrow. You know, the Beatles song 'Dear Prudence'? Bobby was plugging her."

"Mrs. Durst told you that?"

"Yeah, she said Prudence would call her at home demanding that she let Bobby go. It fucked her up."

"Is this recent?"

"Maybe a few months ago. I think Bobby was pretty hot and heavy with Farrow. At least that's what Kathie said. She had enough. She wanted out. But she wanted some money out of it and Bobby said no. She had nothing, not even a dime. She wanted a settlement, but he wouldn't even give her money to live on. She's married to a millionaire and begging her friends for a few bucks. It was pathetic."

"I understand you told one of Mrs. Durst's friends to just leave her alone, that—what were your words?—that 'she's had enough.' "

"I told that to Gilberte Najamy. She kept pushing Kathie to get a divorce. She was a wreck. She thought Bobby would kill her. I wish I knew where Kathie was right now. I'd tell her to stay there."

Struk nodded, closed his file, and thanked Burns for coming in. Burns left the precinct with the understanding that he might be called again for more questioning.

Upstairs, in the squad room, Gibbons was ending his phone conversation with attorney Dale Ragus. Struk had called her earlier in the day at her office, wanting to talk about the documents Jim McCormack had sent her.

Gibbons handled the interview with Ragus himself, one of the many reasons he was so well liked by his men. Interviews and other legwork were usually left to the rank and file. But Gibbons was different. He didn't mind getting his hands dirty. Instead of telling Ragus to call back later, he grabbed a notebook and pencil and began asking questions.

Ragus said she was with the firm of Milbank, Tweed, Hadley and McCloy, a major New York law firm, and had been Kathie's attorney since June 1981. Kathie was in the midst of a protracted negotiation on a divorce settlement, a negotiation that was heavily one-sided.

"She wanted what she thought to be a reasonable settlement given they were married for eight years," said Ragus.

"How much?"

"Around four hundred and fifty thousand dollars."

That was a drop in the bucket for a guy like Bobby Durst, thought Gibbons. Why would he hold out?

Ragus couldn't answer that question. She said that in recent months Kathie had feared for her life, and relayed to Ragus harrowing stories of beatings and mental abuse.

"She thought he would kill her," said Ragus.

"Can you tell me about the documents her brother sent you?"

"Lieutenant, I wish I could, but that's attorney/client privilege. I can tell you this, Lieutenant. Kathie was scared. She was very scared of her husband. And for good reason. Do you know about the dogs?"

"What dogs?"

"Kathie said her husband has a dog, Igor. It's a husky, or something like that. Igor is the fifth or sixth dog he's had. The others died. Kathie said they all died from mysterious deaths. One choked, another accidentally drowned, and so on."

"Did she say he killed them?"

"She didn't know. But the way she told the story, if I was a dog, I wouldn't want Bobby Durst as my master."

8

OF the approximately two hundred assistant district attorneys working in the office of Robert Morganthau, the district attorney for New York County, Mike Struk trusted but one, Roger Hayes.

An affable fellow, Hayes had developed a sterling reputation as an effective prosecutor, having joined the DA's office in 1971, three years after graduating from the New York University School of Law.

At thirty-eight, Hayes had already served as the chief of the frauds bureau and chief of legal systems analysis. He was now chief of the trial division. When Struk called him several days earlier, the first words out of Hayes's mouth were, "I see you're up to your ears in that Durst shit."

Struk laughed, then asked Hayes for a meeting.

"This *is* about Durst?" said Hayes.

"Yes, but we'll talk about it in your office," said Struk.

Struk's call to Hayes followed a disturbing visit from Gilberte Najamy, whom Struk immediately determined to be one of the least attractive women he'd ever met.

Gilberte was thin, with long, dark, stringy hair, wore

black combat boots, and had a very direct, confrontational manner. Struk took her for an adult version of a tomboy.

Gilberte had called earlier, saying she had some important information but could only deliver it in person. When she arrived at the Twentieth Precinct later that morning, she sat down next to Struk's desk and handed him two pieces of paper.

"Where did you get these?"

"On Sunday. I broke into the house."

"You did what?" said Struk, sitting back in his chair. He remembered the front-page story the day before in the *New York Post* about a break-in at the Durst's South Salem house, the paper surmising it had something to do with Kathie's disappearance. Bobby wouldn't talk to the *Post,* but the paper reported that his younger brother Doug subsequently changed the locks on the house.

"What possessed you to pull a stunt like that?"

"Something's wrong," said Gilberte. "Bobby's been hitting Kathie and threatening her. I really feel something happened, and we just can't sit by. We have to do something."

"We're not sitting by. This is an active investigation, and you're not a police officer, so I would suggest that you stay on the sidelines and let us do our work. I don't think it's helpful if you're breaking into people's homes. That sounds pretty extreme."

Gilberte wasn't listening to Struk's lecture. He wasn't telling her what she wanted to hear. She thought there would, at the least, be a congratulatory comment like "good job." But Struk was stern in his warning to stay away from the South Salem home.

"What else have you done that I should know about?"

"Well, I took the same train Kathie took that Sunday night. The nine-seventeen out of Katonah. I boarded it after I broke into the house. There were only two cars and I had pictures of Kathie. But no one recognized her, not the conductor or anyone else on that train. And most of the people who take that train are regular commuters," said Gilberte.

Struk looked at the two papers. One was a receipt from a shoe store. Bobby had used his credit card to buy a pair of $300 boots on Wednesday, February 3.

The other paper had "itinerary" written on the top.

The handwriting was scribbled, but Struk could make out each word.

Mon	10 a.m. Ridgefield coffee
	2 Marshall Bradde
	4—apt get hat
	5—office
	7—film or whatever
Tues	2 am S Salem
	—7 am leave house
	—drive
	8—garage
	8—apt-Oscar mail
	9—sleep
Wed	10 am bought boots
	11 am kennel
	12 am home
	2 pm lunch
	4 PO box

"Both pieces of paper were in the garbage," said Gilberte.

"Throwing out her mail?" said Struk.

"Yeah, some bills and junk stuff. They were never opened. And the house, it was really clean. I'd never seen it so clean," said Gilberte.

"What's that tell you?"

"I don't know. But something isn't right here. That itinerary. That's Bobby's handwriting. Why would he write down where he was all week?"

"That's a good question. But a question for me to find answers to."

Before leaving, Gilberte asked Struk if he heard the Peter Schwartz story.

Struk said yes, and that he checked Bobby's records for any prior arrests, but there were none.

"That's because the charges were dismissed. Peter had sued Bobby and they settled. Kathie went nuts. She called Peter the night she disappeared, when she was at my house before. She didn't know it was over. She couldn't believe it. All she kept saying was the Dursts always win."

Struk thanked Gilberte for bringing the papers to his attention and reminded her to stay away from the South Salem home. As Gilberte left the precinct, she was convinced that Struk was a dimwit.

Struk studied the itinerary, then returned to a report from the task-force detectives. They had interviewed the couple who lived in the adjoining penthouse on Riverside Drive, Kevin and Ann Doyle, and they had a Kathie Durst story that was, at the least, disturbing.

The Doyles reported that the previous November they had been lying in bed watching television when they heard a pounding sound. It was Kathie Durst, and she was banging on their window, in her pajamas, sobbing uncontrollably and screaming for help. They let her in and sat her down. She explained that she had jumped out of a window in her apartment, climbed over a wall that divided their patios, walked along a balcony, and sought refuge. She and Bobby had been arguing about a woman he was seeing, Prudence Farrow, and he had hit her twice, his hand curled into a fist. Kathie remained with Ann and Kevin until midnight, when Kevin went next door to speak with Bobby, who acknowledged that he and Kathie had argued, but said he never hit her.

Struk could only shake his head when he read that Kathie had gone back to Bobby after assuring the neighbors that she'd be fine.

The Doyles stood in the hallway after Bobby closed the door, expecting to hear a loud outburst.

There was none.

After talking with Gilberte Najamy, Struk called the New York State Police and spoke with Investigator Stan Roman, who agreed to meet him at the home of Bill and Ruth Mayer, who lived in South Salem next door to the Dursts' home.

The Mayers had known Bobby and Kathie since 1976, when the Dursts bought the cottage. The new neighbors became friendly and socialized on occasion, though the Mayers had no idea they were socializing with the heir to one of New York's great real estate empires.

Bobby insisted on maintaining a low-key lifestyle, driving older cars, wearing old clothes. And when Bobby and Kathie entertained, they served hot dogs and cheese.

During the summers the Mayers would see Bobby in his canoe, paddling on Lake Truesdale. He was nice enough to make small talk, though their conversations usually didn't last long.

Kathie was far more personable. Always cheerful, she would stop over for long conversations. The Mayers had a young daughter, just a toddler, who adored Kathie, who'd take time out to play with the girl.

Kathie had wanted children of her own, but confided to Ruth that Bobby made it clear he didn't want any. She told Ruth about her pregnancy in 1976 and how Bobby demanded she have an abortion.

Within a year the Mayers learned of Bobby's wealth, and as summers came and went, they watched their neighbors' marriage disintegrate. They heard through Kathie that Bobby was having an affair with Prudence Farrow, and Kathie confided to Ruth that she, too, had an affair going, with a medical student at Einstein. Kathie was also indulging in drugs and drinking and socializing with her cleaning lady, Janet Finke. Finke was younger than Kathie, blond, and just as pretty. One summer afternoon, during a chat while sitting on the grass behind the Dursts' home, Kathie told Ruth that she and

Janet had gone to a party hosted by Hugh Hefner. It was at the Playboy Mansion in Los Angeles.

"She said it was wild. I asked her what did that mean, lots of sex and drugs? She would only smile and say it was absolutely wild," said Ruth.

The last time Ruth saw Kathie was a week before she disappeared. She had come up to South Salem for the weekend, alone. Ruth was hosting a small afternoon party and invited Kathie to come over. As soon as she arrived, she began drinking full glasses of wine, chugging them down like soda pop.

"She was just excessive on the wine and coke. She looked lost and distraught," said Ruth.

Early that evening Ruth said she and Bill, along with another couple, the Picards, decided to have dinner at a local restaurant.

"Kathie asked if she could join us. You could see she was scared to be alone. She came along and all she did was drink and talk, talk all night long about Bobby. She drank two bottles of champagne. Then she said she did something she shouldn't have done," said Ruth.

"What was that?" said Struk.

"She said she told Bob she was going to reveal family secrets if she didn't get more money. Stuff about Bob signing their tax returns and her stock transfers. She wanted a settlement. But the second she told us, she knew she crossed the line. You could see it. She was terrified."

"And she was too drunk to drive home," said Bill. "When she ordered the champagne she told us not to worry about it, that she'd pay for it. But when the check came she just put on her coat and walked out of the restaurant. I wouldn't let her drive, so I took her car and Ruth followed."

"When was the last time you saw Bobby?" said Struk.

Bill and Ruth looked at each other.

"He came by Thursday afternoon, the day before he reported Kathie missing. He stopped by to ask if we had seen Kathie," said Bill. "He said she was missing and he didn't know where she was."

"I heard that and said, 'Oh, my God.' I knew something had happened," said Ruth.

"What do you think happened?" said Struk.

"Oh, God. The way Kathie was talking, she was terrified. And Bobby has a horrible temper. I don't want to even think he could have done something to her," said Ruth.

Roman, the investigator with the state police, joined the meeting after taking a walk around the outside of the Durst home. He sat down next to Struk and said he hadn't seen anything unusual, except for the broken window on the back door.

Struk knew this was the work of Gilberte Najamy, so he didn't pay much attention.

Ruth continued to talk, telling Struk she remembered seeing a strange blue light coming from the room downstairs, near where the door was broken.

"It was a couple of days before Bobby reported Kathie had disappeared, which was—what? A Friday? I must have seen the light that Tuesday, it was in the middle of the night. I'd never seen it before, and I haven't seen it since," said Ruth. "Are you going to look in the house?"

"It's my understanding two state troopers were inside the house and didn't see anything unusual. Besides, she made it into Manhattan," said Struk, who showed the Mayers the composite of the mystery man who had visited Kathie that Sunday night.

The Mayers didn't recognize him.

Struk had shown the composite to all of Kathie's friends and family, but no one could identify the face. They couldn't even suggest someone who looked familiar.

The mystery man was just that, a mystery, as were the whereabouts of Kathie Durst.

WHEN Struk arrived at Hayes's office downtown on Tuesday, February 16, accompanied by two detectives from the Detective Bureau of Manhattan and a third detective from the Manhattan Task Force, he and Hayes exchanged warm handshakes. After Struk settled into his chair, he got right to the point.

"Roger, I want to drop Bobby Durst's phone lines. I think something's screwy here. I need paper," said Struk.

Struk asked Hayes to subpoena Bobby's telephone records at his two residences at 37 Riverside Drive and 12 East Eighty-sixth Street. He also wanted the records from Bobby's office at the Durst Organization's headquarters at 1133 Avenue of the Americas. In addition, Struk wanted the records from Jacobi Hospital, where Kathie was admitted in January.

"The guy came to us to report his wife missing, then says he thinks she's having an affair with some drug dealer. I'm now thinking it's all bullshit. Their marriage was on the rocks, she wants a settlement, he's not giving in. He's having an affair with another woman and he's apparently beating the shit out of his wife, who's all coked up thinking he's going to kill her. I need paper."

"You know she could just be paranoid from all the cocaine. How much was she doing?"

"A couple of grams a week, maybe more."

"Jesus," said Hayes, who agreed there was probable cause and said he'd sign off.

The two men shook hands and promised to get together for a beer in the near future.

Struk was happy. He had his paper.

He headed uptown to the Riverside Drive penthouse. Bobby agreed to allow the Crime Scene Unit to examine the apartment. Unlike a walk-through, like the one Struk had taken before, this would be a complete search. The CSU investigators brought luminol, a chemical used to find trace elements of blood, spraying it in a sweeping motion in various spots. If blood was present, it would glow.

Bobby was there, and handed Struk what he said was a ransom note.

It was postmarked February 10, 1982. The letter was vague, demanded an unspecified amount of cash, and instructed Bobby to stay by his phone for further instructions. Struk didn't think much of the letter, which seemed to be a prank.

Bobby watched as the CSU team visited each room. He was his usual aloof, quiet self. If he was distraught, as Struk had read in the papers, he was doing a lousy job maintaining that appearance.

"I read you hired a private eye. Any luck?" said Struk, trying to engage Bobby in casual conversation.

"No. I'm sure if he comes across any information he'll pass it along to you," said Bobby.

As the CSU team searched through the bedroom, Struk excused himself and walked back into the living room. He looked over toward the closet by the door, but the coat was gone.

It was the weirdest thing. A Burberry raincoat, something he'd noticed earlier in the week when he entered the penthouse with Mary Hughes, Kathie's sister, and Mary's friend Geraldine McInerney. Mary had a key to the penthouse and was desperate to look inside after learning that Bobby tried to sublet the East Eighty-sixth Street apartment on February 4, the day before he reported Kathie missing. Mary also discovered, from one of the building maintenance men, that Bobby had tossed Kathie's belongings from that apartment down the building trash chute. He threw so much stuff down there, a building employee had to remind him the trash disposal was for garbage only. Mary then called Struk, who agreed to accompany the women to the penthouse.

Mary knew the doorman, who told her that Bobby had left for work that morning. She told him she was taking her sister's jewelry. The doorman recognized Struk and let them pass through.

Mary, Geraldine, and Struk walked through each room, and the only odd thing they noticed was the coat that hung on the closet door. Geraldine said it was an expensive coat, and it looked like it had been placed in a washing machine, which didn't make sense.

"You don't wash a coat like that," said Geraldine, who estimated it to be worth around $600.

But now the coat was gone. Struk walked over to the closet and opened the door. It wasn't there either.

The CSU team finished up its search of the apartment, which was clean, though Struk had known the outcome in advance. He thanked Bobby for his continued cooperation during this very difficult time and said he'd be in touch.

When he returned to his office there were more than two dozen messages waiting for him. Some were from people he knew, others were people calling with information on the Durst case. The Durst calls had come in at a steady clip since the stories in the *Daily News* and *Post*. People were reporting "Kathie sightings" all over town. Two detectives were sent to a coffee shop on Thirty-ninth Street, where a waitress claimed Kathie had had breakfast after she supposedly disappeared. Even the Secret Service called, saying some of its operatives had found a disoriented woman at the World Trade Center who fit the description of Kathie Durst. Struk also heard from several psychics, one of whom said she "saw" three men drop garbage bags into the East River. Kathie Durst's body was in those bags, the psychic claimed.

The sightings were quickly discounted. The investigation pressed ahead, though little new information was coming forward. To make matters worse, by the middle of March, Bobby Durst stopped returning Struk's calls.

9

THE tears rolled down Mike Struk's cheeks, rushing to his jaw and falling from his chin.

He was sitting in the bathroom, the door closed, crying quietly. He could hear the police scanner in the background, the voices interrupted by loud squawks and beeps.

His thoughts were with his children, who were up in Middletown with their mother. He missed them terribly, and there were plenty of days when he'd tell someone he was going to the can when in fact he'd sit on the bowl, close the door, and cry his eyes out.

One particularly long sobbing session ended with Struk waiting several minutes for his eyes to clear before leaving the bathroom.

Gibbons, like the rest of the squad, knew about Struk's divorce, but never pried. Convinced that Struk had made it out of the bathroom in one emotional piece, the lieutenant handed him an envelope.

It was the medical records Roger Hayes had subpoenaed from Jacobi Hospital.

Struk's longing for his kids was quickly replaced by

his longing for the information that was in the file, which he consumed.

It was the first bit of new information to come along in several weeks. The investigation had all but stalled, even after Struk and a host of other detectives from the Twentieth Precinct and the Manhattan Task Force had tracked down every lead, followed up on every phone call, and even spoke with soothsayers and psychics. Struk studied the records, which stated that Kathie had checked into Jacobi Hospital during the early afternoon of January 2, 1982. She told the doctors she had been beaten by her husband. An examination determined she had a history of blunt trauma to the left side of the face.

When the doctors pressed her for information, Kathie admitted that she wasn't just slapped, but punched, and several times. She was bruised, but the outward markings were faint. She had pressure and tightness over her left cheek and eye. The doctors gave her Tylenol and advice to find a new husband.

The records confirmed what everyone was saying, that Bobby was beating his wife. And not just slapping her, but using her as a punching bag.

A real scumbag, thought Struk, who felt the strong urge to go down to Bobby's Sixth Avenue office in the middle of the afternoon, police lights flashing, the press surrounding the front entrance, and march Bobby out in handcuffs. But Gibbons called him into his office.

Struk was told to set up a meeting downtown at police headquarters.

———

"WHAT'S your name?"

"Eddie Lopez."

"What's your occupation?"

"I work as a building employee at Thirty-seven Riverside Drive."

"Were you working the evening of Sunday, January thirty-first?"

"Yes."

Lopez sat in a darkened room at One Police Plaza, answering questions from Millie Markman, the NYPD's hypnotist.

Mike Struk sat off to the side, in the darkness and out of view, his head resting on one hand, his eyes closed.

He had driven Lopez downtown at the request of Gibbons, whose superiors had suggested hypnosis. The New York media continued to cover the Kathie Durst story, running pieces every week, theorizing that Kathie met foul play at the hands of a mystery man who entered her apartment that Sunday night, the last day of January. Was he a friend, a lover, or perhaps a drug dealer?

The brass were still paying attention, and "suggested" hypnosis.

Struk thought it was a colossal waste of time.

"You fucking kidding me?" he said when Gibbons told him to set up the appointment with Markman.

Struk hated the idea, but realized he had no choice, so he agreed to draw up the questions. They were all standard. Did you ever see the man before? Can you describe him? What did Kathie say when she opened the door? Did she look drunk or sick?

He wanted to add a few other questions. Are you really hypnotized? Do you know who killed JFK?

As Lopez was "put under," Struk sat there, unimpressed, privately wondering if Markman could hypnotize a banana.

Lopez's story, supposedly under hypnosis, was the same as it had been before: he took Kathie up to her apartment around 11 P.M. and soon after a white male, about thirty-five, clean-cut with a good build and short black hair and a neat black mustache, paid her a visit.

Struk thanked Markman for her wasted efforts, drove Lopez to Riverside Drive, then returned to the Twentieth Precinct.

"How did it go?" said Gibbons.

Struk was flippant. "We solved the case," he said, walking straight to his desk.

Gibbons said nothing, wondering only what Struk would do next.

―――――

MARY Hughes's East Side apartment was filled with family and a few close friends. The mood was somber, conversation reduced to a whisper. Mary's husband, Tom, a New York City fireman, handed Jim McCormack a beer while Ann McCormack sat on the end of a sofa, paying little attention to the discussion that centered on her son-in-law.

Ann was lost in thought. Kathie was her youngest daughter, her baby, the teenage runway model who left her Long Island home when she was nineteen to begin a new life in Manhattan working as a dental assistant.

Kathie had always been spunky, and prone to rash behavior, especially after her father died in 1966 when she was just fourteen. So it wasn't surprising to Ann when Kathie announced not only that she had found an apartment, but that she had a boyfriend, an older man. Ann didn't know what to make of Bobby Durst. He seemed nice enough. He was quiet, reserved, though he never showered Kathie with affection. He was also Jewish, which didn't quite endear him to Ann's heart. She was Irish-Catholic and believed in family and the Church, and not necessarily in that order.

So when Ann finally asked Kathie what it was she saw in her new boyfriend, Kathie smiled and talked about how sweet and kind and sensitive Bobby was.

"And Mom," said Kathie. "He's rich."

When Kathie announced in January 1972 that she was moving with Bobby to Vermont after only two dates, Ann was less than thrilled. Catholics don't live together, she said; they get married. But Kathie moved anyway, and for the next year she helped Bobby run his health-food store in Rutland, which he named All Good Things.

Bobby liked the rural setting, away from the city and his father's hand. Kathie enjoyed managing the store. During their free time they would go for long walks in the woods, and long drives through the back roads of Maine and New Hampshire.

When Bobby decided to sell the store in December, they returned to New York and moved into a home in Westchester County that Bobby's father, Seymour, owned. They didn't stay there long, deciding to pick up and drive south in Bobby's Volkswagen bus, traveling through South Carolina and Florida. The young couple would spend their nights at low-budget motels or camping spots, making love in a sleeping bag.

Sometimes Bobby would go out on his own, leaving Kathie alone for hours. She'd ask him where he'd been, but he was usually evasive, saying he just needed some quiet time to himself.

In 1973, after returning to New York, the couple decided to marry, though Ann remembered the "popping of the question" was more like a "let's try this out."

The only real commitment Bobby made, aside from saying "I do" was "if it doesn't work out in three years, we'll get a divorce."

Kathie didn't mind the arrangement. And she didn't even mind the small, low-key wedding ceremony in Bedford, New York, on April 12, which was Bobby's birthday. Only Seymour and Ann were present when the couple exchanged their vows before a justice of the peace, the foursome then celebrating at a restaurant in Greenwich, Connecticut.

Kathie didn't complain when her mother paid for her own meal.

The honeymoon was another motor tour, this time a six-month journey cross-country. Bobby wrote off part of the trip as a business expense, saying he stopped off to examine Durst properties, though the Dursts didn't own any properties in Middle America. He also confided to Kathie during one of their long daily drives that he didn't have a Ph.D. in economics from UCLA, as he had claimed. He asked Kathie not to tell anyone, including his family. It would be their secret.

The McCormacks were happy for Kathie. She was

young, and she was now wealthy. Her new husband went to work for his father while Kathie attended nursing school in Connecticut. They ate out three, four times a week, usually at fine restaurants, and they traveled often, to the Caribbean, Europe, South America, and Asia.

Despite Kathie's good fortune and new life, there would be problems in her new marriage, and they centered around her unpredictable, erratic husband.

While Ann McCormack knew her daughter was not happy in her marriage, sister Mary was privy to the deepest, darkest secrets. And now Mary was sitting there, across from her mother, immersed in her own thoughts.

Mary knew things could have been different. That Kathie, like the Irish girl that she was, wanted to have children. But Bobby had made it clear that this wasn't an option. He didn't want to be a father, even though for some reason he gave in to Kathie's desire to investigate the possibility of adoption. It was a whim, he thought, something she'd get out of her system, and he didn't object when she made an appointment for an interview.

But making the appointment was one thing. Talking during the interview was another, and while driving home after the interview Bobby suggested that Kathie should follow his lead at future meetings. He didn't like the tone of the conversation and didn't want to make any kind of commitment. When Kathie disagreed with his suggestion, he poured a water bottle over her head as he was driving.

Kathie said nothing that night, and remained quiet two years later when, in 1976, she learned she was pregnant, telling only her sister Mary.

"Congratulations," said Mary when informed she'd be an aunt. She gave Kathie a hug and a kiss, but saw that Kathie wasn't enjoying the moment.

Kathie was dour. Bobby had insisted she have an abortion. He had no idea how Kathie, who used a diaphragm, could have become pregnant. He was angry.

"He said he did not want to be a father and if I have the baby he'll divorce me," said Kathie.

There was but one decision, and in March, Kathie sadly terminated her pregnancy. She fell into a deep depression, crying all hours of the day and night.

Mary tried to raise her spirits, but Kathie fell into a deeper funk in May when she learned that her husband of three years was having an affair.

The news came to Kathie in an unusual way. Bobby had announced that he changed their home phone number and the key to the mailbox, claiming he was being threatened at work and was doing this as a precaution. Two days later Kathie happened to pull a book from their bookshelf and some Polaroid pictures fell out. They were photos of their medicine cabinet and bedroom closet. Kathie was puzzled. Why would Bobby take pictures of a closet and cabinet?

Kathie confronted Bobby, who admitted to having an affair. Kathie sat stunned as Bobby explained that he changed the apartment around to give the impression that he was single. When the woman left, he used the photos to place everything back in their normal spaces.

Kathie asked who the woman was, but Bobby would only say she didn't know her.

Kathie was devastated, and repulsed. Her husband, the man she loved, was using their home for his extramarital dalliances.

Mary didn't know what to say when Kathie told her the news, crying on her shoulder that spring afternoon. Mary had already developed an opinion of Bobby Durst, and it was less than flattering. He was arrogant and cold and displayed a deep and obvious disdain for Kathie's relatives, ignoring them at family functions or, if he was in a good mood, barely acknowledging their existence.

Mary told Kathie that perhaps she'd be better off without Bobby, but Kathie didn't want to hear it.

She was married to a Durst, and it was going to stay that way, even when Kathie claimed to have learned that Bobby was embezzling from his father's company, as she told Mary during a late night phone call. Kathie's brother-in-law Douglas told her that Bobby was taking rent checks and depositing them into his own account. Bobby denied this at first, but she later claimed that he admitted to taking some checks on occasion.

"I don't know what he's doing," Kathie said to her sister. "Sometimes I just don't understand him."

Mary said nothing. She knew her sister wouldn't listen to reason. Besides, she was coming out of her funk. And she and Bobby agreed to buy a pretty little stone cottage on Lake Truesdale, in South Salem. It was a bargain, said Kathie. Only $86,500. It would serve as their summer and weekend retreat and Kathie could stay there when attending nursing classes at WCSC in Danbury. Kathie even held out the hope that this would add a new dimension to their relationship. Weekends away, together. It would be like Vermont. They could go for walks, and talk, and take long drives upstate or into Connecticut.

Mary remembered that it seemed to work for a while. A couple of years at least. But after Kathie entered medical school, Bobby became more abusive, first raising his hands, pretending he would swing at Kathie, and then finally, in 1979, smacking her to the ground during a vicious argument.

Kathie tolerated the abuse. She was now a student at the Albert Einstein Medical School, a beneficiary of the Durst Organization's largesse, and she still very much enjoyed the life Bobby's money and family made possible. Along with the travel to exotic locations, there were the fabulous parties and formal affairs. At one event, a fund-raiser for New York mayor Ed Koch, Kathie was the queen of the ball, the center of attention, a true trophy wife. She was smart and witty and could carry an intelligent conversation. Even Seymour looked on approvingly as Kathie, who was to be the first Durst doctor, made her way through the room, smiling and completely engaging.

Her own family was proud of her, never quite imagining that the baby of the family would one day bear the title M.D.

But behind the glitter and glamour and privilege, Kathie's life was failing. In 1980 she began taking tranquilizers, prescribed by her doctor, to help deal with the stress of living with Bobby, who was now questioning her every purchase and refusing simple requests like spending $200 to fix the air-conditioning on their Volkswagen bug, which Kathie drove to school. And despite the rigorous schedule and pressures of her studies, he even demanded she fulfill her "wife duties," or chores, on her days off.

Kathie had completely unraveled over the last year, and as the McCormacks sat there in Mary's apartment, they talked not just about Kathie, but about their frustrations with the police. Mike Struk wasn't telling them much, if anything, and the McCormacks didn't know if the police were taking the case seriously, or perhaps had been compromised by the Durst family.

It wasn't out of the question. The McCormacks weren't naive. That much was certain after their utterly strange encounter with a man who called Mary and introduced himself as John Vigiani. He said he was a private investigator and offered a unique solution to the case, but needed to deliver his proposal in person.

Jim and Mary agreed to meet Vigiani at a diner on Third Avenue, near Mary's East Fifty-first Street apartment. Jim and Mary sat on one side of a booth, waiters and waitresses busily walking by, their arms filled with plates. Vigiani appeared, on time. He was surprisingly small, no more than five seven. He had short, dark hair and a nose that protruded out from a thin face. He was very businesslike, wearing a smart, firmly pressed dark gray suit and tie. He appeared to be no more than fifty years old and walked with a noticeable limp.

Vigiani introduced himself and sat on the other side of the table, facing the siblings. He said he was a former employee of a government agency, which he would not identify, and said his limp had resulted from being shot.

Jim and Mary said nothing as Vigiani explained that it was obvious that Bobby Durst knew what had happened to Kathie, and that there was only one person who could reveal that information. Bobby Durst himself.

"I can help you," said Vigiani. "For ten thousand dollars, arrangements could be made to interrogate Mr. Durst and get the information you desire."

Jim looked at Vigiani, not quite sure how to respond. Interrogate Bobby? Was this guy kidding?

"Just how are you going to get Bobby to talk to you?" said Jim.

Vigiani folded his hands together and moved forward, closer to Jim and Mary, and spoke softly but clearly.

"Do you know how easy it is to get taken off a street without anyone seeing it happen?"

Mary could feel her stomach turn as she pinched Jim's leg under the table. They said nothing, but continued to listen as Vigiani described his plan to kidnap Bobby Durst.

"It would involve the use of dogs. Doberman pinschers. They would walk up and gently place their mouths around the wrists and escort a person, in this case Mr. Durst, into a waiting vehicle. Have you ever heard of a technique called the Red Room?"

"No, can't say that I have," said Jim.

"Well, by the administration of certain drugs, the person would become disoriented and by the use of a red light a person can become so disoriented as to not be able to tell if they are upside down on a chair or floating in a room. If they are questioned properly, information can be obtained successfully," said Vigiani.

Jim and Mary didn't know what to say. Was this guy a crackpot? Was he really suggesting that they pay money to kidnap Bobby Durst?

"Nothing will happen to him," said Vigiani assuringly. "There will be no trace. He will be returned home, but you'll have the information you need to find your sister."

As bizarre as it sounded, Jim thought for what seemed like the longest second, or two, that it could be possible. Nothing else was working, and the police investigation seemed to be going nowhere. Jim let out a deep breath, and his better sense overcame him as he shook his head.

"First of all, we don't have ten thousand dollars. Second, I'm not going to solve one crime by committing another crime. What you're suggesting is pretty extreme," said Jim.

"Extreme circumstances require extreme measures," said Vigiani.

"Thanks for suggesting this, but I think we'll pass," said Jim.

Vigiani unfolded his hands, took a sip of water, rose from his seat, and reached into his back pocket, pulling out his wallet.

"If you change your mind," he said, handing Jim a white card with nothing but a phone number on it.

Vigiani left the diner, limping out the door onto Third Avenue.

Jim took his card, ripped it down the middle, and tossed it on the table.

As the family discussed the bizarre meeting, it was agreed that, at the very least, someone was trying to help the McCormacks.

Less could be said of the Durst family.

Bobby had broken off all contact with the McCormacks. The Dursts, as a family, had all but spurned any contact with Kathie's family. In the six weeks since Kathie disappeared, not one Durst family member, brothers Doug or Tom or sister Wendy, called Jim or Mary or any of the other sisters. And Bobby wouldn't answer Mary's questions about why he was throwing her stuff out of the East Eighty-sixth Street apartment and the house in South Salem. Even worse, none of the Dursts had reached out to Kathie's mother. Not even Seymour, the all-powerful real estate mogul, who, with one phone call, could give Mike Struk another twenty or thirty or forty detectives to work on this case. Indeed, with his money, the elder Durst could have hired his own private detectives.

But Seymour remained conspicuously quiet, and as the McCormack family talked more about the Dursts, their anger rose to the surface.

They decided it was time to approach the mogul.

A call went out, the strength to make it fueled in part by alcohol, and a meeting was demanded. Surprisingly, Seymour agreed, and the McCormacks hurried down to Seymour's town house on West Forty-eighth Street.

They were greeted by a doorman, who brought the group up to the second floor. As they made their way up the steps, Jim noticed that every inch of every wall was covered by a book or photograph. He heard about Seymour's mythic collection of memorabilia and literature on New York City, and now he was looking at it.

The McCormacks were taken into a room, shaped like a railroad car, but extending from the front of the town house to the back. A long, rectangular-shaped wooden table occupied the middle of the room in which the McCormacks were seated.

There were no offers of coffee, or tea, or soda, or even water.

A side door opened and Seymour slowly walked in and took his position at the head of the table. Like his son Bobby, Seymour was a smallish man with a thin, rodent-like face. He offered a weak hello, then sat back as the questions came quickly.

What is happening? Can you do anything? Can the police be pushed to do more? Why won't Bobby cooperate?

The McCormacks were desperate, and the questions seemed to be coming from every part of the room.

Seymour listened and nodded his head, but said little.

"The police are doing the best that they can," he said. "We need to be patient."

"Seymour, please, we know you can help us," said Mary. "I think Bobby can help us."

Seymour remained evasive and was becoming increasingly frustrated with the tone of the questions, which now turned into an interrogation.

What is Bobby hiding? He has to know something? Can you hire private detectives?

As the questions continued, a door opened on the other side of the room and in walked Tom Durst, Seymour's youngest son. He had just returned from a trip to California and was surprised to see the family of his brother's wife inside his father's home.

"What's going on here?" he said, not even taking a moment to say hello.

Seymour told Tom that the McCormacks had come over to talk about Kathie, and he told them there was little he could do, that the police were doing everything they could.

Tom looked down at the McCormacks.

"Meeting's over, you'll have to leave," he said abruptly.

"Wait a second," said Jim. "We're talking to your father. We need his help!"

"I said the meeting is over," said Tom.

Seymour just shrugged his shoulders and stood up from his chair. The McCormack family quietly exited the room in single file, resigned in the fact that the Durst family had given up on Kathie.

10

GILBERTE Najamy continued her Sunday-night garbage runs for seven weeks, swiping Kathie's medical books, clothes, and other personal effects Bobby had tossed out of the South Salem home.

Each week, Gilberte would take someone along. One night it was Ellen Strauss, who didn't quite fancy herself as a garbage picker but was nonetheless focused on the task at hand.

Ellen and Gilberte and Eleanor Schwank had spoken almost every day since Kathie was reported missing, discussing various theories, trying to locate clues.

After seven weeks Eleanor was convinced that Kathie had been the victim of foul play. Ellen tended to agree with Eleanor, though she held out the slight hope that Kathie could be alive in some mental institution, the victim of a total breakdown.

Ellen even traveled to Boston to visit the psychiatric ward—Bullfinch 7—at the Massachusetts General Hospital, where she spent two hours checking beds and the hospital computers after getting a tip that Kathie might have been admitted there under a different name.

Ellen stopped at every bed in the ward, but as she

expected, Kathie wasn't there. She later sent pictures of Kathie to a hospital in New Hampshire to check another lead. This one involved an amnesia victim. The description of the victim offered faint hope: a woman, around thirty years old, about five feet three inches tall, weighing a hundred pounds, wearing a Lord & Taylor jacket. But like all the other leads, this one went nowhere.

Desperate, the women even drove to Southington to meet with a private eye, Jim Conway, a former New York cop. After four hours sipping soda with Conway at a Howard Johnson's, the best he could offer was a suggestion to hire a psychic.

The Dursts? Conway wanted no part of this.

"You can't go head-to-head with that kind of family. Too much money, too much power," said Conway.

Rebuffed by the private eye, Gilberte talked Eleanor into taking a late-night stroll along the grounds of the estate owned by Bobby's brother Douglas, who lived in Westchester County.

The women weren't sure what they'd find as they walked gingerly through the estate grounds, their path illuminated by the moonlight. They quietly searched the carriage house, gardens, and tennis courts.

As they huddled behind a row of bushes, preparing to make their way off the grounds before they were discovered, Eleanor tried to convince Gilberte that this was all fruitless.

"But she's not dead, she can't be," said Gilberte, who still held out the belief that her friend was either in the witness protection program or lost and unidentified in some hospital.

"Gilberte, stop with the witness protection program stuff," Eleanor said, thoroughly annoyed that the other woman could not, or would not, face what she believed to be the awful truth.

Eleanor was well aware that the past few years with Kathie had been heady times for Gilberte, times when she'd join Kathie and Bobby, perhaps for dinner at Elaine's and then dancing at Xenon or Studio 54, when Bobby would walk right in, past the velvet ropes, like

Moses parting the Red Sea, his entourage right behind him. Because of his wealth and family standing in New York, it was exciting to be with Bobby, even more exciting for a woman like Gilberte, who had no business hanging out with Bobby Durst or any his close friends.

Without Kathie, Gilberte would have been left at the door, waiting outside the velvet ropes like the rest of the bridge-and-tunnel crowd, hoping against hope that she would be extended the exclusive privilege of socializing with the rich and the powerful, if only for a few hours.

Bobby had his own small circle of friends, which included Doug and Rachel Oliver, journalists Judy Licht and Julie Baumgold, comedian Laraine Newman, and writer Susan Berman.

The Olivers, like Bobby, lived off of real estate money, and lots of it. They owned a town house in Manhattan filled with priceless works of art, sculptures and paintings. Rachel was the daughter of Abe Hirschfeld, a maddeningly colorful character and real estate baron whose sanity had been questioned for years.

Doug was considered a weird sort with a short fuse. Aside from Susan Berman, no one was closer to Bobby than Doug Oliver.

Baumgold had known Bobby growing up in Scarsdale, while Judy Licht was a local television news reporter who at one time rented the South Salem home for a few months. Laraine Newman was perhaps the most recognizable friend, an original member of the *Saturday Night Live* cast, a comic and one of the few people who could make Bobby laugh.

And then there was Susan Berman, who was considered Bobby's best friend of all.

They had met in the 1960s when both attended UCLA, where Bobby floated through economics classes, pretending he was studying for a Ph.D. after graduating from Lehigh University in Bethlehem, Pennsylvania, with a major in economics.

Like Bobby, Susan was a child of privilege, the

daughter of gangster Davie Berman and a member of the royal family of Las Vegas.

"Davie the Jew," as her father was called, was by Bugsy Siegel's side as Las Vegas rose from the desert of Nevada.

Following Siegel's violent demise, Davie became a kingpin. He adored his only daughter, bringing in Liberace to perform for a birthday party, and inviting the children of other mobsters, kids Susan didn't even know.

Davie died when Susan was twelve, the cause of death determined to be a heart attack. Susan lost her mother a year later. She was told her mother swallowed a handful of barbiturates.

Susan survived the loss of her parents, and as a young adult she was intoxicating. She looked exotic, her almond eyes slightly slanted in the corners, her jet-black hair combed straight down past her shoulders.

She was drawn to Bobby's quiet way, his innocence. Susan sensed that Bobby carried a deep pain. Like many other women she felt a need to mother him, nurture him, care for him.

By the mid-1970s Susan developed a reputation as an up-and-coming writer in San Francisco, eventually moving to New York and taking a cramped, one-bedroom apartment in Beekman Place with a shower but no bath.

She soon took a job with *New York* magazine, and joined Bobby on his outings throughout the city. Susan loved New York and all its trappings. She had little money, yet still found a way to host fantastic dinner parties in her tiny apartment, and she didn't blink at paying a $300 bill following a meal for eight at a trendy New York restaurant. She could be demure and charming; at least she thought she was. She thought nothing of running into the next-door apartment of a friend, Steven Silverman, at all hours of the day and night to take a bath. He could have been butt naked on the floor, engaged in a romantic liaison, and she'd burst in, not even think to apologize, and run into his bathroom.

Others who crossed the headlights of Susan's life

thought she was more like a Sherman tank. She could be venomous, kissing you on the lips one evening and spreading rumors and gossip about you the next day. She lived in a surreal world in which she was the queen and all others, except for Bobby, were her loyal subjects.

She was proud to be a gangster's daughter. It was a badge of honor and caused people to react with fear. Cross her and she'd readily remind you that she was *the* daughter of Davie Berman. It didn't matter that Davie had died long ago and most people didn't have a clue as to who or what he was.

While others were drawn in or tossed out of Susan's life without so much as a good-bye, Bobby was always different. They were soul mates. It was Bobby—Susan called him her brother—who threw her a party to celebrate the publication of her first book, *Easy Street,* which detailed the life of a gangster's daughter.

They had fun that night, Susan and Bobby, holding each other and posing for pictures, cheek to cheek. Kathie remained in the background, as she always did when socializing with Bobby's friends. Out of sight. Seen but not heard. Kathie emerged only when socializing with *her* friends, Eleanor or Kathy Traystman or Gilberte. Kathie liked Susan—or at least she pretended to, since she knew very well how her husband felt about her. It was plainly evident that Bobby and Susan shared something Bobby could never share with Kathie. It was a deep loyalty that clearly surfaced after Kathie was reported missing. It was Susan who called Kathie's friends, asking if there was any news to report, digging for information. Everyone knew she was calling for Bobby, especially after Susan became Bobby's unofficial spokesperson, answering questions for the media.

She'd tell the press that Bobby was heartbroken, and unable to cope with the disappearance of his wife.

"He's completely distraught and is clinging to the hope that Kathie is alive," Susan told the *Post.* "He loves her very much and he's terribly worried."

Those close to the case, like the McCormack family,

Mike Struk, and Kathie's friends, thought otherwise.

Susan relished the spotlight. And she was protecting a friend. Her best friend.

She was still a gangster's daughter, and she wore that distinction like a medal.

As much as Bobby loved Susan, he despised Gilberte Najamy.

To Bobby, Gilberte was a name-dropper, a hanger-on, a social climber. Gilberte was some caterer from Connecticut to whom Bobby would never have given the time of day if she hadn't befriended his wife in nursing school. Bobby had little use for most of Kathie's friends, especially Gilberte, whom he blamed for fueling Kathie's cocaine use and for pushing the divorce.

Gilberte wasn't attractive, and Bobby questioned her sexuality, though Kathie always told him that Gilberte liked men.

Bobby knew the main attraction was drugs. When Kathie and Gilberte socialized, the cocaine often flowed like champagne. Bobby suspected that Gilberte was dealing, though Kathie would deny that, too. During one especially outrageous party in Connecticut, instead of bringing a bottle of wine, Gilberte presented Kathie, a coke spoon tied loosely around her right arm, as her gift. Gilberte would stand behind Kathie and direct her through the crowd, and partygoers would stop them, reach for the nose spoon, dip it into a cellophane bag Kathie held in her left hand, and snort away.

It was a novel idea, and it made for quite a sight. The partygoers loved it, and Gilberte loved the attention. She relished her relationship with Kathie. She would tell anyone who would listen that she was Kathie's best friend, which was far from the truth. Kathie had lots of friends, and after spending two years in medical school while her life was falling apart and her drug use was increasing, her choice of friends mirrored this contradiction. Some she did drugs with, others she didn't. From the latter she'd keep her drug life a secret and maintain the illusion that, at heart, Kathie was still an Irish-

Catholic girl from Long Island, the kind who grows up, marries, has children, worries about paying her mortgage, and lives happily ever.

While Gilberte absorbed Kathie's pain like a sponge, giving ear to every single story and event, Eleanor Schwank had grown tired of listening.

When they'd met at nursing school, they hit it off immediately, their competitiveness and desire for good grades forming a bond. Eleanor was especially impressed when Kathie once challenged the statement of a professor, something about potassium and osmotic pressure. Kathie had argued the point so intelligently, Eleanor thought.

Eleanor knew she had found a female soul mate when Kathie challenged the administration's rules on the wearing of those little white caps that have long identified nurses. Women had always worn those caps, so it was a great surprise when Kathie Durst questioned why.

"Men don't wear medical caps, and caps have contaminants," was Kathie's argument.

Eleanor, a former flower child and self-professed radical, joined Kathie's crusade, and the two women signed a letter, written by Kathie on Durst Organization stationery, to President Jimmy Carter, protesting the cap-wearing requirement, claiming it was a violation of their civil rights. The letter caused an uproar, and WCSC gave in, fearful it would lose its federal funding. Kathie won the battle, and Eleanor, her co-conspirator, couldn't have been happier.

But Eleanor never understood why Kathie, a member of the wealthy Durst family, was in Connecticut taking nursing courses in the first place.

She'd broach the subject with Kathie, and the reply was always the same: her husband wanted her to have a career, and he made it clear that just because he had money, he wasn't going to support her.

Eleanor thought this made little sense. Married to a multimillionaire and you're taking nursing courses because he doesn't want to give you money? Don't get me wrong, she'd say, but that's not my kind of guy.

What she really wanted to say was "what a cheap fuck."

Her poor opinion of Bobby was cemented when the two women set a date to meet at a restaurant in Connecticut with their husbands. Bobby was barely sociable, introverted and quiet. Eleanor could plainly see he showed little affection for Kathie, and it didn't appear that he showered his wife with money and gifts. At Kathie's graduation party in 1978, held in the backyard of their Lake Truesdale home, Bobby once put his arms around Kathie, but not as an expression of love or affection. Instead, Eleanor had the distinct feeling that he was showing his guests that Kathie was his possession. This little rich man with the poor personality owned this pretty, personable woman.

Kathie didn't seem to mind. It was the most she expected to get from Bobby, a man whose wealth, she would say, prevented him from completely trusting people.

Besides, Kathie would add, it was tough for a man who'd seen his mother fall to her death when he was a kid to show great emotion to a woman.

Eleanor didn't quite understand what Kathie was talking about during another marathon session on the phone when Kathie reported this traumatic incident.

"His mother, she fell off the roof of their home up in Scarsdale. She jumped, committed suicide," said Kathie.

"He saw that?"

"Yes. He was only seven. It really screwed him up. He had a lot of psychological problems. He was sent to several doctors when he was a child, but they couldn't treat him. He really hated his father. I have a letter. It describes what was wrong with him. It says something about a 'decomposing personality,' or something like that. I'll show it to you one day."

"Kathie, you're telling me that your husband had some major psychological issues as a child? Don't you think he still has them now?"

"He has issues, but nothing I would worry about. We have our problems, but he's really very soft and sweet. Deep down, I feel kind of sorry for him."

Eleanor couldn't respond. She knew Kathie loved being a Durst. She was part of a powerful family. People saw her differently. Imagine if she was still Kathie McCormack? Or perhaps married to a cop named O'Reilly? That wouldn't get her into Studio 54, not by a long shot, or medical school. And it sure wouldn't serve as a ticket to the dozens of political fund-raisers and black-tie events she routinely attended, socializing with the Helmsleys or Trumps or Rudins or any other members of New York's real estate royalty.

And there were the parties that drove Eleanor insane.

One of which was hosted by the waste-management cartel. The garbage industry and its unions were owned by the mob, and they had a stranglehold on New York's commercial garbage business.

The party was filled with men wearing slick silk suits and pinkie rings. Seymour and Bobby moved easily through the crowd, and Kathie was like a kid in a candy store, oblivious to the politics and people she was socializing with.

For her part, Eleanor knew better.

"Kathie, what are you doing?" she'd say. "Do you have any idea who these people are?"

Kathie's innocence and naïveté prevented her from making the obvious connection, while the Dursts—Seymour and Bobby—knew very well whom they were partying with. And so did Eleanor, who'd grown up in New Jersey, the daughter of Jimmy Calabrese, a tough union leader whose mornings consisted of a cup of coffee, a loving kiss for his daughter, and a thorough inspection under the hood of his car.

"Kathie, you really have to smarten up," Eleanor would say, especially after she first noticed changes in Kathie's behavior two years into medical school.

Kathie was soon going to have a real career, and Bobby seemed to have a problem with that. He became possessive, his possessiveness manifesting itself in anger, the anger becoming abusive.

There were times, in the months before Kathie disappeared, when Eleanor would be talking with her friend on the phone and she could hear growling noises—*grrrrrrrrrr, grrrrrrrrr*—in the background. It sounded like an animal, but it wasn't.

It was Bobby.

"What's he doing? He sounds like a rabid dog," Eleanor would say.

"We just had a fight. He's over in the corner staring at me. Don't worry about him," was Kathie's standard reply. "Remember, he studied Primal Therapy with John Lennon, he's supposed to growl."

Eleanor didn't buy it. Primal Therapy? A grown man growling?

Kathie would later whisper on the phone, "He's crazy." But after hanging up, she'd go back to the same bed with him.

Eleanor recalled Kathie's drug use picking up during her second year in medical school. She first told Eleanor she was taking Valium to help her get to sleep at night. Soon after she said she was using small amounts of cocaine to help her stay awake. Medical school was difficult, but the drugs were helping her to manage. Besides, she said, most of the students were snorting coke, so it couldn't be that bad, just a tweak here and there to get through the long days.

Eleanor later realized that Kathie's drug use had become far more than recreational during the year before her disappearance. Kathie was clearly on a downward spiral, a 747 that had lost its engines. And the drugs led to other questionable activities. Eleanor saw this for herself during one St. Patrick's Day in Manhattan when she accompanied Kathie to the home of some friends.

Rachel and Susan Berman were supposed to be there, but when Eleanor and Kathie arrived, they found a friend entertaining another man, and a suggestion was put out to the women that the four go upstairs to the bedroom and undress. There was plenty of coke to fuel the sex, and the friend couldn't take his eyes off Kathie, who in turn looked at Eleanor to see if she'd be willing.

Eleanor declined.

"I don't even want to know what they had in mind," Eleanor said as they walked down the block after leaving the apartment. "And please don't tell me you're sleeping with these guys just for cocaine."

Kathie would only smile, like she always did. But it was a smile tinged with sadness. The rigors of medical school were taking their toll, and Kathie was lonely. Her relationship with her husband had soured, any real love for him a faded memory.

There was a period in early 1980 when Kathie seemed to perk up again. Eleanor thought she had a boyfriend, and asked her about it. Kathie's cheeks turned beet red, and she denied anything was going on, but later admitted she was, indeed, involved with someone.

"His name is Alan Schreiber and he's the chief resident at Jacobi Hospital," said Kathie. "I'm in love with him."

When Schreiber left New York that summer for Colorado, Kathie was despondent. Eleanor tried to assure her that she was not in love, that it was just a fling. In time, Kathie realized Eleanor was right. And deep down, she still held on to some hope that Bobby would change, that they could work out their problems and somehow remain a couple.

But then came Prudence Farrow, who would call Kathie at home, demanding that she let Bobby go. Kathie wouldn't budge. But as the marriage crumbled even further, as the beatings became more intense, Kathie finally realized that it was over, and she decided she'd file for a divorce and seek a modest settlement to go with it.

She broke the news to Eleanor, who thought it was about time. Kathie told Gilberte during a winter vacation in Puerto Rico.

The trip was Gilberte's idea. It was February 1981. Gilberte had bought the tickets and paid for the hotel.

After they arrived Kathie told her friend she was going to divorce Bobby. Gilberte was thrilled. Things couldn't have worked out better. Kathie was at an emotional low, and she was here, alone with Gilberte, who envisioned holding Kathie in her arms, comforting her, caressing and kissing her.

But Kathie had other plans, and they didn't include Gilberte. Each night Gilberte waited patiently for Kathie to return to their room, but Kathie was off with a man she'd met the first day they arrived.

Gilberte was infuriated.

When they returned to New York, Gilberte reminded Kathie how much she owed her for the trip, and she'd appreciate a check. Kathie said fine. The check never came.

That summer Kathie hired attorney Dale Ragus and moved forward with her decision to seek a divorce. As the summer turned to fall, Bobby resisted, adamantly refusing to give Kathie any substantial settlement. He made her life a living hell, often waking her up in the middle of the night to argue after a long day at school. He denied her access to cash and cut off most of her credit cards.

Three months before she disappeared, Eleanor knew Kathie was a wreck. She was becoming paranoid, snorting as much as three grams of cocaine a week.

She wasn't sleeping and her studies were suffering. She had no money, and had even turned to Seymour for a handout. Seymour knew his son and pretty wife were having problems, but it wasn't his business, and he wouldn't interfere. He couldn't. He knew his son all too well. Bobby was the heir apparent, and conducted his personal life the same way he conducted his business affairs, privately.

As Kathie pressed for the divorce, she made it clear she wasn't going to step aside without a settlement.

"Eleanor, I have papers. I have information. Stock transfers. Income-tax statements. He forged my name! I have information on Bobby. I'm not coming out of this marriage without anything!" said Kathie.

"You don't need his money!" Eleanor would argue. "Drop it. You're dealing with something you just can't win. It's much bigger than you realize. These are powerful people."

But Kathie thought she was back in college, fighting the administration over the nursing caps.

"I'm going to win this, Eleanor. I'm going to win."

Instead, Eleanor received a call on January 2 from a sobbing Kathie, who said she had been beaten yet again.

"Get to the hospital. You have to get this documented," said Eleanor, who hoped this was the final straw.

Three weeks later Eleanor learned that Kathie had disappeared, and she was the first of Kathie's friends to say that she was dead.

———

ELLEN Strauss didn't know what to think when she heard the news that Kathie was missing. Ellen was a law-school student with modellike beauty and a brain to go with it. She, too, had been a student at WCSC before turning her attention to the law. She was older than Kathie, by eight years, and was married.

Ellen carried herself well, and she knew it. She was very attractive—thin, shapely, with light, golden brown hair that curled under her chin. She was meticulous and extremely organized, to the point where her friends thought she was beyond obsessive. Every meeting, every conversation would be written into a calendar book, to be recorded forever. Ellen was friendly with Eleanor Schwank and had met Gilberte only once or twice before Kathie disappeared. Ellen was one of Kathie's non-drug friends, and was unaware of Kathie's cocaine use. She knew only that her friend was the member of a wealthy family and a medical student who had severe marital difficulties. So severe that Kathie would call Ellen, at all hours of the day and night, seeking advice on how to work through the divorce and get a just settlement.

Ellen would remind Kathie that she was only a law-school student, not a full-fledged attorney, but Kathie would ramble on, hours at a time, and Ellen would patiently listen.

Meanwhile, after weeks of trying to find the answers, and with little word from the police, the patience of Kathie's friends was running out. Eleanor, Ellen, and Gilberte decided to drive into Manhattan and pay a visit to Mike Struk.

At 7 P.M. on Friday, March 19, the three women were led up to the third floor of the Twentieth Precinct station house and into the detectives' squad room. They were lucky. Struk was there, though he didn't seem pleased to see them standing there, waiting at the front gate.

Struk had already met Gilberte. He was immediately smitten with Ellen. Struk pulled two more chairs over to his desk, and the women sat down. But before the detective could offer a single word, Eleanor jumped on him, the questions coming rapid fire.

"What is going on?" she demanded.

"What do you mean?"

"Why hasn't Bobby been arrested?"

"We're conducting an investigation."

"You know Kathie feared Bobby would kill her and told all of her friends, what are you doing about it?"

Ellen, the budding attorney, tried to intervene, attempting a little diplomacy. But Eleanor, the rabble-rouser, had already pounced and drew first blood.

"I'm telling you Bobby murdered Kathie, and if you're conducting such a thorough investigation, why didn't you trace their phone calls? You would have seen that I was on the phone with Kathie for hours and you would have called me for an interview. Instead I have to come here and ask why haven't you called me, and why aren't you searching the South Salem house? Bobby's throwing her stuff out, her books and clothes, everything!"

Struk paused while Ellen cringed. She could see that

the detective's eyes were afire. And any thought Ellen had that Struk would at the least be pleasant to these women, who had barged in unannounced, went through the ventilator shaft and out onto West Eighty-second Street.

Struk wanted to put his thoughts into words, spew them out, then throw these women out of his office. *Criticize me? I've been working this case day and night with a dozen other detectives for two months, and you're going to come into my building and tell me I'm fucking incompetent?*

He was simmering, but regained his composure. His face, which turned a slight shade of red as Eleanor delivered her speech, returned to its pale color. Struk managed to get ahold of his emotions.

He looked at Ellen and spoke slowly, so they would all understand.

"I'm conducting an investigation, and I'm conducting it the way I think it should be conducted," he said calmly. "I know about the clothes, and I know he beat his wife, and I know a lot of other things, but I'm not going to divulge any information to you or anyone else. As for the South Salem home, it's not in my jurisdiction. My business is in New York City. And New York City is where she was last seen alive."

Struk wasn't about to tell these women that he believed them, that he believed Bobby Durst knew more than he was saying, that he wanted to arrest Bobby. He could taste it. He dreamed about it. But he just couldn't do it. Not yet.

And he couldn't tell them about the things he knew. A week after Bobby reported Kathie missing, Struk had received a call from a Dr. Marcia Naveh, who was a resident at Einstein working in Jacobi Hospital. The chief resident, said Naveh, was Alan Schreiber, and it was common knowledge that Schreiber and Kathie Durst were having an affair. The suggestion was that Schreiber might know where Kathie was.

Struk called Schreiber in his Denver, Colorado, office

several days later. Schreiber had been in Colorado since the summer of 1980 and he didn't say much to Struk, except that he had met Kathie during his residency and hadn't seen her since he left for Denver. Struk didn't press the doctor about the affair.

Struk rose from his seat and extended his hand to Ellen and Gilberte.

"Sorry, but there's not much more I can tell you," he said, turning to Eleanor, grabbing her hand, and tightening his grip so hard her fingers were crushed together. It was uncomfortable, but didn't hurt. Still, the message was delivered: don't fuck with me.

As the women walked out of the precinct, Eleanor thought she'd just met a Neanderthal.

"They're incompetent. All of them. I don't understand it. We all know Bobby did it," said Eleanor.

Ellen said little. She was trying to be more pragmatic. As a budding attorney, she knew that evidence, not theory, was all the police could go on. She didn't like the way Eleanor attacked Struk, trying to intimidate him into doing something. Ellen needed to make it up to him, get him on their side.

Struk was still angry after the women left. He walked to the back of the room and poured himself a cup of coffee. He was tired and frustrated, having spent a solid seven weeks searching for Kathie Durst. He put the coffee down on his desk, fingered through his Rolodex, and stopped at *H*.

11

ROGER Hayes was sitting in his downtown office, sporting a wide smile.

Hayes always smiled, especially when he was preparing to deliver bad news, which was one of the reasons why Mike Struk, who was making his case for arresting Bobby Durst, liked him so much.

Struk's hard exterior hid the fact that he had been shaken by the meeting several days earlier with Ellen Strauss, Eleanor Schwank, and Gilberte Najamy. Despite his anger, he agreed with them. He wanted to arrest Bobby. Or at the least bring his evidence, though circumstantial, before a grand jury.

"I have the hospital records, his own interviews, which were filled with lies, mistruths, and discrepancies. I don't know what to make of that itinerary and the boot receipt yet, but I have Kathie Durst's friends, all of whom can testify that she lived in terror of her husband," said Struk. "He was beating her pretty regularly, Roger. And now the prick won't even talk to me. I know you think we've got something here. Can we go to the grand jury?"

Hayes smiled as he shook his head no.

"Mike, you know we could indict him if we wanted to. That's the easy part," said Hayes. "But what do you think is going to happen here?"

Hayes methodically laid out the scenario.

"Let's say Bobby is arrested. The next day it would be on the front pages of all the local newspapers. There will be crazy headlines, like 'Son of Real Estate King Indicted for Murder of Wife!' Your picture will be on page one, Mike, leading Bobby in handcuffs into a waiting police car. It would make a big splash, and everyone would be happy, for a little while."

Hayes paused for a moment, reloading his thoughts.

"But the reality of the case is that all we have is circumstantial evidence, no matter how compelling we may think it is. It just isn't enough. We either need a confession, which we know isn't coming, or physical evidence, a body, a body part, body fluids."

The smile was gone from Hayes's face as he leaned across his desk toward Struk.

"Let's think about this. Bobby would be indicted, and then hire the best criminal attorneys in town. They would destroy our case, and they'd do it by attacking his wife. Yeah, they'd bring in her drug use, her affairs, her problems at school. And who's she hanging out with? Some guy you're telling me is a drug dealer? And a woman who claims to be one of her best friends and may also be dealing? If we go to trial and Bobby is acquitted, which would be highly likely, then what? He couldn't be prosecuted even if they found Kathie's body. Double jeopardy would come into play."

"And that would be that," said Struk.

"And that would be that," said Hayes. "So you see, my friend, indicting Bob Durst would not be the smart, or prudent, thing to do. I would suggest you get a confession, or find a body."

———

ON his way uptown Struk pulled his car over and ordered a beef gyro and a soda from a street vendor, the Russian dressing spilling onto his white shirt as he tried to navigate traffic on Eighth Avenue with one hand and eat his fat, sloppy sandwich with the other.

After parking his car and walking up to the squad room, Struk saw he had a visitor waiting for him. It was Ellen Strauss.

Of all the people the detective had met since Bobby Durst walked into the Twentieth Precinct on February 5, Ellen seemed the most reasonable, not to mention that she was very attractive, dressed well, and carried herself like a woman should.

Seeing Ellen lifted his spirits. If it had been Gilberte Najamy or Eleanor Schwank standing there, he would have said he was busy and quickly dismissed her.

But Ellen was different, and he brought her to his desk before excusing himself for a moment to visit the bathroom to clean the dressing from the gyro that remained on his white shirt.

"I see you had a little accident," said Ellen.

"That's what happens when you try to do too much," said Struk.

Ellen understood the double meaning. She could see that the detective was still sore after his last meeting with the three friends. And unlike the other two, Ellen was of the opinion that Struk was spending a lot of time on this case. She reasoned that if he didn't care, he wouldn't have seethed as he had, especially toward Eleanor.

So Ellen decided she would try to make nice, to bring Struk into their fold.

Struk returned from the bathroom, sat down, and asked what he could do for her.

"Listen, I had some business in Manhattan today and I wanted to stop by to invite you to a party I'm having this weekend," said Ellen. "It's going to be me and seventy of my closest friends at my house in Connecticut."

"A party?" said Struk, his tough exterior melting just a bit. He was taken aback, actually surprised and pleased by the gesture. Working the Durst case, along with the problems in his personal life, hadn't left him much time for partying. And he couldn't remember the last time he'd received an invitation to attend a party in Connecticut, of all places.

His first thought was to accept, but he knew this was still an active case and perhaps it wouldn't be proper.

Ellen assured him there would be no drugs at the party, something she always insisted upon, and that plenty of pretty, available professional women would be in attendance.

"You're not married, are you?" asked Ellen.

"Separated," said Struk. "But I'm not really looking."

"I took the liberty of writing this down," she said, handing him directions to her home. "If you're free, please come up."

"Okay," said Struk. "If I can make it, I will."

Struk watched Ellen as she left the room. Lieutenant Gibbons walked over to the detective, whose eyes remained on Ellen.

"That," he said, "is one nice-looking lady."

"That's Ellen Strauss. She just invited me to a party at her house Saturday night. Whaddaya think, lou?"

"Will it help the case?"

"Let's call it a covert operation," Struk quipped. "Actually, she said there'll be seventy people there. Maybe I'll bump into someone who has something to offer."

"Okay," said Gibbons. "Just make sure you sign out that you're going to Connecticut. And take someone with you."

———

THE cardboard sign taped to the front door of Ellen Strauss's Colonial home in Westport read NO TOKING, NO SMOKING, NO JOKING!.

The house had been hard to find. Struk had grabbed another detective, Rocco Marriotti, told him they had a tough job that night, and headed up to the Bronx, to the Hutchinson River Parkway north to the Merritt Parkway and into Connecticut. It was about an hour's drive from Manhattan. It was dusk, and as Struk drove up Route 53 in Weston, he could see some of the homes that lined each side of the road.

They were large Colonials and Tudors, and even a mansion or two. Struk realized he was out of his territory, and even out of his league. Ellen's street was in a wooded area, where the homes were somewhat smaller but still attractive. Cars lined the gravel road and filled Ellen's small driveway. People were milling around outside, some smoking marijuana. He saw others, farther away, their hands reaching up to their noses.

Ellen had said her home was drug-free, but that hadn't stopped some of her guests from indulging outside in the darkness.

The red-and-black-trimmed two-story home was, as Struk had imagined, complete with dark, hardwood floors and antique furniture. The house was bulging with people and Struk's six-foot-three-inch frame towered above most guests. He caught a glimpse of Eleanor Schwank, who was making her way through the crowd from the other end of the room, heading straight for Ellen.

"Do you see who's here!" said Eleanor, pointing over to Struk, who stood awkwardly by the front door. "What the fuck is he doing here?"

Ellen grabbed Eleanor's arm.

"Take it easy. I invited him. I didn't like how our last meeting ended and we need him on our side," she said.

"You've got to be kidding me," said Eleanor, then stormed into the kitchen area. She had no use for Struk. She didn't like his investigation, she didn't like his attitude when they met, and she sure didn't like his handshake.

Ellen made her way through the crowd and walked over to the detectives, who were still standing by the front door.

"I'm glad you came," she said, smiling, holding out her hand. "Did you have any trouble finding the house?"

"No, we just followed the cars. That's a long line down the block."

"Yeah, there's a lot of people here. I do this every once in a while. There are a lot of nice people here, some lawyers, some doctors. The bar is over there," she said, pointing toward the kitchen.

Ellen walked Struk and Rocco over to the bar, where they opened a couple of Heinekens and smiled as Ellen introduced them to some of her friends, who asked the two detectives about the status of the Kathie Durst case.

Struk told them what he could, that they were still searching but were somewhat frustrated. There'd been no sign of Kathie for nearly three months.

The night was supposed to be official business, but Struk found he was enjoying himself. He felt at ease, lost in the loud music and good humor. And Ellen was right: there were plenty of beautiful and available women walking by, smiling and sometimes stopping to chat. Word quickly traveled through the house that two New York City detectives were in attendance. Struk was popular, if only for a few hours. The night passed quickly, and Rocco decided to join about a dozen other inebriated people who were sleeping on the floor. Struk thought it best to leave, and gave one of Ellen's female guests a ride home.

———

CHIPS was on Columbus Avenue and West Sixty-ninth Street, directly across from WABC-TV's studios. The restaurant and bar served as a hangout for the reporters and anchors from the station, which aired on Channel 7 in New York, and was also a friendly watering hole for some detectives from the Twentieth Precinct, including Mike Struk and Lieutenant Robert Gibbons.

It was early on a Monday night, and the two men decided to meet for a drink, a bite to eat, and a talk about the Durst case. Something was bothering Struk, only he wanted to hash it out outside the precinct, and Gibbons agreed to meet.

As they sat at the bar, they could easily hear the laughter coming from the back of the restaurant from some of WABC's newspeople, who had gathered after wrapping up the 6 P.M. news.

One of them, a producer, recognized Struk and walked over to say hello and ask about the Durst case. Struk could only say that he was still investigating. He introduced the producer to Gibbons and ordered another beer.

After the producer rejoined his group, Struk leaned over toward Gibbons, his elbow on the bar and left hand on his forehead.

"Here's what's bothering me, in a nutshell. This guy is loaded, right? Has a ton of money. Everybody knows who his father is, and if they didn't know before, they know now. My question is: Where is this guy? Where is Seymour Durst? You and I and some of the other guys have been humping on this case, but other than the first week, I don't see any pressure on us to find this lady. My question to you is, and I want you, as a friend, to tell me: Are we wasting our time here?"

"What you're asking me is, are we chasing our tails?"

"You know what I'm saying," said Struk.

"No one has pulled me aside and said to lay off. That's never happened to me, period. Do I think it's weird there hasn't been more pressure coming down to find her? Yeah, maybe," said Gibbons.

"That's what I'm saying," said Struk. "You'd think Nicastro—fuck, you'd think the commissioner would be on our asses about this. But they're not. I haven't heard anything about Nicastro since the first week. Have you?"

"No. I give the captain updates, and word travels downtown."

"And what about the old man—Seymour? Where the fuck has he been? If that was my daughter or daughter-in-law, I'd be doing everything I could to find her. But this guy hasn't done shit. He even tossed the McCormack family out of his house."

"And what does that tell you?"

"It tells me they know what happened to her. And it's not good. Jesus, I've got people telling me that Kathie was threatening the family. That she had tax returns and stock transfers and information on the Dursts they wouldn't want anyone to know about."

"So you think the family had her bumped off?"

"No, I'm not saying that. I think Bobby Durst has a bad temper and he hit her one too many times. He's tossing all of her stuff out. He wants nothing to do with her. Not even a memory. He's not acting like a bereaved husband, right? Actually, I think he's got a couple of screws loose. But I don't know where to go with this, and if I'm at the end of the line, then we're done. Finished. She's gone, forever."

"What about the phone records?"

"Still waiting."

"And Bobby won't talk to you?"

"I've been trying. He's not returning my calls."

"Why don't you try him again. Maybe it's time to get him in for a polygraph. See if he'll cooperate. Aside from that, we'll wait for the phone records and see what we get from that."

The two men sipped their drinks and ordered dinner.

THE following morning Struk left another message with Bobby Durst, asking him to return the call. An hour later, his phone rang.

"Detective Struk," he answered.

"Hey, Mikey," said the voice on the other end of the line. "How ya doing!"

Struk didn't recognize the voice.

"Who's this?"

"It's Nick, Attorney Nick Scoppetta. I've been retained by Robert Durst to represent him. I know you've been trying to contact him in regards to his wife. I'd appreciate it if all calls concerning Mr. Durst now go through me. Okay, Mikey?"

Struk recognized Scoppetta's name but couldn't quite

Kathie and Bobby,
New Hyde Park, New York, Christmas, 1979.

Courtesy Jim McCormack

Kathie with Igor at Seymour Durst's Katonah,
New York, estate, circa 1978.

Courtesy Jim McCormack

Graduation day, Western Connecticut State College,
May 1978. Kathie Durst kneeling on left,
Eleanor Schwank on far right.

Courtesy Eleanor Schwank

Ellen Strauss, 1981. The would-be attorney kept her notes and documents on the Durst case in a safe-deposit box.

Courtesy Ellen Strauss

Eleanor Schwank, Nantucket, 1981. Eleanor blamed Bobby
soon after learning of Kathie's disappearance.

Courtesy Eleanor Schwank

Mike Struk, detective NYPD.
Lead investigator on the Durst case, 1982

Courtesy Mike Struk

Joe Becerra, investigator, New York State Police, 2001.
Becerra reopened the Durst case in 1999 after receiving a tip.

Private investigator Bobbi Sue Bacha in her Webster, Texas,
office, 2002. Her relentless work on the Durst case
exposed more of Bobby's secrets.

Courtesy Bobbi Sue Bacha

Bobby Durst at his extradition hearing in Easton,
Pennsylvania, January 2002.
Courtesy Wideworld Photos

place it. The call took him by surprise, and Scoppetta's "Hey, Mikey" greeting didn't earn him any points.

"Well, yeah, I've been trying to contact him. There are a couple of things I'd like to discuss with him," said Struk.

"Are you going to arrest Mr. Durst?"

"I didn't say that. I just want to talk to him."

"Well, I'm advising Mr. Durst not to talk to anyone at this point. He really wants to help you, but he's very busy and there's nothing more that he can add than what he's already told you."

"Would Mr. Durst be willing to sit down for a polygraph test?"

"Absolutely not. He's done nothing that would warrant him to be embarrassed like that," said Scoppetta. "But we do have something you would be interested in. Drinking glasses with what appears to be a powdery residue on the side. We think it's cocaine. The glasses belonged to Mrs. Durst. We'd be happy to give them to you. Perhaps you could run them through for prints? Mr. Durst has said all along that he believes his wife may have gotten in trouble with drug dealers. That sound good, Mikey? And should something else come up relevant to this case, feel free to call me, okay, Mikey?"

Struk could hear the click on the other end of the line, and he slammed his phone down onto the receiver. At the moment he didn't know what he was more upset about, the fact that Bobby hired an attorney or being called Mikey.

He got up and walked over to Gibbons's office.

"Bobby's lawyered up," said Struk. "He's got some guy, Nick Scoppetta, representing him."

"Scoppetta?" said Gibbons. "He's a player. A criminal attorney. Bobby's bringing out the first team."

Gibbons knew all about Scoppetta, a New York City insider, a member of Mayor John Lindsay's administration in the 1960s, a former deputy mayor and city investigations commissioner who knew just about everyone within city government, and everyone knew him.

"He says there's no way Bobby will talk to us, and no way he'll sit down for a polygraph. Does that shut us down?" said Struk, knowing there was no chance he'd be talking to Bobby Durst anytime soon.

"For now, until we get the phone records," said Gibbons.

Bobby had dropped the bomb. All Struk could do was sigh.

"Damn," he said.

A month later, as promised, Nick Scoppetta produced two glasses containing what appeared to be a white, powdery residue. As a matter of routine, Struk had the glasses examined, and the residue tested positive for cocaine, though there were no identifiable fingerprints.

Struk was back working other cases. A murder here, a burglary there. There'd be occasional calls from Kathie's friends, particularly Ellen Strauss, seeking updates, but there was nothing to say and nothing to report. The only leads that trickled in were false sightings or crazed psychics claiming they'd seen Kathie's body buried under a tree, or under the Meadowlands parking lot in New Jersey, next to Jimmy Hoffa.

In early June, the *New York Post* reported the Bobby Durst affair with Prudence Farrow. Bobby was even quoted in the story, saying that Kathie was doing badly in life, flunking medical school and having a problem with drugs, particularly cocaine. He said Kathie came home the Sunday night of her disappearance from Gilberte Najamy's home in a foul mood, and he blamed Gilberte.

"She'd come home from Gilberte's yelling and screaming and giving me a tough time over lawyers and why I do this and why I do that. It was a tirade," Bobby told the *Post*. "Gilberte Najamy from the very beginning has been trying to get us to break up. For whatever reason, she never liked me."

Bobby also admitted publicly that Kathie was using

cocaine and wondered if her drug use was the reason for her disappearance.

"All I want to know is that she's someplace and she's all right," said Bobby. "I'm not trying to drag her back."

The *Post* story quoted anonymous officials saying they didn't know if Kathie was murdered or had run away and assumed a new identity. Struk had no idea where they'd gotten that information, but he was amused that Bobby would talk to the *Post* but not to the New York police. For a man who had nothing to hide, he wasn't saying much.

The day the *Post* story was published, Kathie's sister Mary Hughes parked herself in front of Bobby's apartment, waiting with reporters for Bobby to emerge. He did, late in the morning, with his dog, Igor, and Mary called out to him, asking why he and the Durst family were ignoring Kathie's family.

Mary called Struk later that day. She had been crying.

"I told him, 'I know you killed her!' But he just looked at me as if he didn't even know me and said, 'I have nothing to say to you.' That's it. He's married to my sister for nine years and that's all he can say? Isn't there anything you can do?"

"Mary," said Struk, "I don't know what to say. I wish I did, but I don't."

12

CENTRAL Park was awash in color, and Mike Struk was enjoying the view. He always liked the autumn months, the cool weather a welcome relief from the stifling, humid summer heat that turned the Twentieth Precinct into a super-oven.

Summer passed by quickly for Struk, who took a respite from the frustrations of the Durst case and spent some much-needed vacation time with his children. He even found himself a girlfriend.

As he stood on the corner of Central Park West and West Eighty-sixth Street, having returned from a court appearance to testify in a burglary case, he took deep, full breaths, inhaling the cool, fall air. He felt pretty good. Better than he had in months, with the the Durst case and all its problems placed somewhere in the back of his mind.

The case was cold; frozen was more like it. The last newspaper story had appeared in June. Even the calls from the psychics were few and far between.

Struk took one last deep breath then walked west toward Columbus Avenue.

When he returned to the precinct, he saw Gibbons in

his office, focused on paperwork laid out on his desk.

"Whatcha got there?" said Struk.

Gibbons looked up, his expression a mixture of seriousness and excitement. "We got the phone records."

There they were, Bobby's phone records, subpoenaed months ago by Roger Hayes and finally delivered courtesy of New York Telephone.

Struk pulled a chair up to Gibbons's desk.

"Look," said Gibbons, who'd spent the last hour studying the records, pointing to a listing of calls made to Bobby's office on Tuesday afternoon, February 2. "Collect calls, all of them, from Ship Bottom, New Jersey. It's down the coast, on Long Beach Island. Just north of Atlantic City. That's our boy, isn't it? Isn't that his MO, making collect calls?"

"You bet," said Struk. "That cheap fuck wouldn't put a dime in a pay phone if someone gave it to him. Look at this."

There were dozens of collect calls to Bobby's office, but only on that one day did any calls originate from Ship Bottom.

"Where did he say he was that day?" said Gibbons.

"In Connecticut, on business," said Struk.

Struk ran over to his desk, pulled out his Durst file, and removed a copy of Bobby's itinerary, the one Bobby had tossed into the garbage and Gilberte Najamy found.

"Here, look. He wrote down that he arrived in South Salem at two A.M. that Tuesday morning and left at seven A.M. It doesn't say where he went, but he drove back to Manhattan at eight that night," said Struk.

"What's that say?" said Gibbons, pointing to a single word scribbled between the "7 A.M. leave home" and "8 garage."

"It says 'drive,' " said Struk. "The little fucker wasn't in Connecticut. He went to Jersey."

Gibbons and Struk agreed they needed to check the local property records for any Durst holdings in the Atlantic City area, including and surrounding Long Beach Island.

Struk suddenly sat up in his chair, shocking himself with his brilliant thought.

"The Pine Barrens."

"The what?"

"The Pine Barrens. This is near the Pine Barrens."

The Pine Barrens were 1.1 million acres of sandy expanse and thick forests between Atlantic City and Philadelphia known chiefly as the last resting place for assorted mobsters; the fine, loose dirt was easy to dig up any time of the year, even in early February.

"How would he know to go to the Pine Barrens?" said Gibbons. "Hit men and serial killers go to the Pine Barrens."

"Maybe he had help. I don't know," said Struk. "What I do know is I better get down there."

———

THE cold November wind slapped Struk's face as he stood on the shore in Ship Bottom on Long Beach Island, watching the breaking waves of the Atlantic Ocean. He stood in the sand, looking like an overgrown seal in his black trench coat and black shoes.

Struk was deep in thought. The instant he saw the Laundromat he made the connection. He tracked down the collect calls to Bobby's office on February 2. They came from two pay phones. One here, on Long Beach Island Avenue near the beach, and one across the bridge on the mainland, in Manahawkin, which was right in front of a Laundromat.

Struk remembered the coat. That expensive Burberry raincoat hanging on Bobby's closet, the one he'd apparently washed and ruined.

He washed it here, that Tuesday.

As Struk stood on the beach, his eyes closed, seagulls circled high above him.

He was convinced that Kathie Durst was down here. Somewhere. Bobby supposedly owned property in the area, and Struk was prepared to get a backhoe and dig through every inch of ground. But the Ocean County courthouse didn't have any listings for property owned by a Robert Durst, or any Durst, for that matter.

And Struk knew that searching the Pine Barrens was pointless. Finding a body in such an expanse would be like searching for a golf ball on the moon.

On the drive back to Manhattan, up the Garden State Parkway, Struk decided it was time to pay a visit to Flo Jones, Bobby's former secretary, who lived on 145th Street.

Somehow, Jones had slipped through the cracks. Struk had wanted to interview her in the early stages of the investigation, back in February. But it was decided it would be better to wait until after he locked Bobby into a story. The problem was, aside from the first two interviews, Bobby wasn't talking, and Jones had been forgotten.

She wasn't pleased to see Struk at her door. But she let him in, and as she began to answer his questions, it was clear she had no love for Bobby, who she said had fired her in April, just a couple of months after Kathie disappeared.

Jones told Struk that she was the recipient of Bobby's collect calls and said he *always* called the office collect, which made it difficult to remember any specific day, like February 2, and know where Bobby might have been. Whenever he called in for messages, he never said where he was, unless he wanted her to know.

And when Bobby was in the office, aside from business calls, he had an entourage of women who called him or came by the office on a regular basis. Jones remembered their names. Judy Licht, Julie Baumgold, Susan Berman, and Joanna Revson. There was also that Farrow woman, though Jones couldn't remember her first name.

"I did like his wife. I felt so bad for her," said Jones.

"Why was that?"

"She told me he was beating her. I said what the hell you doing, get away from that man. He was my boss, but no woman has to take that. You know what I mean?"

And Jones clearly remembered Bobby telling her, before he even reported Kathie's disappearance to the police, that Kathie was gone.

"He said, 'You may as well know, Kathie is missing,' " said Jones. "I said, 'What do you mean?' He said she was gone."

It was at this point that Jones told the detective that she had been fired, nearly three months later, in mid-April, and that Bobby had taken all her logbooks and office notes.

"Why did he fire you?" asked Struk.

"Damned if I know," said Jones.

———

IT was a week before Christmas, and Struk once again made his way downtown to Roger Hayes's office, this time fighting through holiday traffic.

He knew this was going to be his last shot at convincing Hayes to go to a grand jury. Only this time he had the phone records, and the statement from Flo Jones that Bobby had known that his wife was gone before he even filed his report to the police. And, as before, he had the interviews with the friends, Kathie's family, her professors from medical school, the itinerary, and the boot receipt. He felt confident, more than he had at any other time during the investigation.

As he presented his new evidence to Hayes, Struk was forceful.

"He tells me he's in Connecticut, but he's down in south Jersey. Someplace called Ship Bottom. The one and only time any collect calls are made to his office from Ship Bottom is February second. And the calls are made in front of a Laundromat, where he washes an expensive coat. Do we have to guess why?" said Struk. "The next day he buys a new pair of boots and tells his secretary that his wife is gone."

Hayes listened intently.

"Are you certain it was Bobby down in Jersey?" said Hayes.

"Who else could it be? That's his MO: he makes collect calls to his office."

"Did you confiscate the coat?"

"No, but I saw it, along with Kathie's sister and another woman."

"And you saw it entering the apartment illegally, right? You didn't have a warrant. The sister let you in and you tiptoed around the place, right?"

Struk said nothing when Hayes lectured him again on double jeopardy and the simple fact that the Durst family would defend Bobby with the biggest legal guns in New York.

Struk argued that he believed the evidence was more than circumstantial, it was overwhelming, enough to convince a jury. But again, just like the last meeting, Roger Hayes smiled, and Struk knew what was coming.

"I would agree that the evidence is compelling, and I'm talking about the actual evidence you can use in this case. But you know why we can't go forward," said Hayes. "You have to give me more."

Struk didn't answer. He didn't have to. He knew it was over. He'd spent nearly a year investigating the disappearance of Kathie Durst, and he had everything but Kathie Durst.

In the end, he realized he didn't have a case.

As Struk rose slowly from his chair, Hayes extended his hand.

"Mike, you fought the good fight, my friend. You know how these things work. Maybe something will turn up."

Struk reached over, grabbing Hayes's hand.

"Mark my words, this isn't over," said Struk. "One day, years from now, we'll catch some guy doing something and he's going to want to cut a deal. And he's going to tell us that he knows something about what happened to the rich guy's wife."

13

THE smallish man with the laundry bag said nothing as he walked by a group of people standing in the foyer of the four-story house at 18 North Allen Street.

He looked like they did, poor, disheveled, lost— wearing old, crumpled clothing that covered old, tired bodies. They formed a circle, trying to scrounge up nine dollars to buy a pizza, which would serve as their dinner. If they were really lucky, they'd have enough change left over to buy a bottle of soda. As they pulled out pieces of paper and lint from their pockets and counted whatever loose coins they could find, the man with the laundry bag walked up to his room. The room was small, just a bed, a kitchen, and bathroom. The price was $300 per month. Fourteen other rooms like this were sectioned off in the old mansion in Albany, New York, which served as a home—temporary or otherwise—for transients and other lost souls.

Some had jobs with meager salaries. Others were mired in a haze of drugs and alcohol, collecting a monthly check from the state. All had barely enough money to pay their rent, eat every now and then, and maintain a steady supply of cigarettes.

Some of the people living here stayed for years, others only a week or two. Most arrived without a destination, looking only for a cheap place to sleep. The landlord was a lady named Pearl who had been born during the Roosevelt administration—the Teddy Roosevelt administration. She had to be around ninety years old, yet was as sharp as a woman thirty years her junior. She knew how to quickly size up prospective tenants, making sure they had the first month's rent, cash or money order, and had them sign a lease, which didn't really matter because she knew most of them would be long gone in a matter of weeks.

As long as she collected that first month's rent, she was fine.

When the man with the laundry bag arrived two days earlier in the old rental car, he paid his rent in cash. Pearl eyeballed him up and down. He appeared quiet and unassuming. He kept his hair short, wore an old T-shirt, and upon close contact, Pearl could detect a faint smell of marijuana on his breath. That didn't bother Pearl, who had a decidedly different opinion if she smelled Scotch or Ripple. When Pearl accepted his cash she noticed his hands. Unlike the other residents, these hands were smooth, clean. He wasn't a laborer, that much was certain. She watched as he walked up the stairs to the second floor and to his room, which he entered, dropping his laundry bag on the bed. He remained there for only a few minutes, washing his face and brushing his teeth. He then headed back outside, past a man sitting on the second-floor landing with a radio in his lap, listening to a Yankees baseball game. Don Mattingly had just hit a home run, and the man lit up a Marlboro in celebration.

As he walked out of the house, by the people in the foyer, the man could see they were counting their change. It was the end of the month. For some of them, it was another day or two before the next check came. He stopped, reached into his pocket, and pulled out a crisp ten-dollar bill, handing it over to a woman who was standing with the group.

Now they had their dinner money. With the change and few dollar bills they managed to scrounge, they even had enough for a soda and salad.

They were all grateful, each offering a heartfelt thank-you.

"Would you like to eat with us?" said one of the men in the group.

The man smiled back.

"Maybe later," he said, the words coming out in a slow drawl. "I'm sure we'll see each other again later."

He walked outside, and faded into the darkness.

———

JOE Becerra sat behind the wheel of his idling unmarked police cruiser, fumbling through papers that lay scattered on the passenger seat, looking for the one sheet that had a description of the South Salem home that had once been owned by Robert and Kathie Durst.

Becerra knew the house was here, on this block, but there had been no addresses back in 1982, and he didn't want to attract attention by knocking randomly on doors.

Frustrated, he gave up searching for his written sheet, closed the folder, and peered through the car window. Becerra had spent two weeks studying the Kathie Durst file, absorbing each interview and concluding early on that Kathie Durst hadn't just vanished. His curiosity had brought him here, to Hoyt Street, and he was now searching for a stone facade.

To his right were the older lakeside homes, which were small, some quaint, with backyard decks that extended down onto piers that stretched out onto the still waters of Lake Truesdale. On the other side of the street were several large Colonial homes, some of which were new. Christmas decorations adorned a few of the homes, while others displayed menorahs in celebration of Hanukkah.

The block ended in a cul-de-sac. To its right Becerra noticed what appeared to be a stone wall. The house behind the wall was the second from the end, its stone facade covered by dormant shrubbery.

Becerra drove slowly down the block, stopping in front of the stone wall. He stepped out of his car and walked toward the front door. He pressed his hand over his tie, making sure it was straight against his crisp white shirt and freshly pressed dark suit, and knocked on the thick, wooden door.

A young woman answered, and Becerra identified himself, showing his badge, apologizing for the intrusion and stating that he was searching for a house once owned by Robert and Kathie Durst.

"This is it," said the woman, who identified herself as Gabrielle Colquitt.

She was young, maybe thirty-ish, thought Becerra. He explained that Mrs. Durst had disappeared long ago and he was researching her case. He didn't want to tell her too much, but Colquitt said she knew about the missing woman. Becerra eagerly accepted the invitation to come inside, where Colquitt offered him a soda. They sat down on her sofa.

"The neighbors told me about Kathie Durst after I bought the house. I thought that was over with," said Colquitt.

"Well, it was. Sort of," Becerra said. "We received some new information and I wanted to come here and see the house."

Becerra tried to stay focused on Colquitt but couldn't stop himself from looking around, catching glimpses of the kitchen, dining room, and living room. There was a bedroom toward the rear, past the stairs that led down to a bedroom and a mudroom.

Colquitt said she had never met Robert Durst, having bought the house in 1994 for $400,000 from the previous owners, Carmen and David Garceau.

The Garceaus, said Colquitt, bought the house from Durst in 1990.

"It's funny. They told me that when they bought the house there wasn't a stick of furniture here except for a cot downstairs in front of the crawl space. Seems Mr. Durst was sleeping down there. But I don't know what you would find here. I'm sure the police searched the house back in 1982," said Colquitt.

Becerra put his glass down, his mind racing to find a way to soften the news he was about to deliver.

"Actually, they didn't," he blurted. "That's why I'm here. You see, Mr. Durst reported his wife missing in Manhattan, and the police there had several eyewitnesses who placed his wife in the city before she disappeared. So they never thought it important to search up here."

"Excuse me?" said Colquitt, jumping to her feet. "I thought this was all done with, that they searched the house and the property. I was told the police were up here."

"A couple of troopers did come inside the house, but they never searched it."

"And I'm guessing you're here to get my permission to do just that," said Colquitt, standing, her arms crossed against her chest. "Do you really think you'll find anything? I mean, it's what, almost eighteen years?"

Becerra paused for a moment, unsure what to say next.

Colquitt then rushed her hand to her mouth.

"Oh, my God, you don't think her body is here, do you?"

Becerra stood up. He wanted to be forthright, but he didn't want to scare her.

"Listen, I don't know what we would find, if anything, but with your permission, I'd like to look in the house, on the property and in the lake. It will take some time—months. I'd have to wait until spring to search the property and lake. I'll try not to inconvenience you. But in the end we'll clear any doubts that something may have happened inside this house."

Colquitt appreciated Becerra's honesty, and to his surprise she didn't hesitate in agreeing to the search. She even promised not to tell the neighbors about Becerra's visit or the investigation.

THE White Plains office of Westchester County district attorney Jeanine Pirro was large and intimidating, a rectangular room filled with upholstered furniture, an oversized conference table, Oriental rugs, and photos of the beautiful district attorney with former President George Bush, Henry Kissinger, and New York Cardinal John J. O'Connor.

Pirro had decorated the office herself after winning her first term in 1993, and it resembled the office of a partner at a top New York law firm, not someone on the public payroll.

Joe Becerra was led into the office by a secretary and took a seat at the table that filled the center of the spacious room. He sat with one of Pirro's assistants, John O'Donnell, a senior investigator in charge of homicide investigations.

Becerra had a good relationship with Pirro, who was Westchester County's first female district attorney, having bulldozed her way through the male-dominated ranks of local politics. She was smart, resourceful, well-spoken, and possessed the kind of dark-haired, brown-eyed beauty that melted men in their shoes.

At forty-seven years of age, she looked at least ten years younger, thanks to a daily regimen that included an intense workout at 6 A.M. The hard work had paid off in many ways, and her glamorous appearance earned her inclusion in *People* magazine's "50 Most Beautiful People of 1997."

Added to her package was her husband, Al, a well-known real estate attorney and influential Republican Party insider, a major fund-raiser and good friend of New York governor George Pataki. Her husband's wide influence had helped Pirro win her first bid for office in 1993, and he'd been there again for an easy reelection campaign in 1997. During her tenure in office she developed a reputation as a no-nonsense prosecutor who pioneered the first domestic violence unit in the county and placed greater importance on hate and environmental crimes. Pirro's conviction rate, at 97 percent, was by far the highest in Westchester County history.

She was also known as the district attorney who never met a television camera she didn't like. Pirro had an insatiable thirst for press coverage and self-promotion, courting the local and national media and appearing frequently as a guest commentator on programs like *Nightline, Geraldo,* and *Larry King Live.*

As an assistant district attorney, she was known to have walked over a few of her fellow assistants—and the DA himself—in order to shine the media lights on her cases. She served as a Westchester County court judge prior to her election as district attorney. After taking office, she let it be known throughout all of law enforcement that she, and she alone, would speak to the press. Many considered her arrogant, interested only in her own gain, to the point where she would take personal credit for high-profile cases, leaving the police who actually solved the crime cursing on the sidelines. Her own assistant district attorneys, 118 of them, walked the halls in fear, hoping they would never anger their boss.

It was also no secret that Pirro was politically ambitious and eyed bigger and better things. She'd once been a Republican candidate for lieutenant governor, and following her reelection victory in 1997, she was considered a prime candidate to replace Democratic senator Daniel Patrick Moynihan when he retired in 2000.

Pirro was a political star and would have thrown her hat into the Republican primary ring against New York mayor Rudy Giuliani, who was also eyeing the seat, if it hadn't been for the problems encountered by her husband, who was contesting very public and embarrassing allegations of income-tax evasion.

In early 1999, U.S. attorney Mary Jo White alleged in a sixty-six-count indictment that Al Pirro had fudged his federal income taxes from 1988 to 1997, hiding $1 million in income.

He allegedly did so by claiming assorted personal expenses as business deductions, including his Ferrari and his wife's Mercedes-Benz. He also claimed Caribbean vacations, furnishings for a Florida vacation home, and a Mercedes for his mother-in-law, along with cigars and fine wines, as business expenses.

What made things even more interesting was that Al had the kind of political and social connections most lawyers could only dream about. He was considered the number one real estate attorney in Westchester County and lobbied for the likes of Donald Trump, New York City's self-proclaimed master builder. Al Pirro easily moved projects along through the labyrinth of local zoning and municipal regulations, even controversial projects such as the new $100-million mall in White Plains. If you wanted to build in Westchester County, you turned to one man, Al Pirro. His wide influence extended deep into Republican political circles. He was a major party fund-raiser, the man future governors, senators, and even presidential hopefuls turned to for help to fill their coffers.

The couple enjoyed their standing in Westchester County and lived accordingly in a $1.7-million home in Harrison, an upscale community, with Pirro contributing her $136,700 salary to pay the house bills.

Jeanine Pirro herself wasn't named in the indictment, even though she had signed many of the joint returns. She said she trusted her husband, and claimed that the charges were politically motivated, given that there was a Democrat, Bill Clinton, serving as president.

There was a strong feeling among Pirro's supporters that if a Republican had been serving in the White House, the U.S. attorney would never have filed the charges.

Unfortunately for Pirro, that wasn't the case. And it wasn't the first time her husband had been in trouble.

In 1986 Pirro withdrew as a candidate for lieutenant governor of New York following questions about her husband's dealings with a waste-disposal company that allegedly had ties to the mob. In 1995, after successfully defending himself against charges that he offered a $5,000 bribe to a local planning official to support a planned entertainment center, Al Pirro found himself the defendant in a paternity suit. The plaintiff, Jessica Marciano of Indiana, claimed that she and Al had a torrid three-month affair seventeen years earlier when both were working on a condominium project in Florida. The affair led to the birth of a daughter. Al denied the claim for three years, until a court-ordered DNA test in 1998 determined that Al was indeed the father of the now sixteen-year-old girl.

To his wife's embarrassment, Al publicly acknowledged that the girl was his daughter and announced that he had placed $10,000 in a trust fund. That didn't assuage Marciano, who was looking for more zeroes, claiming past child support.

The recent charges by the U.S. attorney alleging income-tax fraud only added to DA Pirro's woes, and what with her husband's trial approaching, she had other things on her mind when she entered her office to sit down with Joe Becerra.

Pirro walked over to one end of the table, her legs exposed up past the knee, thanks to a fine-fitting business suit. Becerra had to continually remind himself that he was talking to the district attorney and hoping to gain her blessing to reopen the Kathie Durst investigation.

Becerra didn't think there would be a problem. He had a track record with Pirro, having brought other investigations before her, and they had a good relationship. But thanks to her husband's troubles, the district attorney sat there with Joe Becerra and a deputy, picking up only bits and pieces of the conversation about the missing wife and Becerra's intention to begin a new investigation.

Pirro ended the meeting quickly.

"Go ahead," she told Becerra. "Just keep us informed."

BECERRA wasted no time in lining up his interviews with the family and friends of Kathie Durst. He found all the names in the file. Some had been interviewed back in 1982, others were merely mentioned. All were still alive and most were still living in the New York area. Eleanor Schwank, who now used as a middle name Joy, was living in Matagorda, Texas, a coastal town south of Houston. Becerra figured he'd begin the investigation by reaching out to Kathie's family.

When the phone rang at Jim McCormack's home in suburban Sparta, New Jersey, he was working at his desk in the basement fielding some paperwork for his sports merchandising business. His wife, Sharon, answered the call.

"Get up here, you have to get up here," she called down.

Jim didn't quite understand, but looked up the stairs and saw his wife standing at the doorway, holding a phone, frantically waving, so he figured it must be something important.

"Who is it?" he whispered.

"An investigator with the New York State Police," she said, her hand over the phone. "He says he wants to talk to you. He wouldn't say why."

Jim grabbed the phone and listened as the voice on the other end of the line explained that his name was Joe Becerra, that he was reopening the investigation into the disappearance of Jim's sister Kathie Durst, and that he'd like to interview members of the family.

Jim's immediate thought was to tell this investigator not to waste his time. The NYPD had tried it, not just once but three times, with detectives knocking on his door as late as 1986. Nothing ever came of it, except the reopening of old painful wounds and the resurfacing of terrible memories.

"My sister didn't disappear," said Jim.

"I know," said Becerra. "I read the file. I have a lot of questions, but I need to speak with the family to start getting some answers."

Jim paused for a moment.

"You said you were with the New York State Police, right? Can you give me your number and I'll call you right back."

A thought occurred to Jim that perhaps he wasn't talking to a New York State trooper. So he took Becerra's number and dialed. The voice on the other end of line answered, "State police, Somers barracks." Jim asked for Joe Becerra.

"Sorry about that," said Jim. "I just wanted to be sure you were who you said you were. You have no idea what we've gone through over the years since my sister disappeared."

Becerra said he understood, then continued the conversation, asking if Jim and his siblings would be available for interviews.

Jim felt more relaxed now that he was certain he was talking to an investigator with the New York State Police, but he wondered why, after all this time, the New York State Police was interested in this case.

"What are you going to do that the city police didn't do before?" said Jim.

"Mr. McCormack, I'm interested in the house, the one your sister owned in South Salem. It's in my jurisdiction. I read the NYPD file, and I know about the discrepancies in Mr. Durst's statements. And I know your family believes he killed your sister. If you can give me your cooperation, I promise you, I'll get some answers."

Jim agreed to meet with Becerra, a renewed sense of hope overwhelming him. He handed the phone back to his wife, walked into his kitchen, pulled a beer out of the refrigerator, and took a long gulp.

Sharon followed him into the kitchen.

"They're investigating again? Why, why now?"

"He says he read the file and there were things that didn't add up. He wants to search the South Salem home," said Jim, taking another long swig.

"After all this time," said Sharon, who took a seat by

the kitchen table. "You know your sisters are not going to be happy with this. And neither is your mother."

Jim rolled his eyes, finished off his beer, and walked upstairs.

Sharon remained at the table, a tear falling down her cheek, her own memories rushing to the surface.

She was only twenty-three when she began dating Jim, who was nine years older. She had heard about the McCormack sister who married a millionaire and was nervous when Jim told her Kathie had invited them to a party at the Westchester home of Doug Durst, Bobby's younger brother.

Sharon remembered walking up to the front door of the estate, surprised that a family like the Dursts would keep their property in such a state of disrepair. The lawn grew wildly and was in desperate need of a trimming; the driveway pavement was cracked and broken. Home is where the heart was, thought Sharon, and this home was in desperate need of a coronary transplant.

But Sharon wasn't there to visit with the Dursts; she was there to finally meet Kathie, Jim's little sister, who was at the party with her husband, Bobby.

Sharon had heard so much about the youngest sister with the rich husband, and it was Kathie who opened the front door, offering a wide, beautiful smile and hug for her big brother and a warm hug for her brother's pretty new girlfriend.

Kathie was beautiful, so fine, Sharon had thought. She wore a long Indian skirt with sandals, her hair twirled into French braids that hung down to her shoulders. By the end of the afternoon Sharon was certain that Kathie was the classiest woman at the party. She even looked at Jim a different way after meeting his sister. If he could have a sibling as warm and pleasant as Kathie, then there must be something good and decent and warm about Jim.

It had to be in the genes, she thought.

As for the hosts, as good as Sharon felt about Kathie, she felt equally repulsed by the Dursts, who were cold and arrogant throughout the afternoon, remaining in their little cliques. It was always Kathie who handled the introductions. Bobby was there, but said little. He remained in a corner, a beer in his hand, quietly talking to his friends—Susan Berman and Doug Oliver.

Sharon felt like an intruder and couldn't wait to leave, and she couldn't wait to see Kathie again.

THE message on Gilberte Najamy's answering machine left her breathless. She put her hand to her chest, mouthed "Oh, my God," and dialed the pager number left by Joe Becerra.

Five minutes later her phone rang.

Gilberte was stunned when Becerra explained that he was reopening the Durst investigation. So surprised, and paranoid, was Gilberte that it took several minutes for Becerra to convince her that he really was an investigator with the New York State Police.

"You know, I spent thousands on hiring private detectives. I spent so much money I eventually lost my catering business," said Gilberte. "They even robbed my house, stole documents that Kathie had given to me."

Gilberte was spitting out information, going far too fast for Becerra to follow.

"You need to slow down, okay? Now, you were saying something about documents?"

"Yes, tax returns and stock transfers and Durst company papers on properties they owned or were going to buy around Times Square. She gave it all to me and told me to hold on to it. A year after she disappeared, my house was robbed and the papers were taken."

"Did you report that?" said Becerra.

"No. After Kathie disappeared I didn't trust the police. I didn't trust anyone. The Dursts have so much money, I didn't know who to trust."

"Well, right now you can trust me, okay?"

They talked on the phone for more than an hour with Gilberte telling Becerra that she thought about Kathie every day, that she had always known the truth would finally emerge, and that she wanted to help any way she could.

Gilberte immediately determined that she liked Joe Becerra and was beside herself with delight when Becerra said he was going to search the house in South Salem.

"That's what I told that idiot Mike Struk after Kathie disappeared! I told him to go there, but he wouldn't listen to me! I told him she never got on that train that night, and I told him I broke into the house and it didn't look right, and I told him Bobby was throwing Kathie's stuff in the garbage! I told him all that and he ignored me. He was bought off, I know he was. The Dursts got to him!"

Becerra didn't say a word as Gilberte spewed nearly eighteen years' worth of frustration. When she was finished, Becerra said he wanted to schedule a meeting at the barracks to review the case.

Gilberte agreed, asking if she could bring along another old friend, Kathy Traystman.

Becerra agreed, and asked Gilberte to keep quiet about his call.

After hanging up the phone, Gilberte turned to her partner, Andrea.

"I can't believe it," she cried. "They reopened the case. They're going after Bobby. After all this time, they're going after Bobby."

———

ENDLESS traffic jams made the drive from Westchester to Long Island difficult, first on the Cross Island Expressway coming off the Throgs Neck Bridge, then on the Long Island Expressway heading east toward New Hyde Park.

When Becerra finally entered the modest home of Ann McCormack, she was sitting in her kitchen, gazing out a window, and offered little reaction when he broke the news to her.

Ann didn't want to meet with the investigator, and did so only after a long discussion with her daughter Mary, who spoke with Becerra and wanted her mother to give him a chance to explain what he was doing.

"I can't do this," said Ann.

"I know, Mom. It's going to be hard on all of us. But I spoke with this investigator and he's serious. I have a good feeling about him," said Mary.

Ann was polite enough when Becerra arrived, offering him a drink and something to eat. She was now in her mid-eighties and relegated to spending most of her time at her home. She had learned to come to terms with the loss of her daughter, even though there was no body, no funeral, no grave to visit. There was never a last good-bye—just a call one evening that her precious daughter, a medical student, was missing. That was it. Ann would often finding herself sitting in Kathie's old bedroom, sobbing as she remembered her beautiful baby.

The first few years had been the hardest, particularly after the hearing in 1983, when the courts turned down Ann's request to become temporary administrator of her daughter's estate. There wasn't much there, less than $50,000. But Bobby had challenged Ann, and won.

"I don't think you know what we as a family went through with the Dursts," said Ann. "You're sitting here telling me that you think you can resolve this case, but do you really know anything about it? Do you know we went to court? I went to court, to look over my own daughter's estate, and that monster challenged me and won. Did you know that?"

"No," said Becerra. "I didn't."

"Then you don't know about the stock-transfer documents held in Kathie's name but forged by Bobby, who wanted to sell them. And you don't know that he tried to sublet the East Eighty-sixth Street apartment my daughter had even before he reported Kathie missing. And you don't know that my daughter Mary went to the Riverside

Drive apartment and found all of Kathie's jewelry—her diamond earrings, a watch, a wedding band, and two gold chains—after Bobby told us she was wearing the jewelry when she disappeared. Did you know all of that?"

Becerra said nothing. It was obvious Ann was carrying a deep pain, not just over the loss of her daughter, but a result of the obvious frustrations from years of dealing with a criminal justice system she believed had failed her.

"How can we, Mr. Becerra, this little family from Long Island, ever even hope to fight people like the Dursts? Justice? What justice is there for people like us? We tried it before, and we failed. I really don't have the energy to try it again. My daughter is dead, Mr. Becerra, and I've come to terms with that. If you want to investigate, if you really think you can bring closure for my family, go right ahead. But I can't help you."

———

JANET Finke wasn't particularly happy to receive a phone call from Joe Becerra, and far less thrilled to learn that the state police investigator had found her after arresting her brother, Todd, on New Year's Day. It was a fortunate break for Becerra, who had been having difficulty locating Finke, who was remarried and living under a different name. She was far removed from those crazed years when she was married to Alan Martin, and even before that, when she worked as the Dursts' cleaning lady.

Janet had been only sixteen when she started her home-cleaning service. She was bright, enterprising, and very pretty—tall with long blond hair. The Dursts became clients, and in her early twenties she became friendly with Kathie, who treated her like the younger sister that Kathie had never had. There was a period in the late 1970s when Janet lived with Kathie and Bobby, whom she called Bob, in their Manhattan apartment, and on Kathie's days off from medical school, the two women would socialize, visiting dance clubs and restaurants.

When they were in South Salem they visited the home of Keith Richards, the Rolling Stones guitarist who had a house there. Richards kept peculiar hours, sleeping till four or five in the afternoon, then staying up all night drinking and playing music. Every once in a while Mick Jagger would show up and they'd have impromptu jam sessions in the backyard, which infuriated Richards's neighbors.

Janet and Kathie had even gone together to a party at the Playboy Mansion in California. When they returned, they said little about their trip, but their smiles spoke volumes.

Janet saw the best and worst of Kathie and Bobby. She remembered clearly that Bobby was sensitive and generous, a quiet man who, despite rumors of his cheapness, always paid the bill at restaurants. On occasion he'd even crack a joke. He was as easygoing as they came and exhibited very little ego for a man of his wealth and means. Women loved him. Not sexually, but emotionally. They felt his sensitivity and wanted to mother him.

Kathie was far more pleasant, and exuded a brilliant warmth that drew people close to her.

Best of all, she could talk for hours, and the two women would do just that, talk and talk and talk.

While Kathie was in medical school she talked about working with children, perhaps as a pediatrician, and even mentioned that she still hoped to be a mother one day.

They'd talk about Janet's boyfriend, Kim, an unassuming man who worked as a landscaper. They had gone out for five years, breaking up shortly before Kathie disappeared.

Becerra told Janet that he had begun the investigation two months earlier after speaking to her former brother-in-law, Timmy Martin. Janet was irate to learn that Martin was not in jail and wanted to know who let that "fucking wacko" back on the streets.

"I can't believe he's out on probation," Janet said. "Not only does he burglarize homes and participate in nearly every crime imaginable, but he's also masturbating in front of women—in public! Right now I'd worry less about Bob Durst and more about Tim Martin. He should have been locked up years ago."

Becerra said nothing else about Martin, moving the conversation along to the Dursts. As Janet told her stories of the good times with Bobby Durst, there were incidents she couldn't explain, and behavior she could only question.

She remembered clearly that Bobby would disappear, sometimes for days at a time, without so much as saying good-bye. Upon his return he'd never say where he'd been, offering instead weak excuses that he was scouting a potential out-of-town real estate purchase.

And Janet remembered when Kathie told her about the Polaroids she found in the drawer, the ones Bobby had taken of the apartment, including the closets and bathrooms. The explanation, said Janet, was that Bobby was having an affair. But Janet never bought into that.

"That had nothing to do with another woman," said Janet.

"What's that supposed to mean?" said Becerra.

"Just that, it had nothing to do with another woman. Do you have any idea how weird he could be? Think about it. Changing the inside of a closet and medicine cabinet? That's got nothing to do with a woman."

"What do you think it's about?"

"You don't want to know what I'm thinking," said Janet. "Look, I haven't heard from Bob in years. I have a new husband, children, and a new life. I don't think I can give you much."

But Janet did have a suggestion—that Becerra should have a conversation with Liz Jones. Liz had taken Janet's place and had been cleaning the Dursts' South Salem home when Kathie disappeared.

"Talk to Liz," said Janet. "She'll tell you about the blood."

———

LIZ Jones still lived in South Salem. Like Janet Finke, the police had never interviewed her in 1982, a fact that Becerra found odd.

Liz had been cleaning the Durst home for about a year, given the job by Janet. She was in the house that Tuesday, February 2, two days after Kathie disappeared, and told Becerra that Bobby was gone that day. She didn't recall seeing anything unusual in the house after arriving at 8 A.M. It wasn't until the following Tuesday, February 9, the day the Kathie story broke in all the newspapers, that she noticed something odd. It was a dried bloodstain on the front panel of the dishwasher in the kitchen. She didn't know what to make of it. As she stared at the blood, someone knocked on the front door. It was the police. Two detectives, in suits. She said she couldn't remember if they were NYPD or with the New York State Police. They said they had seen the newspaper stories that day and asked Liz if she'd seen anything unusual in the house. She invited them in and took them to the kitchen, pointing to the blood on the dishwasher.

"They ignored it. They said they didn't think it was anything," said Liz.

"They said that?" said Becerra.

"Yeah. They weren't interested."

Becerra followed Liz's story, writing furiously in his pad. This was something new and unexpected.

"What else?" he said.

"There were the fingerprints."

Liz said she took the two detectives to a closet in the dining room. Above the closet was a removable panel, and Liz said she showed the detectives fingerprints that were visible on the edges. One of the detectives took a chair, climbed up, and pushed the panel in, looking inside. He didn't see anything.

"That was it. They left and I never saw the police again. They didn't seem interested in talking to me or checking out the fingerprints or the blood." said Liz.

"If they did, what would you have told them?" said Becerra.

"That Bobby was weird, really weird. A couple of months after Kathie disappeared I found pictures and letters in the garbage. About a dozen of them. All these women, giving Bobby their bust size and telling him in writing what they'd do to him if he ever called. Real kinky stuff. He put an ad in the paper. A personal ad. Maybe the *Village Voice,* I don't know, but that's what they were responding to. He always scared me. When he placed a singles ad in the paper only weeks after Kathie disappeared, seeing that scared me even more."

———

THE entrance to the Garden State Parkway began at the northern edge of New Jersey at the New York border, and Joe Becerra came off the Tappan Zee Bridge thankful he now had to drive only a few miles over the New Jersey state line to the Paramus exit, then follow the written directions to Mike Struk's house.

Struk was perhaps the most surprised of all when he received a call a week earlier from Becerra, who introduced himself, complimented Struk on his thorough investigation, and asked for a sit-down. Struk was clearly amazed, and pleased, that the case still had life, that someone would actually pick it up some eighteen years later. Then he remembered his conversation years earlier with Roger Hayes, and his prediction that one day someone would step forward. What Struk hadn't figured on was that the guy stepping forward would be another cop. Still, Struk was hesitant to meet with Becerra. Like the McCormack family, he carried old wounds.

He retired from the NYPD in 1985, leaving the job he once loved on the first second of the first minute of the first day of his twentieth year—just enough to earn his pension.

He had remarried and was now father to two more children. At fifty-five, he was still thin, though the pencil mustache was gone. He had a head full of short, gray hair. He thought he was a little old to be starting over again, kids and all. But he enjoyed his life with his new family in New Jersey, playing house dad, working as a private investigator, and serving as a technical consultant for the television show *Law & Order*.

His old friend David Black, who'd authored Struk's book on the Met Murder, was one of the original screenwriters for the show and had brought Struk in as a consultant. The work was good and kept Struk busy, though there were days his mind would wander back to Manhattan, the Two-0, and the Durst case. He'd never show it, of course. He was still a tough guy. But the wounds were deep, still fresh as the day that Bobby Durst walked into his squad room. Resolving the case would certainly have meant a promotion, and maybe even prolonged his career with the NYPD. But like the Met Murder case, there had been no promotion, and Struk couldn't wait to file his retirement papers.

He now lived on a quiet, dead-end suburban street in a small, bi-level house surrounded by much larger, two-story center-hall Colonials, chauffeuring his two young children to their basketball and baseball games. He led Becerra downstairs to a family room. The two men sat on matching black leather sofas while Struk's two white Lhasa apsos jumped onto Becerra's lap.

"C'mon, get outta here," said Struk, waving his hand at the dogs.

Becerra, the dog lover, held them on his thighs, and petted them behind their ears, the smooth strokes quieting the dogs.

"So," said Struk, getting right to the point. "Whaddaya got?"

Becerra told him that he'd read the file, several times, and was developing a theory, a premise based on the possibility that Kathie Durst had never made it into Manhattan.

"So you're buying into what the friends were saying, especially that one nut, what was her name? Gilberte. You're thinking that maybe they were right?"

"I'm thinking that Bobby Durst lied about the whole thing, that he ran into New York to report her missing to keep your investigation there. I'm thinking he's an extremely shrewd guy who thought this out and didn't want any attention placed on the house in South Salem."

"You read the file," said Struk. "You know our witnesses said they saw her in Manhattan before she vanished."

"Mike," said Becerra, leaning forward, the dogs still on his lap. "I found Eddie Lopez."

Struk thought for a second before it came to him. "Lopez? The elevator guy?"

"Yeah. He says now he doesn't remember if he really saw Kathie Durst that night or that other guy who came later. The mystery man. He said he could have been mistaken."

Struk fell back into his sofa.

"He said that? Fucking guy. We even put him through hypnosis. I sat there for that whole bullshit session. I even told my lou it was garbage. But the brass wanted it. He repeated everything he told me the first time I interviewed him."

Struk clasped his hands together and rested his palms on his head, elbows out.

"What about the other employees?" he said.

Becerra said they were reinterviewed, and all said that Lopez had a drinking problem.

"They said it was normal for him to disappear for a few hours. They figure he was off drinking Scotch somewhere and lied about taking Kathie to her apartment to keep his job."

"Why didn't they tell me that before?"

"They were scared. I'm told this was a big deal back then, in all the papers. No one wanted to talk. And no one wanted to lose their job."

"Damn," said Struk. "I got to tell you, Joe, do you

know how hard we humped that case? We focused everything on the city based on what Lopez told us and the other witnesses. Did you talk to them, too?"

Becerra took his hands off the dogs, reached for his notebook inside his jacket, and flipped several pages.

"The dean at the school, Cooperman, he said he was never sure if the woman who called in sick that day was really Kathie Durst. And the other doorman, the guy who thought he saw her get into a cab, he's now saying he doesn't remember ever seeing Kathie Durst that morning."

"So we were chasing our fucking tails," said Struk, shaking his head. "So what are you going to do next?"

Becerra told Struk of his plan to search the South Salem home, the property around it, and the lake.

"I'll bring in forensics. Hopefully we'll come up with something," said Becerra. "I spoke with one of the Dursts' old cleaning ladies, a Liz Jones. She told me a story about some blood in the kitchen, on a dishwasher, a week after Kathie disappeared."

"I don't remember that," said Struk.

"She said two detectives knocked on the door and she let them in. They took a look around. She claims she showed them the blood, but they ignored it. It was the day the story broke in the papers."

Struk paused as if in deep thought. "I was up there that day, talking to the neighbors. There were four of us, me and a partner and two investigators with the state police. We walked around the outside of the Durst house, saw the broken window on the door from Gilberte. But we never went in. Do you think four seasoned detectives would walk into a house like that without a warrant?"

"I'm just telling you what she told me," said Becerra.

"If that's true, then why didn't she come forward back then?"

"Like I said, I'm just telling her story. Maybe she has an ax to grind. I don't know. She wasn't particularly friendly with Bobby Durst. She also said she showed the two detectives fingerprints on a panel above a closet. They looked inside, but didn't find anything."

"I don't know what the fuck you're talking about. Never heard that before," said Struk.

Becerra could see that Struk was clearly shaken with some of the new details in the case, especially the information about Eddie Lopez. He'd hung his entire investigation on Lopez's sighting of Kathie Durst. And Becerra didn't know what to make of Struk's denial about the blood in the house. He was right, thought Becerra, experienced detectives wouldn't have gone into the home. But Jones was believable.

Struk quickly regrouped, and rattled off some names, like Jim McCormack and Gilberte Najamy, asking Becerra if he'd spoken with them or anyone else.

"All of them," said Becerra, "including Najamy. She didn't think too highly of you."

"She was a pain in the ass," said Struk, who clearly remembered Gilberte, the novice detective who broke into the South Salem home and picked through Bobby's garbage. The woman with a hundred theories.

"I didn't know what her problem was back then, but there was more to her than I cared to find out. She was totally out of control. I think she was a caterer or something."

"She's working as a counselor at a women's shelter and living with her girlfriend in Connecticut."

"Girlfriend? She's a dyke?" said Struk.

"Looks that way."

"Now that I remember, someone said she may have been into women. I never figured out why someone as pretty as Kathie Durst would hang out with a Gilberte Najamy," said Struk.

"You don't think she and Gilberte . . . ?" said Becerra.

"No. Kathie was into men. That prick of a husband she had ignored her, so she took up with a bunch of different guys. Never in a million years would she hook up with someone like Gilberte, even if she were gay."

A young voice called down to remind Struk that he was late for a basketball practice, and Struk looked at his watch.

"Three o'clock. Time to go. Duty calls."

The two men rose from the couches and shook hands. Struk then reached over and took a brown notebook off the top of his television set and gave it to Becerra.

It was his personal notebook, and it included detailed thoughts and notes about the Durst case, all written during Struk's investigation.

"Listen, if you need me for anything, call," said Struk. "Right now all I can say is you have what I had, and that's nothing. I would search that house upstate. See what you come up with. Maybe you'll pull an O.J. and find your bloody glove."

Both men laughed at the obvious reference.

"Remember," said Becerra. "He got off."

14

THE dried mud on the outer edges of the old cupboard was rock hard and reddish in color, yet stood out like a shining beacon.

The cupboard was square, roughly two feet on all sides, and was inserted into the wall in the dining room. It had once been pulled out from the wall for some unknown reason, then put back in, the person pulling it out apparently leaving their partial handprints on the edges. Behind the wall was a space that opened wide at knee level. The only way to search inside the wall was to tear it down.

As forensic specialists gazed at what appeared to be partial handprints, once hidden in darkness and long forgotten, one of them told Becerra the reddish color appeared to be blood that was mixed in with the mud.

It was the first clue they had found in the home, and Becerra hoped there would be more.

Gabrielle Colquitt had given Becerra permission to search every last crevice in her pretty little home, and with the arrival of spring, he didn't waste any time. He brought in the special units, including divers to search the murky waters of Lake Truesdale, where they waded through the water in grids, marking off sections of the lake. The lake bottom was soft, the divers' feet sinking into the mud like quicksand.

Becerra didn't hold out much hope that the lake would turn out to be the last resting place for Kathie Durst. She had disappeared in late January, a time when the surface was usually frozen solid.

And like the lake, the property around the house had been frozen and digging a grave would have been all but impossible. But he brought in the cadaver dogs anyway to remove any lingering doubt that Kathie's remains were buried somewhere near the house.

Becerra thought he knew where Kathie Durst was. He just wanted to be sure.

Over the course of the spring and summer, Becerra quietly visited Hoyt Street more than half a dozen times. The forensics team examined the mud prints and searched downstairs in the crawl space, delicately digging through the loose dirt, a painstaking search that lasted more than six hours.

Each visit was a stealth mission. When the lake was dredged, nosy neighbors were told the police in the water were conducting an exercise. And when the house was searched, investigators used unmarked vans and plainclothes.

Becerra would come back to the house yet again and examine the living-room floor. Colquitt had told the investigator months earlier, during their first meeting, that when she bought the home in 1994 from David and Carmen Garceau, they had told her of the mysterious holes.

Becerra eventually found the Garceaus, who repeated their story to him.

Robert Durst had agreed to sell the house to them in February 1990, but only on the condition that they lease it back to him for three months.

Bobby had never given a reason why. The Garceaus were barred from entering the house until the last day of May.

It was an odd arrangement, said David. Even odder

was the condition of the house, which was in a shambles. It hadn't been cleaned in years.

The Garceaus intended to refurbish the house, which included replacing the dirty and stained carpeting on the main floor. When they removed the old carpeting, they found three holes in the wooden subflooring that were patched with plywood.

The living room, said David, was above the crawl space.

And there was more. When they agreed to buy the house, they saw but one piece of furniture, a cot, which was downstairs next to the entrance to the crawl space. Bobby had been sleeping on the cot; the Garceaus couldn't figure out why. The crawl space was so small a person had to crawl on his belly to get in. The floor of the crawl space was made up of loose dirt. The couple used it as a wine cellar.

The Garceaus said they knew nothing about Kathie Durst or her disappearance until told by neighbors bearing newspaper clippings. Like many other people, they mistakenly believed that the police had long ago searched the house.

Becerra looked on as Colquitt's furniture was moved and the carpet lifted, and he could see, right there in the center of the floor, three pieces of plywood that obviously didn't belong. The plywood was lifted, and the holes turned out to be old heating vents.

The forensic team turned its attention to the kitchen, particularly the dishwasher, which to Becerra's surprise was the same dishwasher the Dursts had used when they owned the home. Luminol was sprayed on the dishwasher and floor, and Becerra waited for the old blood to glow.

―――――

THE chatter that filled Jeanine Pirro's conference room quieted for just a second as Pirro poked her head in to say hello but left quickly. The district attorney wouldn't take part in the meeting called by Joe Becerra on Wednesday, November 8, 2000.

It was nearly a year since he began his investigation and Becerra was sitting around the large conference table along with other representatives from the state police, John Anderson from the New York City police, John O'Donnell from Pirro's office, two assistant district attorneys, and several guests, including Mike Struk, Gilberte Najamy, Jim McCormack, Kathy Traystman, and Ellen Strauss.

Struk was invited by Becerra, a specific request to share his expertise on the case. Struk didn't recognize Gilberte Najamy, whom he remembered as thin, with wild, dark hair. She had since filled out and was now a large woman with short, manageable hair. She wore old clothing and no jewelry. Struk did recognize Ellen Strauss, who to his eyes looked much the same as she had twenty years earlier. Ellen had aged well, and looked every inch the woman he remembered.

All were gathered to discuss the Durst case, which Becerra was still trying to sell to Pirro and her people, who made it clear they were not ready to go to a grand jury to seek an indictment with purely circumstantial evidence.

As people drifted into the room, it became clear that this was the first time in nearly twenty years that some of them had seen one another, and there were plenty of hugs and kisses among Gilberte, Ellen, Kathy, and Jim McCormack.

There was an underlying feeling of excitement in the room, a sense of hope that, after all this time, the McCormack family, along with Kathie's friends, would finally find closure and her killer would be brought to justice. They all looked to Becerra and thanked him for his efforts. Everyone believed they were on the verge of taking a major step forward, particularly Becerra, who thought bringing his evidence before a grand jury seemed more plausible than ever, considering the verdict that had been handed down in a similar case just two weeks earlier.

Dr. Robert Bierenbaum, forty-five, was a New York surgeon who had been convicted of killing his wife, Gail, who disappeared in 1985. Her body was never found, but prosecutors presented enough compelling circumstantial evidence to persuade a jury that she had indeed been murdered. Her husband, it was determined, strangled and dismembered her and took her remains to an airstrip in New Jersey. A pilot, Bierenbaum loaded his wife's body, which was packed inside a duffel bag, inside a Cessna and dumped her over the Atlantic Ocean.

It was a precedent-setting case, considering that Bierenbaum was convicted solely on circumstantial evidence. Judging by the evidence he had, Becerra thought the Durst case was a slam dunk. He knew he had far more compelling evidence against Durst than prosecutors in Manhattan had had against Bierenbaum.

But repeated attempts to nudge Pirro to move forward were greeted coolly. Pirro made it clear she wasn't about to take on a celebrity trial and all the trimmings that would go with it during an election year.

While the public had no idea who Bobby Durst was, and the press had forgotten the story of his missing wife aeons ago, the Durst Organization—the family business—was now worth more than $2 billion, and Pirro knew prosecuting Bobby would turn into a circus.

She also had other, more serious and pressing problems to deal with. Her husband, Al, was convicted on June 22 of tax fraud and was now residing in a minimum-security prison in Florida, having received a twenty-nine-month sentence. Al's conviction was a bitter and embarrassing mark on the DA's reputation and a career breaker. Pirro's designs for higher office were derailed, and she now faced a tough reelection campaign in 2001. Pirro had signed several of the fraudulent joint tax returns her husband was found guilty of submitting to the IRS, and the questions from her critics were simple: How could a woman, as bright and tough as Pirro, not know what was going on in her own home?

Pirro declined to answer any questions about her husband following the verdict. She knew the issue would be a main topic of discussion during the upcoming campaign.

The meeting concerning the Kathie Durst investigation lasted about ninety minutes. Becerra directed the conversation, going around the table, listening to everyone from Ellen to Kathy to Jim to Gilberte.

Gilberte did most of the talking, relaying again the story about Kathie's last day at her house along with a bizarre story about her encounter with a man named John Vigiani and his plan to kidnap Bobby Durst.

Kathy Traystman rolled her eyes as soon as Gilberte began to tell *that* story, knowing Gilberte's propensity to embellish, but she was utterly astonished when Jim McCormack rose from his chair to say he, too, had met the mysterious Vigiani. He shared his story about the meeting in the diner with his sister Mary.

"You see, you thought I was crazy," said Gilberte, pointing a finger at Kathy. "Vigiani was real. I told you he was real. You should have believed me. It was Dale Ragus, Kathie's attorney. She brought me up to her office and left me in a room with that guy. He scared the hell out of me."

Gilberte remembered that Ragus had said there was someone she, Gilberte, should meet, only she admitted that Ragus would deny ever making the introduction and deny knowing Vigiani.

"She just left the room, closed the doors, then in walked Vigiani," said Gilberte. "When he told me what he wanted to do, I was shaking. I just ran out of there."

As she continued her story, Jim nodded again and again, verifying everything Gilberte said about Vigiani, the little man with the sharp business suit and noticeable limp. Only Jim was unaware that it had been Dale Ragus, Kathie's attorney, who was behind the meeting.

"Vigiani told us about the dogs and the drugs and the ten thousand dollars," said Jim. "The police didn't seem to be doing anything at the time, so at first I didn't think it was such a crazy idea. But then I realized this was nuts, and we said no."

Gilberte felt vindicated. She told several stories during the meeting, each one raising eyebrows throughout the room. She said Kathie had given a folder containing damaging information on the Durst family to a New York senator, but the senator passed the folder along to Seymour Durst. Her implication was that Kathie's disappearance could be a conspiracy involving the Durst Organization.

There were two senators at the time, Daniel Patrick Moynihan and Jacob Javits, but Gilberte wasn't sure which one Kathie had approached.

Few in the room believed that story, so Gilberte moved on to tell about a burglary at her home a year after Kathie disappeared; the only items taken were papers and documents given to Gilberte by Kathie.

"They were the tax returns and stock documents she said Bobby forged," said Gilberte.

Kathy Traystman confirmed this story, saying her apartment had also been burglarized, around the same time as Gilberte's, and similar papers kept in a clothes drawer and given to her by Kathie had been stolen.

Neither Gilberte nor Kathy reported the burglaries to police, claiming they were spooked by the whole ordeal.

"It could have been a conspiracy," said Gilberte. "Kathie was threatening to expose Bobby, and I believe the information was embarrassing, and threatening, to Seymour Durst."

Becerra and the other law enforcement officials at the table said nothing, writing notes on their pads. They were listening, but weren't necessarily believing any of this.

But Gilberte continued on, telling everyone how the loss of her friend had ruined her life.

"I lost my business and my money. I should never have let Kathie leave my house that night. You don't know how guilty I feel over that. She told me if something happened to her, it was Bobby."

"She said that to all of us," said Kathy Traystman. "We told her to leave him. What else could we have done?"

Struk, for his part, remained quiet, but was redeveloping a strong dislike for Gilberte. She was running off at the mouth again, acting like she had in 1982, as if she were the detective and she knew the answers. Gilberte had gone overboard in 1982, breaking into the South Salem home and sneaking off with Bobby Durst's garbage. And her stories today were just as wild and out of control as the ones she'd told in 1982.

Struk didn't believe any of the conspiracy talk. He knew Gilberte was obsessed back then. And she seemed obsessed now. Perhaps it *was* guilt, he thought. But guilt over what? Letting Kathie leave her house that night? Here she was, years later, rambling on like she did back then, talking in a direct and accusatory manner, spitting out preposterous theories, and pointing an accusing finger at the NYPD, which amounted to pointing the finger at Struk.

For a moment the ex–NYPD detective wished Gilberte was a man, so they could go outside and settle this once and for all.

Becerra decided he'd heard enough from Gilberte and turned toward Jim McCormack, who had little to add other than questioning the role of the Durst family. It was apparent that the police weren't buying Gilberte's conspiracy theory, but Jim didn't rule it out completely. Aside from that one meeting with Seymour Durst, the McCormacks had never heard from him or the Durst family again. The McCormacks were forgotten, discarded. Kathie had been a Durst for nine years, but was no more important to them than some house cat. She was disposable.

"I never understood that," said Jim. "How callously and coldly they reacted to Kathie's disappearance. I always believed they knew something. Or they were protecting Bobby. Take your pick."

———

THE meeting ended around 3:30 P.M. with a reminder to everyone not to contact or speak to the press. Becerra had managed to keep his investigation under wraps for nearly a year, and he wanted to keep it that way. There would be one last search of the South Salem home next week, and then he said he would finally call Robert Durst, who had no idea a new investigation had begun.

But Becerra had another problem. No one knew where Bobby was.

Bobby had gone back to work in 1983 but left the Durst Organization in a huff ten years later after Seymour selected Bobby's younger brother Douglas to take over the business. Seymour, who was then in his eighties, had drawn a clear line of succession, and Bobby had been passed over. When he was informed of the news, Bobby stormed out of the Durst offices, cutting all ties with his family and close friends.

He wouldn't see his father again until two years later, in 1995. Seymour was on his deathbed, and Bobby visited him after assurances that no other family members would be present. He said his good-byes there, alone with his father, later skipping the funeral.

For the past five years Bobby had remained virtually out of sight, listing addresses in New York, Connecticut, California, and Texas. Just what he was doing, nobody seemed to know. There were rumors that he was involved in several real estate transactions, but it appeared that he had just dropped off the face of the earth, contacting no one. Not even his closest friends, like Doug Oliver, heard from him.

Bobby maintained a New York phone number, but the only way to reach him was to leave a message and hope he'd return the call.

Becerra figured he'd eventually track him down and even surprise him, hoping to sit him down and lock him into another story. He even spent the summer preparing the questions. Let him explain his way out of buying the shoes, or making the phone calls from Ship Bottom, or the itinerary he drew up, or the Burberry raincoat, or the records from Jacobi Hospital, or, of course, the handprints on the cupboard and blood on the dishwasher. And what about the rental car, the Rent-A-Wreck he drove some 450 miles to God knows where a month after Kathie disappeared. What was that about?

All Becerra wanted was ten minutes alone with Bobby Durst, and then he figured he'd have his man.

———

ON a Saturday morning, three days after the meeting in Pirro's office, Becerra had run his usual four miles, fed his dogs, and had just sat down in his living room when his phone rang.

It was Henry Luttman, his newspaper-reading colleague at the Somers barracks, and he asked Becerra if he'd seen the morning papers yet.

"No, I'm getting dressed. What's up?" he said.

"The Durst investigation, it's in the papers. Everything. And even worse, they talked to Durst himself."

"Jesus," said Becerra. "What did he say?"

"He said he didn't know anything, and he wouldn't have any comment."

Becerra had had an idea something was wrong when he received a call the day before from Barbara Ross, a reporter at the *New York Daily News*, who asked about the investigation. Becerra said, "What investigation?"

Ross pressed Becerra, who said that the Durst probe was still a missing-persons case and hung up.

But someone had talked, someone at that meeting on Wednesday had leaked word about the investigation. And not only to the *Daily News*. The *New York Times* ran a lengthy story the same day, including a Durst family statement: "Robert Durst continues to maintain his innocence."

And there was even more bad news. Both papers

credited Becerra, not Pirro, with reopening the case, which was true, but here in Westchester County, that's not how things were done. In Westchester County, this was Pirro's investigation; Becerra just happened to be along for the ride.

Becerra cursed his bad luck, and he cursed the media. He knew Bobby wasn't going to talk, not now, not after the world knew that police had searched the house in South Salem. Bobby would lawyer up again and say nothing.

As he sat there on his couch, Becerra rolled his head back and closed his eyes, trying to figure out who was the one who had leaked the story to the press.

15

ON November 15, 2000, four days after the revelations about the renewed investigation into the disappearance of Kathie Durst were reported in the New York papers, Klaus Rene Dillman of Galveston, Texas, received a phone call from a man with a pleasant voice who said he was an assistant to a deaf-mute named Dorothy Ciner.

Dillman had placed an advertisement in the local newspaper for an apartment he had available in a home he owned at 2213 Avenue K in Galveston. There were four apartments in the home, including the two in the front of the house, that had been available. Dillman had just rented one of them to an elderly man named Morris Black.

The assistant, who did not give his name, said Ms. Ciner was in her fifties and was interested in renting the two-room apartment.

The caller agreed to the $300 monthly rent and said Ms. Ciner would pay three months in advance upon her arrival, which would be in several days.

The assistant said Ms. Ciner traveled often, and would have someone come by from time to time to maintain the apartment during her absence.

The assistant spoke smoothly and assuredly, had a slow drawl, and paused before each sentence.

Dillman agreed, and the apartment was rented.

―――――

ELLEN Strauss was sifting through two large folders, both several inches thick, as a curious Gilberte Najamy anxiously looked on.

Ellen, the meticulously organized attorney, had always kept fastidious notes, some going back as far as 1978. She'd write daily accounts of meetings and conversations with friends as well as the time of day they occurred. The notes were maintained in books stamped with each year.

The women were in Ellen's home going through the thick folders, hoping to find some information on Susan Berman.

As Ellen scrolled her finger down each page of each book, she'd stop at any mention of a phone conversation with Kathie Durst, even the late-night calls that had come in long after Ellen had fallen asleep, when Kathie wanted to talk about her never-ending problems with Bobby.

Some of Ellen's friends considered her obsessive-compulsive, but it was just part of her nature. Along with the phone logs, there were notes and assorted documents, numerous news reports, and pieces of scrap paper, all contained in two manila folders that Ellen had kept over the years, hiding them in various parts of her home—under her bed, in a closet.

Just in case, she figured.

After hearing Gilberte and Kathy Traystman relay their stories about the burglaries in their homes, Ellen had decided to put her folders in a safe-deposit box.

During the meeting at Jeanine Pirro's office two weeks earlier, Ellen had whispered to Gilberte that she had plenty of old documents and newspaper clippings, and Gilberte wanted to see them, saying there could be something that might help the investigation along, the intensity of which had grown immeasurably now that the press had the story.

Ellen's papers and notes were now spread out on an antique wooden table. It was only 10 A.M. on a dreary Saturday, and it was wet outside. As they worked through the folders, a steady rain pelted against the windows. Ellen, as usual, looked like a million bucks. Her hair, makeup, and clothes were all in order, as if it were 10 P.M. and she was dressed for a late dinner.

Gilberte arrived wearing a wrinkled gray sport coat and sweater.

As she sat at the table, Gilberte raced through each document, ignoring the little scraps with random notes like "gay massage parlor" and "Mike Burns."

"Is any of this making sense?" said Ellen. "And who was Mike Burns?"

"Oh, nobody. Just some guy who hung around with Kathie," said Gilberte, who quickly dismissed the question and continued to shuffle through the papers, stopping dead in her tracks when she pulled out the doctor's letter.

"Oh, my," said Gilberte, hastily reading every line. "How did you get this?"

"I don't remember," said Ellen, looking over the table at the document. "I'm not sure if Kathie gave it to me or not."

Gilberte held the letter up, moving it over the table so Ellen could see. "You know, if this ever gets out he'll plead insanity when he's finally arrested. They'll put him in a nice, safe mental institution, not a jail cell where he belongs. We can't have that. Do you understand?"

Gilberte wasn't just pleading; she was issuing an order.

Ellen hemmed and hawed. She remembered the letter, but hadn't read it in years.

"I know what you're saying, Gilberte, but I think we should forward a copy to Joe Becerra. I think he should be aware of this."

Gilberte was adamant.

"No, Ellen, no. Let's hang on to this for a while, keep it here. I don't want anyone to know about this, at least not now. Okay? At least not now."

As she made her forceful plea, she grabbed Ellen's arm. Ellen decided there wasn't any rush to bring the letter to Becerra's attention, so she acquiesced, taking it from Gilberte's hand and placing it back into her folder.

Gilberte looked down at the table, at some of the other papers lying before her. She studied each of them closely, making sure nothing escaped her eyes. The letter had been a shock. What else did Ellen have? she wondered. It didn't take Gilberte long to find another piece of paper. Her eyes opened wide for a split second when she recognized it, a time line, written down by Gilberte and Ellen several weeks after Kathie disappeared. It traced Kathie's movements that last Sunday when she had visited Gilberte's house.

Ellen was trying to slip the doctor's letter into a clear, plastic covering when Gilberte held up the small piece of paper.

"And you can put this away, too," she said, holding it up high. "You can't show it to anyone, not the police, reporters, or anyone, okay?"

Gilberte wasn't as dogmatic in her tone as she was with the letter. She spoke softly and directly.

Ellen leaned over and took a quick look at the paper. "Is this significant?"

"No, but let's just put it away. No one needs to see this," said Gilberte, now leaning over the table and looking directly into Ellen's eyes. "This is about putting Bobby in jail, not tainting Kathie's memory. Promise me that no one will ever see this."

Ellen shrugged her shoulders and agreed, placing the paper back in the file.

The two women searched through what was left on the table, Gilberte paying careful attention to every little scrap. She was unnerved by what she found so far. She didn't want anything else to escape her attention.

The two women were also hoping to find something, anything, that would be useful in their search for Susan Berman.

Because Susan had been considered Bobby's best friend, Gilberte, Ellen, and Kathy Traystman had made it clear at the meeting that they thought she should be interviewed. Susan loved Bobby. He was her "brother," and if he were in a bind, she'd be there to help him. That was the nature of their relationship.

At the meeting, the women told those gathered that it was Susan who had served as Bobby's mouthpiece to the press during the weeks after Kathie's disappearance, and it was Susan who called Kathie's friends, wanting to know what was going on behind the scenes and what people were thinking.

It had been obvious that during many of those calls Bobby was right by her side, waiting to hear what new information Susan managed to glean.

And most important, it had to be Susan, they theorized, who had made the phone call to the dean at the Albert Einstein Medical School pretending to be Kathie.

The last anyone knew, Berman had moved to California. She had written several books, and she claimed to have made some money selling the film rights to *Easy Street,* her chronicle of the life of a mobster's daughter.

She drove off to California in a brand-new convertible soon after Kathie's disappearance, looking forward to a life as a screenwriter and esteemed member of Hollywood society. It was a life she had envisioned for herself all along.

Becerra had feigned immediate interest in Berman. She was one of Bobby's friends, and Bobby's friends were last on his interview list. Then Ellen did her own search, finding five Susan Bermans in the Los Angeles area. She E-mailed all of the information—complete with Social Security numbers, addresses, and phone numbers—to Becerra, who thanked her for her efforts but did nothing with the information. He was more interested in the *People* magazine story on the Durst investigation.

When it was published in early December, the *People* story was long, five pages, with happy pictures of Bobby and Kathie from the old days, the house in South Salem, and even Gilberte Najamy, sitting in a diner looking old and forlorn.

The *People* reporter contacted Becerra, but the investigator had had little to say. Privately he hoped that with its millions of readers, the *People* story would produce a witness—or several witnesses.

If he was really lucky, he thought, he'd get a good, unexpected break. Something totally out of the blue. Perhaps Bobby himself would read the story.

If anything, Becerra reasoned, it would make Bobby nervous.

———

THE barking wirehaired terriers had always been an annoyance to the neighbors on Benedict Canyon Road, but even more annoying today because it was Christmas Eve, 2000. Those damned dogs from that run-down house at 1527 had been barking all morning long. One of them, Lulu, was even running up and down the block.

The Los Angeles police were called, and upon arriving, they found the front door unlocked. They called into the house, but there was no answer. Two officers went around to the back and discovered a door that had been opened. They looked inside and saw red paw prints speckling the floor. They pulled their guns and slowly entered the house, following the paw prints to a back bedroom. There, lying facedown on the floor wearing only sweatpants and a T-shirt, was a woman, probably in her fifties. She had been shot, a single bullet to the back of the head. There were red paw prints all around the body, particularly around her blood-matted head.

The policemen searched through the remainder of the house, and everything seemed in order. It didn't appear that the woman was the victim of a robbery. They found her identification. Her name was Susan Berman.

16

THE holiday season had, thankfully, come and gone and Joe Becerra was ready to get back to work on the Durst case. He didn't have a wife or kids to awaken with on Christmas morning, and that in itself was depressing. He spent the holidays at his parents' home, spoiling his nieces and nephews.

Returning to work for Becerra was a godsend, lifting his spirits. He didn't even mind following up on calls he'd received weeks earlier, the result of the *People* story, from professional psychics and others who claimed to be clairvoyant. The calls at first were amusing, then distracting, and Becerra returned them all.

By Friday, January 5, 2001, he was ready to finally begin interviewing the friends and family of Bobby Durst, and he was going to start with Susan Berman. He downloaded the E-mails Ellen Strauss had sent him one month earlier, with the addresses of five Susan Bermans in the Los Angeles area. He then called the Los Angeles Police Department to let them know, as a matter of courtesy, that he was interested in talking to someone within their jurisdiction.

Five minutes later, Becerra was frantically trying to

reach Jeanine Pirro to give her the shocking news that Susan Berman was dead. Executed was more like it. At least that's what the L.A. cops said. Even more mind-boggling, she had apparently known her killer.

The L.A. police explained that based upon their preliminary investigation, Berman was notoriously fearful and paranoid, always expressing fears that she was in imminent danger of being harmed. Neighbors and friends said she always kept her doors locked, and she would never invite an unknown visitor inside her home.

Becerra was told there had been no forced entry, and Berman was apparently leading the killer to the rear of the house at the time of the murder. It appeared that whoever had shot her lifted up a gun, pointed it at the back of her head and fired one shot.

Berman had had no idea that her life was about to end.

The entry wound was small, and homicide detectives determined the gun to be a small-caliber weapon, maybe a .22, or a nine-millimeter. It was hard to tell because the bullet fragmented on impact.

Upon hearing the news, Pirro, like Becerra, was dumbstruck, but quickly realized what had been a somewhat sleepy investigation into an eighteen-year-old mystery now had new juice—and the juice was flowing. A key potential witness is slain? And during an election year, no less.

For their part, the Los Angeles police were interested in what Becerra had to say about his investigation. They didn't know anything about Bobby Durst or his missing wife or that he had been a good friend of Berman. They were intrigued by the possible connection, but never publicly considered Bobby a suspect. He was but one of many people of interest the L.A. police said they wanted to talk to. Aside from that, they were tight-lipped, unlike Pirro, who seized upon the opportunity, telling her subordinates to remind the state police that her office, and her office alone, would handle all media queries concerning the New York investigation.

Pirro also let it be known in a very public way that

prior to Susan Berman's death, Pirro's office had been preparing to interview the woman in connection with the Durst case, and that it was more than coincidental that she was now dead.

Pirro used phrases like "her death is very questionable" and "the timing is extremely curious" to subtly implicate Bobby.

Becerra was miffed. He hadn't mentioned Susan Berman's name until after he found out she was dead. And he hadn't made any effort to interview her until he placed his phone call to the Los Angeles police earlier that day. But Becerra kept his mouth shut and booked a flight to Los Angeles, where he was dispatched with John O'Donnell to debrief police there on the Durst investigation and find out more about Susan Berman and her murder.

Becerra knew little about Susan, only what Gilberte and Ellen and Kathy Traystman had told him about her thick bloodlines to the Las Vegas mob and her close relationship with Bobby Durst.

By week's end Becerra heard all he needed about Susan Berman and her hard-luck life: how she had arrived in California in 1983, supposedly flush with cash after selling the film rights to her book, and married a twenty-five-year-old writer, Mister Margulies, in 1984.

The wedding was a lavish affair at the Hotel Bel-Air. Susan paid the bill. Bobby was there, and even gave her away, beaming like the proud brother he'd always been.

But the marriage dissolved almost as quickly as the romance had began, and Margulies died just months later from a heroin overdose.

Susan's cash stash had all but run out when she met Paul Kaufman in 1987. He was a financial adviser with two teenage children, Sareb and Mella. Susan became close with the children, particularly Sareb. And she remained close with Sareb, who considered Susan his mother, after her relationship with Kaufman went south.

In 1992, broke and virtually homeless, Susan declared bankruptcy. Her fortunes changed a bit two years later thanks to a television special and a new book project about Las Vegas. But by 2000 she was broke again, owed tens of thousands to friends, and was being evicted from her home. That summer, desperate, she tried to call Bobby for help, but his line was disconnected. She wrote him a letter in care of the Durst Organization in New York, but got no response.

That fall, out of the blue, she received a warm letter from Bobby, along with a $25,000 check. In December, she received another check, again for $25,000. Bobby had reappeared in her life, and in a big way.

Susan used the money to pay her bills and began work on a new book on the Las Vegas mob. She had found a source, the wife of an old mobster, who was willing to talk, providing the kind of inside detail even a mobster's daughter would salivate over.

Susan was ecstatic following the interview, so happy that she told her friend, actress Kim Lankford, that she had information on a story that would "blow the top off of things."

Kim had no idea what Susan was talking about, and Susan wouldn't tell her.

When the rabid press got hold of that quote, immediate speculation was that Susan was going to tell all about her dear brother, Bobby.

It made for great headlines, but Susan still lived by the old code. She was a mobster's daughter, and she'd never get Bobby in trouble. Even when she agreed in mid-December to an interview with the *New York Times,* there was no way she'd incriminate Bobby. But Susan never got to speak with the *Times.*

By Christmas Eve, Susan wasn't talking to anyone.

17

THE remains of six dogs were now visible in their shallow graves, the dirt removed to expose their large frames.

They were Akitas, and Joe Becerra, the dog lover, stood over them wanting to know who could be so cold to kill six beautiful dogs and bury them here.

They were found by a woman who was walking her own dog on a dirt path in Goldens Bridge. The smell was overwhelming. It was late March, and the winter snow had long melted away. The woman's dog followed the unbearable scent and dug up one of the dead dogs.

Becerra was on duty at the Somers barracks when he received the call. He examined the site, unearthed the remaining five dogs, then decided to load them all onto the back of a pickup truck and take them for autopsies at the necropsy department of Cornell University.

Becerra had the time to investigate the deaths of six dogs because the Kathie Durst trail had gone cold, even after the shocking news about Susan Berman.

It was now three months after Susan had been found facedown in a pool of her own blood with a hole in the back of her head, and the media had drained every last word they could out of the story. The L.A. police were investigating, but remained close mouthed, sharing little with anyone, particularly Jeanine Pirro, who, in their opinion, talked too much.

Pirro had brought grandstanding to a new level, taking Susan Berman's death and pushing herself to the front and center, sopping up every last bit of exposure she could find. CNN, MSNBC, *Geraldo,* all the networks, even the local New York stations. The Westchester County DA was everywhere, looking so attractive and confident, saying Susan Berman's death seemed more than a coincidence and she was hot on the trail of Robert Durst.

"The Kathie Durst case is very much a priority," was her standard line.

The focal point of Pirro's newfound attention, Bobby Durst, remained out of sight. He was spotted once in Los Angeles in January, in a hotel, waiting to attend Susan Berman's memorial service. But he didn't attend the memorial, never leaving the hotel, saying his lawyers advised him to stay put. He checked out soon after.

Aside from Pirro's statements, Becerra had little to discuss with Kathie's friends or family, though the investigator would call Jim McCormack on occasion. Jim, for his part, didn't want to hear any details or inside information. He was on a need-to-know basis. He was hopeful; judging by Pirro's statements, it appeared she was prepared to move forward with her case. Becerra cautioned McCormack. He knew the pain his family had suffered, and he didn't want them to believe that closure was around the corner.

Becerra also stayed in touch with Gilberte Najamy, who was furious that Berman had died before she could talk.

"I told you, I told you last year to talk to Susan Berman," she said. "She was the key. She knew everything."

Becerra agreed with Gilberte; it was an opportunity lost. But he couldn't explain why he hadn't been ready to approach Susan. He had figured Susan would run to

Bobby, telling him everything about any interview she had with Becerra, what questions were asked, what information the police might have had.

This was how investigations were conducted, one piece and one interview at a time. Becerra had still been focused on the house in South Salem. Susan Berman had to wait. But Becerra knew losing Susan was a crucial blow to his investigation, and he kicked himself for not trying to reach out to her back in November.

As headlines about the Durst case once again faded from view, Becerra the dog lover would use the dead Akitas investigation to keep him away from Pirro, away from the Durst case, and busy for the next few weeks.

The autopsy results revealed that the dogs had been asphyxiated, strangled with some type of cord or wire. That much was certain. Becerra had an idea, a gut feeling, that only a breeder would have six dogs he wanted for some reason to kill. So he worked the phones, and by early April he had tracked down every Akita breeder in the Westchester County area.

On the morning of April 12, 2001, he made one last call to a breeder in Brewster, then took a drive to the gym to lift weights and clear his head.

Midway through his workout, as he was lying on a bench doing presses, his cell phone rang.

Becerra looked down and recognized the number. It was Gabrielle Colquitt.

He could hear she was hysterical, screaming into the phone.

"He's here! He's here!"

"Who's there?"

"Durst! Robert Durst! He was in my backyard!"

"Are you sure?"

"He was here! Down by the water! Please, you have to come here now!"

Becerra ran to his locker, barking out orders into the phone.

"Stay in the house. Lock the door. I'm calling for help. I'll be there in a few minutes."

He hung up with Colquitt and called the Somers barracks, telling them to get police units over to the house on Hoyt Street in South Salem immediately.

When Becerra arrived fifteen minutes later, several New York State Police cars were parked in front of the house and in the driveway.

Bobby was nowhere to be found.

Becerra walked into he house and saw Colquitt sitting on her sofa.

"Are you okay?"

Colquitt was shaken. She'd had no idea how her life would change when the news of the Durst investigation broke five months earlier. Her phone never stopped ringing, with calls from the media coming all hours of the day and night, not to mention the television crews camping out in front of her house and the satellite trucks taking up most of the space on the small street.

This wasn't what Colquitt had bargained for. She liked Becerra, and she had thought she was doing him a favor when she let him into her home at least half a dozen times.

But this was unacceptable. Bobby himself showing up on her property. At her house.

Colquitt was angry and scared, for herself and her young daughter.

As she sat in the living room, a glass of water in her hand, Becerra knelt down on one knee in front of her.

"Can you tell me what happened?"

Colquitt took a sip from the glass then paused to gather her thoughts.

"I was going to the store and pulled out of the driveway when I noticed this blue car, it was parked in front of the house, idling," she said.

"Did you see anyone inside the car?"

"No, the driver was bent over onto the passenger side. I thought maybe it was another reporter hanging out in front of the house. I drove about a mile and decided to turn back. I'd had it with those people. I wasn't going to let him sit there in front of my house. I was angry, so I turned around. When I got back to the house, the car was in my driveway."

"Do you know what kind of car it was?"

"It looked foreign, like a Saab, I think. I didn't see anyone in the front of the house. I wrote down the plate number, got out of the car, and walked to the back, and there was this man, standing there, looking out onto the lake."

"Did you know who it was?"

"Not at first. He was just standing there. He looked lost, like he was deep in thought. I called out to him, demanding to know what he was doing on my property. I told him to leave, but I don't think he heard me. I saw my dog lying on the grass. She wasn't moving. I kept walking toward him. He wasn't a big man. He was small. I kept yelling out to him and got within a few feet when he finally turned around. I knew who he was. I was so scared."

"Did he say anything to you?"

"Nothing. He just looked at me with this blank face, and walked right by me, got into his car, and drove away," said Colquitt. "I ran into the house and called you."

Becerra ran a check of the license-plate number, and the car, a Saab, was registered to Robert Durst. The date, April 12, was of significance. It was Bobby's birthday, and the day he married his long-lost wife, Kathie.

———

THE flight from Denver landed in New York on June 10. As soon as Leonard Ammaturo exited the plane, he walked into the waiting arms of Joe Becerra, who handcuffed him and took him to Westchester County, charged with killing six Akitas, hanging them from a bicycle rack in his garage and then burying them.

Ammaturo was a dog breeder who had moved to Edwards, Colorado, in November 2000. Becerra had tracked him down, finding his Colorado phone number and calling him up in his home. Ammaturo acknowledged that he had killed the dogs. He said he couldn't bring them with him to Colorado and didn't know what to do.

Detectives in Colorado, at the behest of Becerra, interviewed Ammaturo, took his statement, and sent it back to New York. Becerra had his man.

A day after Ammaturo was arrested, a story appeared in the *Journal News,* the local newspaper in Westchester, citing Becerra's investigation and crediting him with the arrest.

The story, short in length, nevertheless caught the attention of Jeanine Pirro, who was furious. She told her people to call reporters, informing them that *she* would be holding a press conference on Tuesday morning to announce the arrest of Leonard Ammaturo, which she did, telling the local media that Ammaturo was being charged with six counts of aggravated cruelty to animals.

Even though the victims were six dogs, it was still a gruesome, shocking crime and local residents were repulsed at the news that six innocent dogs had been strung up and hanged in a garage. Justice was demanded, and the credit for the arrest would go to Pirro, not some investigator with the New York State Police, even if it was the investigator who found the dogs, took them for autopsies, and tracked down their killer.

Still, it came as a great surprise to Becerra when he was informed that he would be working weekends that summer, that Pirro had called his superiors to remind them that she—and she alone—would speak to the media, that she alone would render justice in Westchester County, and that she alone would be credited for this, even in the case of six dead puppies.

Becerra reported to work the following Saturday afternoon.

18

JIM McCORMACK, his family, and a few friends surrounded the television in his Sparta, New Jersey, home, preparing to watch an hour-long *ABC News* special on the disappearance of his sister Kathie Durst.

It was late July and the refrigerator was full of beer and soda, and there were plenty of chips and pretzels to complement the cold drinks. It was almost a festive occasion, this being the first network special devoted solely to the story of Kathie Durst.

The special was called *Vanished,* ABC having taken a particular interest in the case following the death of Susan Berman. The interviews had been conducted in the spring, with Jim, Gilberte Najamy, Kathy Traystman, and even Mike Struk sitting down for lengthy interviews at ABC's studios in New York.

As the hour progressed, the point of view of the program was obvious: Bobby Durst had killed his wife, and the NYPD had blown the investigation in 1982.

Jim had high hopes that the program would not only shed new light on the case of his missing sister but produce new witnesses as well. Someone, he figured, would have to see it and come forward. He knew that having a whole hour on network television devoted to one subject—the disappearance of Kathie Durst—was an incredible opportunity.

Jim was pleased with his performance, the protective big brother who now served as the family spokesman.

One hundred miles away in Hamden, Connecticut, Gilberte Najamy was more than pleased with how she came across. She was tickled pink. She felt, with all certainty, that by the end of the program, she had emerged as the single most important source in the story.

On camera she denied rumors that Kathie had a drug problem or was in danger of flunking medical school, and recounted the last, sad details about that Sunday afternoon at her house, just as she had told it for the last nineteen years: that she had been hosting a quiet family get-together when Kathie called from South Salem, Kathie's arrival, and her subsequent departure.

And there was Gilberte's last dramatic, emotional moment with Kathie on the front porch, and Kathie's last, fateful words.

Gilberte had choked up when she retold the story.

"She said, 'Gilberte, promise me if something happens to me, you'll check it out. I'm afraid of what Bobby might do.' "

The tears welled once again.

"I made a promise to Kathie, and I'm going to keep my promise," said Gilberte. It made for great television, as did Gilberte's comments later in the program, when she described how she had allowed herself to be photographed by *People* magazine and insinuated that she was the reason why Bobby had apparently gone off the deep end, making an obvious allusion to Susan Berman's murder.

"I wanted Mr. Durst to open up the magazine and know that Gilberte had come back, and then I wanted him to look at me and say, 'Oh, my God, she's talking.' "

Gilberte wasn't the only one talking that night.

It was Kathy Traystman who said, on national television, that she believed Bobby had murdered Kathie.

But in Gilberte's mind, no one else mattered. She was the key. She believed herself to be the person who had nurtured the investigation along, pushed it to the point where Bobby was now acting irrationally. Joe Becerra? He was just a lapdog who followed orders. Without me, figured Gilberte, he'd have nothing.

Along with promoting her efforts to a nationwide audience, behind the scenes Gilberte used the generous time with ABC's producers to hang Mike Struk and the NYPD, comparing them to the Keystone Kops, and worse.

Like the rest of the media, ABC was infatuated with Gilberte. She was articulate, forceful, and direct. Everything that came from her mouth appeared to be truthful and accurate. She was, in essence, golden.

So when Gilberte told ABC's producers during her marathon interview session that Mike Struk was incompetent and that he probably got his job as a technical consultant to *Law & Order* because he cut a deal with the Dursts, they listened intently.

"He had to get something from the Dursts. We told him to search the home in South Salem, but he ignored us," she said.

And Gilberte had other theories. She accused Kathie's sister Mary Hughes of coming to some kind of arrangement with the Dursts that allowed Mary to rent an apartment in the very building that Kathie had lived in on East Eighty-sixth Street.

It was Mary, after all, said Gilberte, whom Bobby accused of trying to blackmail him for $100,000 after Kathie disappeared.

"How could you move into the same building where your sister once lived, and the very building owned by the family that killed your sister?" said Gilberte.

And Gilberte also claimed that the McCormack family was contemplating filing a wrongful-death suit against Bobby, though in reality, filing a lawsuit was the furthest thing from their minds.

"How can they do that without me? I should be part of that suit," said Gilberte.

When reminded that she wasn't a family member, Gilberte scoffed.

"But I was Kathie's best friend," she said. "Of course I would be involved in any suit. How could I not be?"

Her favorite targets, though, had been Mike Struk and the NYPD, and her tirades were venomous.

"He was incompetent, completely incompetent. I'm telling you the Dursts got to him and the entire New York City Police Department," said Gilberte. "They should have searched the South Salem home. We told them to search the South Salem home. It was Seymour. He had the money and the power to make this go away!"

Gilberte's ramblings about Struk struck a chord with ABC. Struk had broken his long silence and agreed to cooperate, sitting down for a three-hour interview. He calmly explained everything about his investigation in 1982, at least all he could explain without jeopardizing Joe Becerra's investigation.

Yet Struk, whose appearance on the program was lengthy, came across as confused on the screen. He faced delicate questions about perceived incompetence from reporter Cynthia McFadden, who seemed incredulous that neither Struk nor anyone else would have thought to search the South Salem home.

Struk tried his best to explain his actions, but he did look incompetent that night, like a rookie working his first shift, not the experienced detective he had once been.

And while the questions came from McFadden, Struk knew they originated with Gilberte. They had to.

"Kathie's friends say they repeatedly told Detective Struk what Kathie had said about Bob's violent behavior. But, they say, Detective Struk did not seem to take them seriously," said McFadden, as the program moved along.

Struk replied that things were becoming redundant,

that the friends weren't offering anything useful, and there were no fact witnesses.

The more Struk talked, the sillier he looked, each answer to each pointed question dragging him deeper and deeper into the abyss.

By the end of the program, Struk, who watched from his New Jersey home, was cursing himself for having agreed to the interview.

And he cursed Gilberte Najamy as well.

19

THE little old man with the fishing hat and Bermuda shorts was leaning against a wall in downtown Galveston, Texas, his hands clutching his chest. He looked like he was having a heart attack when Ted Hanley spotted him as he was driving along Market Street, a stretch of road separated by old cotton mills, factories and empty lots.

"Morris? Morris? Are you okay? Can I help you?" said Hanley, who left his car and walked over to the man, who was waving his hand to go away.

"No, no, go away. Nobody can help me. You have no idea the kind of problems that I have in my life. Nobody would understand. I can never talk about it with anybody."

It was the middle of August and the humidity covered Galveston like a heating pad. Morris was drenched in perspiration, but Hanley knew his ailment wasn't physical.

Hanley had seen Morris Black like this before, back in the spring, standing against the side of a building just a few minutes after handing out eyeglasses to the poor and needy.

Hanley was the director of the Jesse Tree, a way station for the disenfranchised, homeless, and other lost souls who always managed to find their way to Galveston with the other flotsam of humankind. Galveston had a history of being a last refuge of sorts, a stinking-hot, blue-collar, shot-and-a-beer town, some forty miles of island bordered by the Gulf of Mexico, Galveston Bay, and Purgatory. It was a place to disappear.

Hanley had known plenty of people who wanted to vanish, but he had never met anyone like Morris Black, a seventy-one-year-old drifter with a Boston accent who walked around town with a noticeable limp and was best known by the volunteers at the Jesse Tree as that crazy old man with the fishing hat.

Morris first came to Hanley's attention in January 2001, when he showed up at the Jesse Tree unannounced, determined to convince Hanley that he should buy reading glasses off the Internet and give them to the poor.

They were cheap, said Morris, and the poor could use them.

Hanley explained that he didn't have the money to buy the glasses, no matter what the price, and said he wasn't interested. In reality, he thought it was a great idea.

Morris wouldn't take no for an answer, so he ordered the glasses himself and decided to give them away every Saturday morning in downtown Galveston, where the Jesse Tree served free breakfast and offered free medical services.

Each week Morris would arrive, a shopping bag in each hand filled with dozens of pairs of glasses he had bought in bulk. Morris figured it cost him forty-six cents a pair, a bargain. They were made in China and had Walgreens stamped on them.

"You see, Ted," Morris would say. "If you bought these at a store it would have cost you twelve dollars."

Morris would walk up to the people waiting on line, ask each person a few questions, and give away his glasses. He was all business and took his endeavor with great seriousness.

There were times, though, when he felt someone was taking advantage of his generosity. He would then take the glasses back, often in a loud and embarrassing fashion.

One poor fellow had the misfortune of carrying a pack of cigarettes in his shirt pocket. Morris saw the cigarettes after giving the fellow a pair of glasses, reached over, and angrily took the glasses out his hand.

"If you can afford to buy cigarettes then you can afford to buy these glasses!" Morris screamed.

On another occasion Morris thought someone had stolen a pair of glasses from one of his bags and he began to yell and berate those standing on line, his arms flailing.

Then a child walked up to Morris, the lost glasses in hand, asking Morris if he dropped them in the parking lot, where they were found. Morris said nothing as he snatched the glasses from the boy and stomped away.

As the weeks went by, Morris decided to change the eligibility requirements for his free glasses. Instead of being just poor or homeless, you now couldn't be a poor, homeless smoker. Or if he thought you were lazy, you were denied.

"Lazy people don't deserve glasses," Morris told Hanley.

"But how do you know if they're lazy?"

"I can tell. Believe me, I know these people. I can tell."

During the week, Morris would often walk over to the Jesse Tree unannounced and tell Hanley about new listings on the Internet and opportunities to get even cheaper glasses.

On one such day Hanley wasn't interested. He was also busy, and told Morris if he had any further questions he should E-mail him. Hanley knew Morris was computer literate, since he was seen often at the Galveston library working at a computer terminal.

Morris said no, if he had something for Hanley he'd tell him in person.

The following week Hanley saw Morris leaning against the building. Usually quick moving and talking fast, Morris was somewhat lethargic as he gave away his glasses. When he was finished, he slowly walked away, then crouched over as if to vomit.

"Morris, do you need a doctor?" said Hanley.

"No, no. You can't help me. Do you understand? You can't help me. You would never be able to understand the problems I have," said Morris.

Hanley, a Christian in name and practice, put his hand on Morris's shoulder.

"Morris, you know I work with people every day who have all kinds of problems. Very serious problems. There's always somebody who can help you."

Morris remained hunched over, his head shaking back and forth.

"No! No! No!"

It suddenly occurred to Hanley that Morris's problems weren't physical, but mental. Terrible thoughts that totally overwhelmed him. Whatever it was, Hanley determined, it was consuming the man.

"Morris, if you don't want me to help you, then I will pray that you will believe there is somebody there for you to talk to."

Morris said nothing.

Ted offered to give him a ride home and got his car. He helped Morris into the front seat and the two men drove to 2213 Avenue K, where Morris rented an apartment in the front of a two-story home.

Hanley offered to take Morris's bags into the house, but Morris, who remained lethargic during the five-minute ride, exploded.

"No! No! You can't come into my home. You can never come inside. Do you understand?"

Hanley was startled, but didn't reply. Morris bolted from the car and quickly walked up the stairs to his front porch. He turned around, looking out toward Hanley, and waited for him to drive down the block before entering the house.

Hanley saw Morris again the following Monday. He had come into the Jesse Tree enraged over another issue concerning his glasses. Hanley had had about enough and ordered two of his employees to show Morris the door.

Morris returned on Friday, "I'm sorry about the other day," he said.

Hanley let it go. Before leaving, Morris brought up another subject.

"I hear you're looking to buy another piece of property for the Jesse Tree. Would you be interested in a low-interest loan? I know somebody who has a lot of money and could make a low-interest loan available."

Hanley was somewhat surprised by the offer. The Jesse Tree was indeed looking to buy a property nearby. The price tag was $50,000. Hanley had no idea how Morris had learned this, but he would never get involved in any kind of financial dealings with someone like Morris Black.

"Morris, if somebody wants to do something for the Jesse Tree, they just need to talk to me."

Morris nodded and limped out the door.

Hanley was in his office the following Monday when the receptionist walked in to tell him he had a visitor. A strange man, he was told, who appeared to be a deaf-mute and very agitated.

Hanley ran into all sorts of people as the director of the Jesse Tree, but it wasn't often he'd run into an agitated mute.

He walked into the front lobby area and saw, standing there, a short man wearing a gray T-shirt and black-rimmed eyeglasses, the same kind of glasses Morris was giving away. Only the lenses were taped, the right eye completely covered, the left eye covered except for a small area in the middle.

"Are you deaf?" said Hanley.

The man shook his head up and down.

"Do you sign?"

The man shook his head left to right, then nodded toward a room next door, which was used for computer work.

The two men walked into the room, and Hanley closed the door.

The man turned around. "I don't speak to women. I hate them," he said.

"Okay," said Hanley, now knowing that his visitor wasn't deaf or mute. "What can I do for you?"

"I need fifty dollars, in cash."

"Sir," said Hanley. "This is the Jesse Tree, not the Money Tree. I can't spit out cash. What do you need it for?"

"I don't like this place. I want to go to Beaumont. I have to stay in my car and I need money for gas."

Hanley told the man that he could give him a blanket, food, and a gas voucher, but he couldn't give him fifty dollars.

The man exploded.

"So this is like every other goddamn place that gives you the runaround!" he yelled, talking with his hand on his forehead, partially covering his face. Hanley, at first, didn't think much of him, probably just another poor soul with a few marbles floating around somewhere in his head. His short hair was scraggly. He appeared to be in his mid-fifties.

But as his visitor continued to talk, Hanley sensed something about him, and the conversation. He realized the man didn't need fifty dollars. Instead, Hanley felt as if he was being tested, that the visitor was trying to push his buttons, get him riled and excited. For what reason, Hanley didn't have a clue.

The man huffed out of the Jesse Tree without his fifty dollars or any vouchers, and without giving his name.

It was two months later when Hanley spotted Morris slumped against the wall, the same way as last spring, and again asked if he could help.

"No! No! Nobody can help me. I can never talk about it," said Morris. "Just leave me alone."

Hanley told Morris again that he would pray for him, went back to his car, and drove away.

He would never see Morris Black again.

20

JANET Finke's heart began to pound when she saw the name Robert Durst on the caller ID. She hadn't spoken to Bobby in years, and couldn't believe that he was calling her now in late August 2001.

Her first thought was to wonder how he had gotten her home number. No one from the old crowd knew where she lived or what she was doing.

The phone rang three times. Janet hesitated before picking it up on the fourth ring, when the answering machine would come on.

"Hello?"

"Janet?" came the distinctive voice on the other end of the line. "It's Bob."

Janet was terrified. What would she say? And what if it was true, that Bobby had killed Susan Berman? Janet already had her own theories about what had happened to Kathie. Her mouth moved, but the words couldn't come out. She tried to remember the good things about Bobby, the kind, sweet man who had taken her in when she was down-and-out.

"Bob, how are you?" were the only words Janet could nervously muster.

"I'm fine," he said. "Despite what you may have been reading, I've been fine."

The voice on the other end didn't sound like the crazed psychopath described in the media. He sounded like . . . Bob. That quiet, reassuring, pleasant voice Janet had known so well so many years before.

It took but a few minutes for Janet to feel at ease. Bobby was still a friend, a long-lost friend, and in no time the conversation began to flow, with Janet telling him about her new life and Bobby recounting his recent difficulties thanks to the new investigation into the disappearance of his wife, Kathie.

As he spoke, he was more than cordial—he was downright pleasant. The more Janet talked, the more comfortable she felt. They talked about Kathie, with Bobby expressing fond memories for his long-deceased wife, saying he believed all along that drug dealers had sealed her fate. He vehemently denied having anything to do with Susan Berman's murder, saying he felt only grief that his very good friend was dead.

"How can anyone think I could kill Susan?" Bobby said.

"Then why don't you say something?" said Janet. "Why don't you fight this?"

"Because my lawyers told me not to say anything. I have to stay quiet. Believe me, it's not easy. I also think my phone is tapped. Some things I can talk about, others I can't."

Bobby said he had seen the ABC *Vanished* special in July, and the conversation took a stranger, darker turn as the topic shifted to Gilberte Najamy. The pleasantness was gone. Bobby was now angry, and bitter, and Janet could hear the sudden change in his voice when he mentioned Gilberte's name.

"Nobody knows what that woman did to Kathie," said Bobby. "And she sits there on television accusing me!"

Janet said nothing as Bobby ranted on. This was the weird Bobby whom Janet told Joe Becerra about a year and a half earlier. He was still there, deep inside.

The ranting soon subsided, and the questions came, one after another, all focused on Becerra's investigation. Who were the police talking to? What kind of information had they received? Had they found anything in the South Salem home? And did Janet agree to an interview?

Janet was unsettled by the last question. She acknowledged that she spoke to Becerra in January 2000, but said she gave him nothing.

"What could I tell him? I don't know a thing," she said. "All I told them was we were supposed to have dinner that night, you and me and Kathie and Alan. I told them I canceled and you were fine with it, that Kathie was at Gilberte's and you were just going to hang out. Bob, what could I do? They're talking to everyone. I couldn't say no."

"What do you mean talking with *everyone*?" he said, the last word drawn out in a nasal whine.

"Bobby, the police were hounding people. They've either interviewed or are getting ready to interview anyone who knew you. It's what they do, especially now, after Susan's murder. When she was killed, the story was in the papers every day. The district attorney just about said that you did it."

"But I didn't do it!" said Bobby. "How could that bitch say that? And how could I ever do something like that? Susan was my friend. I loved her."

Janet didn't reply. She didn't want to answer any more of Bobby's questions about the investigation. The conversation ended with Bobby asking her if she'd meet him for coffee the next time he flew into New York.

"Are you in town often?" she said.

"No, not really. Every now and then."

"Can you tell me where you are?"

"No, nowhere special. I'm traveling and I was thinking about you. It's been a long time, so I thought I'd give you a call."

They agreed to meet at some future date, though Janet

had no intention of ever meeting Bobby for coffee, or dinner, or anything.

She was scared and unnerved. She knew Bobby was probing her. He was nervous, and that made Janet nervous.

She looked at the caller ID. The area code was 409.

Bobby was calling from Galveston, Texas.

———

THE summer went by slowly for Joe Becerra. The weekend duty played havoc with his social life, which was picking up a bit, with a date here and there. He was working other cases, and aside from infrequent calls to the Los Angeles Police Department for Susan Berman updates, nothing was happening with the Durst investigation.

The L.A. police were being cautious, and secretive, a new tact taken following the O. J. Simpson fiasco. Since then they'd begun to take their time with major murder investigations, saying little, even to fellow investigators from other jurisdictions.

Becerra didn't mind. If detectives in L.A. were being patient, then that was their business. He did learn that Susan had apparently been shot with a nine-millimeter handgun at close range. And he learned that there were two suspects, Bobby Durst and Nyles Brenner. Brenner had served as Susan's manager, and Susan not only owed Brenner money, but was draining the very life force from his body. She'd been calling him at all hours to take care of a host of chores unrelated to being a manager, such as helping Susan move a couch into her house.

Susan was the drama queen of all drama queens, and when she had a problem, no matter how minor, she had called Brenner.

His reaction to Susan's death appeared to be one of relief, as if a great burden had been lifted from his shoulders. Considering how Susan depended on him for most everything, including money, it wasn't hard for many of

Susan's friends to understand why Brenner was less than distraught to hear that Susan had died. Still, many found it inconceivable that Brenner had ended Susan's life over money, or anything else for that matter. And the more the L.A. police studied Brenner, the less they thought of him as a suspect.

Becerra knew what direction the L.A. police were taking, but he remained mum and focused on his own case, though there wasn't much happening.

His days were filled with routine calls, and an occasional homicide. Becerra was making most of his Durst calls at night, from home, on his own time. He'd usually talk with Jim McCormack, who was growing increasingly frustrated with the slow pace of the investigation.

Becerra would also, on occasion, speak with Gilberte, who was decidedly beginning to become a problem.

Reporters would call Becerra seeking confirmation on information passed along quietly by Gilberte, important information like the blood evidence that had been found inside the South Salem home, and the itinerary Bobby had written twenty years earlier, of which Gilberte had a copy.

Becerra knew that Gilberte had become a media darling during the past ten months, the one person reporters would turn to for the best quotes on the Durst case. Her name appeared prominently in *People* magazine, *New York* magazine, the *New York Times,* the *Los Angeles Times, New York Daily News,* and *New York Post*.

And as good as she was in print, she was even better on television, as evidenced by her appearance on the ABC special about Kathie. Gilberte was articulate and could cry on demand. The tears flowed whenever she spoke about Kathie and that last day they spent together at Gilberte's house.

When Becerra did receive a call from a reporter concerning something Gilberte may have said, his standard line was that he couldn't and wouldn't discuss the case. He'd then call Gilberte and tell her to keep quiet.

"You're going to singlehandedly jeopardize my case," Becerra said.

Gilberte would deny everything, saying the reporters were calling her to discuss the information, which they must have gotten elsewhere.

"I bet they got it from Pirro's office," was Gilberte's quick response. "There definitely is a leak, and it has to be coming from someone in her office."

Becerra would sigh, remind Gilberte to be quiet, and hang up. He had begun to distance himself from her, keeping her close enough to maintain a dialogue, but out of the loop of information.

Privately he wondered if it mattered at all if Gilberte was talking.

He'd seen the *Vanished* program, along with millions of others, and, like Jim McCormack, he hoped that it would lead to someone calling with some new information on the Durst case.

The call never came.

As the summer wound down past Labor Day, the Kathie Durst investigation all but came to a stop. And aside from his visit to South Salem in April, Bobby Durst had all but disappeared and Becerra was beginning to believe that Bobby would again escape arrest, just as he had done in 1982. Becerra was resigned to the fact that it would take an incredible break for the case to move forward, a break he now believed would never come.

21

DUSK had yet to settle in Galveston, the sun hovering over the causeway that serves as a conduit to the mainland and an exit sign for the giant supertankers, their hulls filled with fresh crude, as they sailed slowly beneath the bridge toward the Gulf of Mexico.

It was hot and humid, which is how it usually is along the Texas coast in late September.

Not far in the distance, on the Galveston side of the bay, four silver garbage bags floated in the water near a concrete pier while a human torso bumped against a rock jetty, mixed in with some garbage that had washed in with the high tide.

A thirteen-year-old boy, James Avina, was staring down at the water, putting his fishing pole to the side while trying to figure out what something he thought was a dead pig was doing in the water.

Avina lived around the corner, on Channelview Drive, part of a secluded two-block neighborhood of nondescript houses bordered by the bay and a marsh that served as a perfect hiding place for a family of alligators.

The fishing in this part of the bay, off this stretch of

pier, was good, so good that a sign warned anyone who didn't live in the neighborhood to stay away.

James had come to fish at dusk on this Sunday night with his little sister, Elyse, and stepfather, David. Only he didn't realize that he wouldn't need his fishing pole to reel in the biggest catch of his young life.

As he stared down at the water, it soon became apparent to him that the fleshy mass wasn't a pig at all, and he called out to his stepfather.

"Hey," he said. "There's a body over here."

———

THE silver 1998 Honda CR-V was heading east on Broadway, Galveston's main thoroughfare, when Police Officer Gary Jones spotted the car and pulled it over, his lights flashing.

It was 9:30 A.M. on Tuesday, October 9, and Jones had been waiting for the Honda. As the officer approached the car, his gun pulled from its holster and aimed at the driver's side, he barked commands for the driver to step out. The man obeyed, placing his hands and arms over the roof of the car. Jones approached him slowly, looked inside the car to make sure the driver was alone, and then pulled the driver's hands behind his back and slapped the cuffs on him.

The man said nothing and refused to answer any questions. He wouldn't even confirm that his name was Robert Durst after Jones reached into his wallet and pulled out his credit cards.

Durst would now be taken to have a chat with Sergeant Cody Cazalas, a strapping Galveston police detective who sported a buzz cut and a hearty laugh. A thirteen-year veteran, Cazalas was the detective who had been charged little more than a week earlier with investigating the murder of Morris Black, who rented apartment number one at 2213 Avenue K.

Police had found the address because Black's killer had been sloppy, leaving a newspaper with a sticker stamped *Resident at 2213 Avenue K, Galveston, TX* in one of the garbage bags found floating in the bay along with one of Black's legs.

Other items were found in three of the bags, including a second leg in one bag and two arms in another. The fourth bag was empty, but the end of that bag was sliced open wide. Whatever had been inside had fallen out.

Along with the body parts police found a receipt dated Saturday, September 29 from Chalmers True Value, a hardware store on Broadway not far from Black's residence. The time of sale was 4:17 P.M. The receipt listed trash bags and drop cloths; the cost was $22.17. Inside the trash bags police also found wet and bloodied towels, a cover for a Green Thumb twenty-one-inch bow saw, two Metamucil packets, blue plastic cups, a shower flip-flop shoe, paper towels, a blue bedsheet, and underwear briefs.

The body parts were laid out in the morgue after they washed up in front of the Avina family. They hadn't been in the water long, as evidenced by the fresh-cut wounds around the torso. Fish and other marine life would have had a field day had the torso been in the water longer than forty-eight hours.

But the wounds were clean, the torso relatively untouched while in the water, and rigor mortis had yet to set in, leading Cazalas to conclude that the slaying occurred on Saturday, September 29 or Sunday morning, September 30.

Cazalas noticed something else. He was a hunter and knew a thing or two about cleaning animals. Judging by the cuts around the torso, whoever chopped up Morris Black had known what he was doing. Cazalas followed the cut lines and reasoned that the killer first sliced the outer skin, probably with a small sharp knife, maybe a scalpel, then peeled the skin away before continuing to cut through the tissue, blood vessels, and muscle. The arms were easy, like cutting through a wood two-by-four. They were removed right below the shoulder. But severing the legs was much more difficult. Once the killer reached the bone, he had switched tools, using something bigger, with teeth. Judging by the saw marks, Cazalas didn't need an autopsy report to determine that

someone had sweated as he sawed through the thick fe-
mur bones in the center of the thighs, the blood splat-
tering in all directions with each stroke.

The most disturbing part, at least to Cazalas, was the
removal of the head.

His first thoughts were that a person would have to
be not of this world, or at least not of sound mind, to
take a human body and slice the skin around the neck,
then dig deep with a saw, cut through the thick muscle
and spinal cord, and pull the head off.

What the hell did I walk into? thought Cazalas.

His question was partially answered the next day
when he visited 2213 Avenue K.

The brown house, which resembled a two-story Cape
Cod with a front porch, was in the middle of a nondescript block, a church on the corner. Cazalas, along with
Officer Jones, looked around the front of the house and
then walked to the back. They peeked inside a trash can
and found two trash bags, similar to the ones that had
been floating in the bay, packaging for a number four
paring knife, a bloody sock, a Band-Aid, a Bank of
America cash envelope, a .22-caliber handgun, a spent
.22 shell casing, and a receipt for an eye exam for one
Robert Durst.

Cazalas contacted the landlord, Klaus Rene Dillman,
who informed him that he didn't know any Robert
Durst. There were four apartments in the house, and the
two in the front had been rented by a nasty old fart,
Morris Black, and a woman, Dorothy Ciner, a deaf-mute
who traveled often and was rarely seen.

Dillman said Ciner and Black had arrived around the
same time in November 2000. Black was a cantankerous
fellow who was about to be evicted. He argued with
everyone, making life miserable for his tenants. Dillman
just wanted him out.

Ciner, he said, was a bizarre-looking, flat-chested
woman who communicated by scribbling notes. She
paid her rent months in advance, always in cash or
money order. They had an agreement that since she often

traveled Dillman could check on the apartment. With Cazalas behind him, Dillman knocked on Ciner's door, but there was no answer. They went outside and looked through a front window into Ciner's apartment. They could see a drop cloth spread out on the floor.

Cazalas obtained a warrant to search Black's apartment and later that day entered the house with Jones and other police officers. The place was empty. Whatever Black owned, including his clothes, was gone. It was evident that someone had mopped the kitchen floor in a hurried attempt to clean the apartment. The police brought in Luminol and sprayed it throughout the apartment, finding a glowing, bloody trail that led from the kitchen, kitchen sink, bathroom floor, sink and shower, to the carpet in the front room.

Cazalas also found blood in the hallway separating Black's apartments from Ciner's.

It didn't take the police sergeant long to figure out that he wanted to get a look inside Ciner's apartment. He obtained another search warrant, and the next day, October 4, found Ciner's place was just as blood-soaked as the one across the hall.

Cazalas found bloody boots, blood on the carpet, on the kitchen floor, even on the kitchen walls. There was blood underneath the floor in the kitchen, which had seeped up through a small cut in the linoleum.

Police also found a bloody paring knife and a drop cloth that had been spread out in the living room.

It was a slaughterhouse, some sick scene from a slasher movie. Cazalas didn't know what to think at first: Was this the apartment of an elderly woman or Hannibal Lector?

A photo of a man was found inside Ciner's apartment and shown to the two neighbors who lived upstairs. They identified the man as Robert Durst.

Dillman, the landlord, didn't know Durst. All he knew was that he had rented the apartment nearly a year before to Ciner, who had written a note about traveling a lot and about a friend who was to come over to check on the place from time to time.

The other tenants told Dillman that Durst had spent a lot of time in the apartment, engaging in loud arguments with Black, a daily ritual that ended with each slamming his door.

Cazalas took fingerprints from the number one apartment, traveled to the morgue, and matched them to Black.

Durst's name was run through the Texas Motor Vehicles Department and checked for any criminal record; the scan revealed no prior arrests. Cazalas did retrieve a VIN number for a 1998 silver Honda CR-V owned by a Robert Durst.

During interviews, several neighbors said they remembered Durst, whom they described as a quiet and strange man who spent his time sitting on the front porch smoking marijuana and was once seen barking back at a dog. The neighbors recalled hearing a loud *pop* sound around noon on Saturday afternoon, September 29, coming from inside 2213, but didn't think anything of it.

Later they saw Durst loading garbage bags into his car.

He was arrested as he drove down Broadway, on his way to pick up a new pair of eyeglasses, the receipt for which was found in the garbage pail behind the house on Avenue K.

Bobby was now sitting in the Galveston police station, handcuffed, wearing a gray T-shirt. His hair was cut very short, yet looked wild, like thin weeds run amok.

He said nothing, responding to Cazalas's questions with a blank stare, which only served to anger the veteran detective, who was of the opinion that a man who'd just been arrested for murder should be somewhat more agreeable to talking with the police.

"Sir, I'm going to ask you if you are going to cooperate with us," said Cazalas.

Bobby remained silent.

"Can you give me your name?"

"No," said Bobby, staring at Cazalas.

Perhaps Mr. Durst didn't realize he was in serious trouble, or didn't care. Whatever the case, Cazalas was at his wit's end with his suspect.

"Sir, I'm going to take you downstairs and put you in a cell. Do you have any questions?"

Bobby looked up, his casualness overwhelming Cazalas.

"What did I do?" he said.

"What did you do?" said Cazalas, now thoroughly irritated with this little man who was dressed like a refugee from the Salvation Army. "I don't know, you got two hundred and fifty thousand in cash?"

Bobby didn't flinch. He looked into Cazalas's eyes, a faint smile apparent at the corners of his mouth.

"No, not on me," he calmly replied.

The big Texan was rattled. The eye contact Bobby had made was smooth and cohesive. Cazalas knew he was being played. He also knew this wasn't some itinerant, some bum on the street who, for whatever reason, had carved up another human being like a Thanksgiving turkey. He was something more. Cazalas couldn't imagine just what that could be. Maybe a drug dealer?

As Bobby sat there amusing himself at the expense of Sergeant Cody Cazalas, another search warrant was obtained and police combed through the Honda CR-V. Inside they found a nine-millimeter handgun, three joints, yet another bow saw, the key to a Galveston Holiday Inn Express where Durst had apparently spent several nights under the name of Jim Turss, and a receipt from a dry cleaner in New Orleans.

Robert Durst was charged with murder in the second degree of Morris Black and possession of narcotics.

At his hearing, bail was set for $250,000, plus an additional $50,000 slapped on for the drug-possession charge, bringing the grand total to $300,000, which was considered high in Galveston, even for a murder charge.

Judging by his motley appearance, from his sneakers,

shorts, and T-shirt, no one thought Bobby had that kind of cash.

Call it experience, but Cazalas had a hunch that Bobby's cool response to his questioning meant he'd certainly be gone the next day, that he'd somehow come up with the money, make bail, and be off, which is exactly what happened.

Bobby made one phone call that night, to New York, telling the woman on the other end of the line that he had been arrested in Galveston, Texas, and was charged with murder. He needed to post bond.

The call was short, to the point, and the money was there the next morning.

22

GILBERTE Najamy couldn't believe what she was hearing when she received a sudden phone call from Andy Geller, a reporter from the *New York Post,* informing her that one Robert Durst was arrested for murder in Galveston, Texas.

"Are you sure that's *our* Bobby?" she said over and over again.

Geller assured her that it was, indeed, *our* Bobby, that a source had called the *Post* with the information on the arrest, that Bobby was said to have dismembered a senior citizen, and that the *Post* had confirmed it.

In fact, it was the Galveston police, realizing that the bail money had come from New York, who called the New York City police, informing them that one Robert Durst had been arrested for murder. Someone within the NYPD called the *Post* with the tip, and the *Post* called Galveston district attorney Mike Guarino and asked him to send a photo of the man in custody. Guarino refused, so the *Post* sent a picture of Bobby to the Galveston police, who identified the man in custody as the same man in the photo.

There was one other shocking detail.

Bobby had, it seemed, spent some of his time in Galveston walking the streets dressed as a woman, wearing dresses, wigs, and makeup.

"Oh, my God!" said Gilberte, trying to digest the news that Bobby not only stood accused of a horrific murder, but had also become a cross-dresser. "He flipped. That's what happened. He just flipped," she continued. "I knew we'd get him. I knew he'd see my picture in *People* magazine and he'd know that we were onto him. The pressure was too much. He killed Kathie, he killed Susan Berman, and now he's killed again. Oh, my God!"

Gilberte was beside herself, utterly shocked at the latest turn of events, yet at the same time crediting herself with provoking what she described as Bobby's total breakdown.

She was thrilled with the news of his arrest and saw it as a total validation of everything she had said over the past twenty-two months.

And she was pleased with the fact that Geller's first call had been to her. She knew, when it came to the Durst case, that she had the ears of all the major papers in New York.

Gilberte had been the most talkative of Kathie Durst's old friends, and her conversations with reporters, including Kevin Flynn of the *New York Times* and Barbara Ross of the *Daily News,* were clear, succinct, and often patronizing.

When a reporter came up with a theory to run by Gilberte, she'd take a deep breath, as if impressed, and say, "Oh, you're good! I never thought of that!"

She'd also direct reporters in different directions, telling them who they should talk to and who not to talk to.

When one asked about Ellen Strauss, Gilberte said not to bother, since she really hadn't been that close with Kathie and didn't have much to offer.

"She thinks she knows a lot, but doesn't really know anything. I wouldn't waste my time."

A circle of trust developed between Gilberte and the

press, and reporters on the story believed most everything that she said. She was still "golden," perhaps the source of all sources. She claimed to know everything about Kathie and Bobby and offered details to prove it.

So when Geller began working on his story, the first person he called was Gilberte.

Following the call from the *New York Post,* Najamy quickly paged Joe Becerra. When the state-police investigator returned the page, his tone was one of utter disbelief. Texas? A dismembered body? Bobby masquerading as a woman?

"He was cornered. That's what happened, he was cornered. He knew we weren't going to stop," said Gilberte.

Becerra didn't reply. His mind was racing. Susan Berman's death had been a shock, a wild left hook to the chin. But this? It didn't make any sense. Why would Bobby kill some old drifter? And why would he be dressing as a woman, and in Galveston, Texas, of all places? Becerra hung up with Gilberte and called Jeanine Pirro, who was equally stunned.

The Durst case had been all but forgotten following the September 11 terrorist attacks on the Twin Towers and Pentagon. Many of those who died at the World Trade Center lived in Westchester County. Pirro even went so far as to announce that she had suspended her reelection campaign to deal with the tragedy.

But with less than a month to go before Election Day, Pirro couldn't resist an opportunity for publicity. She also realized that this was perhaps the luckiest of breaks, another solid reason to avoid debating her challenger, Democrat Tony Castro, who was clamoring for a chance to meet the incumbent DA face-to-face and run her family problems through the mud and across Westchester County's television screens.

But Pirro would have none of it.

As the news of Bobby's arrest raced through newsrooms across New York, reporters called Pirro's office, asking what the murder charge in Texas meant for the Kathie Durst investigation. Unlike the Los Angeles police, who continued to remain tight-lipped about the Susan Berman investigation, Pirro didn't just speak, she spoke volumes. She even went so far as to say that she saw striking similarities in the death of Morris Black and what she believed had happened to Kathie Durst.

That statement in and of itself was a shock to reporters who had been covering the Durst case. If she really saw similarities and if she meant by this that she believed Kathie had been dismembered, then why hadn't Bobby been indicted?

The next morning, Becerra called the Galveston Police Department. He missed Cody Cazalas, who had risen early in order to make a six-hour drive to New Orleans to trace the receipt with Bobby's name on it—the one that had been found in the garbage pail behind the house on Avenue K—to the dry cleaner who had issued it.

Cazalas was near the Louisiana border when his cell phone rang. It was Lieutenant Mike Putnal from his office, and he had some news.

"How we doing, partner?" said Cazalas.

"You're not going to believe who this Durst guy is," said Putnal.

"Go ahead."

"He's some rich guy from New York. His family has billions. They own buildings in Manhattan. Even better, he's a suspect in the murder of his wife."

"You shitting me?" said Cazalas, pulling the car over to the side of the road.

"No. She disappeared twenty years ago. The New York police opened the case again last year. And there's more. A close friend of his in Los Angeles was found murdered, shot in the head, last Christmas. Whoever killed her used a nine-millimeter, same type of gun we found in his car."

"Where you getting this all from?"

"New York reporters. They've been calling all morning. They're like goddamn buzzards. I told them they had to talk to you."

"Jesus. Where is the little bastard now?"

"Don't know. He made bail this morning. His hearing is set for October sixteenth."

"Damn. I knew it. I could tell last night that he'd get the money. He's not going to show for the hearing," said Cazalas. "No way he's going to show. He's gone."

———

CAZALAS returned to Galveston after midnight. The trip to New Orleans had produced an interesting piece of information: Bobby had driven to a dry cleaners there to have blood removed from a comforter. The clerk at the store didn't remember much about Bobby, and Cazalas couldn't find an address or telephone listing for a Robert Durst or Dorothy Ciner anywhere in the metropolitan New Orleans area.

He was back at his desk the next morning at 7:30 rubbing his tired eyes, with a stack of phone messages waiting to be dealt with, all from the New York media and all inquiring about Robert Durst.

Cazalas ignored the messages. He knew what the main question was going to be: How could he let a guy like Durst go free?

He looked over to Lieutenant Putnal.

"Eighteen phone messages. Can you believe that? Eighteen, all from New York," said Cazalas.

He wasn't about to return the calls. What was he going to tell them, that the Galveston police had run a criminal check on Durst, and it came up clean? That unless there was a capital crime involved, bail had to be set? That's exactly what had happened, but Cazalas knew the New York media wouldn't buy it.

Here we go, he figured. The hicks from south Texas are going to get roasted as a bunch of bumpkins that wouldn't know a multimillionaire murderer from a homeless jaywalker.

"They're going to fry our balls and hand them to us on a platter," said Cazalas, who noticed that one of the messages was from the New York State Police.

"I was wrong. They're not all from the media. There's one here from a Joe Becerra, an investigator from New York. What do you think he's calling for?"

"The dead wife?" said Putnal.

"Well then, let me give him a call and find out," said Cazalas.

———

TED Hanley sipped on a cup of coffee in a conference room at the Jesse Tree while reading the Galveston County *Daily News,* his eyes frozen on the mug shot of Robert Durst, the man who'd been arrested for the brutal killing of Morris Black.

Hanley already knew that Morris was gone; the news of his death had been reported several days earlier. Hanley said a prayer for the troubled man.

But as he stared at the paper, reading about the man who'd been charged with the murder, he suddenly recognized the photo on the front page: this was that creepy guy who'd come into the Jesse Tree during the summer pretending to be a mute and then demanded fifty dollars for gas money to drive to Beaumont.

Hanley read that Durst was a member of a wealthy family in New York, and if this was so, it made absolutely no sense to him that he'd be living in a $300-a-month apartment in Galveston, of all places. Hanley's life was about dealing with the down-and-out, the lost and confused. He knew people, and knew them well. But this, even he couldn't explain.

And what about Morris, that cranky, combative limping fool of a man who aggravated everyone he came into contact with? What could Morris possibly have done to deserve this kind of fate? Hanley noticed that both the accused murderer and his victim lived at the same address. He paused after he finished the rest of the story and went back to the beginning, to the part about Durst having money. Hanley couldn't figure it out, how Morris could have known that Durst had money.

Would a man like Durst tell some crazed fool like

Morris that he had millions? Or was there more to their relationship? It couldn't have been a coincidence that Durst stopped by the Jesse Tree just days after Morris had said he knew someone who could offer Hanley a loan to purchase that new building.

Hanley did come to one conclusion, aside from the fact that Morris and Durst had been living among Galveston's homeless. He realized that Durst had come to see him not in order to borrow money, but to check out the Jesse Tree.

———

JOE Becerra arrived in Houston on Monday, October 15, with John O'Donnell, the senior investigator from the Westchester DA's office, renting a car and driving south on I-45 into Galveston. Jeanine Pirro arrived in Galveston that same day, having taken a separate flight with Lisa DePaulo, a writer who had filed one story on Susan Berman for *New York* magazine back in February and was now on assignment for *Talk* magazine to write another.

Becerra drove over the causeway and made a left onto Broadway, heading downtown and straight for the Galveston Police Department. There, he and O'Donnell met Cody Cazalas and Mike Putnal. Becerra liked them immediately, especially the much-taller Cazalas, who greeted his visitors from New York with warm handshakes and a big smile.

As they sat down to talk, Becerra briefed the Texans on the Kathie Durst case, and Cazalas told him and O'Donnell all he knew about the still-unclaimed remains of one Morris Black, who two weeks into the investigation remained a riddle. He apparently had no family and only one prior address that the police knew about—in North Charleston, South Carolina, where, in 1998, he had been arrested for threatening to blow up a local utility company over a disputed bill.

"The other tenants in the Avenue K house said he was a bitter pill to take. Always arguing, shutting off lights. Being a general pain in the ass," said Cazalas.

Morris was an enigma, said Cazalas, but an enigma with a hefty $137,500 in savings, which police found in six accounts in a South Dakota bank.

"He and Durst lived right across from each other. According to the landlord, they both arrived in November. Durst rented the place around November fifteenth. That date mean anything to you?" said Cazalas.

Becerra thought for a minute. "Yeah, it was a few days after word of my investigation leaked out to the newspapers in New York."

"So let's say Durst heard about your investigation and was on the run," said Cazalas. "If he were running, this was the place to hide. If Galveston is good for something, it's for hiding."

It sounded plausible, said Becerra, that Bobby would have come to Galveston to disappear. But dressed as a woman named Dorothy Ciner?

"We got a call from a Dorothy Ciner," said Cazalas. "She lives in Wisconsin. Says she went to high school with Durst in New York but hasn't seen him since. She also said she's never been to Texas. She heard her name mentioned on the news and called us."

Cazalas looked for a reaction from the state-police investigator, but there was none.

"He also used a phony name, a Jim Turss, renting a room at the Holiday Inn around the time we found Black. Turss is another old high school classmate."

Again, there was little reaction from Becerra.

"You don't look shocked," said Cazalas.

"I'm not," said Becerra. "We know he's used another name. James Klosty. Scarsdale High School. Now that we know he likes to use different identities, let's get down to this question: Why kill Morris Black?"

Cazalas could only shrug his shoulders. Putnal thought Durst was unlucky that Black's remains had been found.

"Had the tide drifted in a different direction, the body

would have eventually sunk to the bottom. As it was, it washed up in shallow water," said Putnal.

Cazalas said that based on his interviews, Black hadn't been the best of neighbors, yelling all hours of the day and night, even going so far as to turn off the circuit breakers in the house when he thought the other tenants were using too much electricity.

"Definitely not the easiest person to get along with. But I don't think that's cause for murder," said Cazalas. "As far as Black and Durst knowing each other prior to Galveston, Joe, that's an interesting theory. The time I spent with Durst, I got the impression he was very smart, very intelligent. Durst left a receipt in a garbage can behind the house on Avenue K. It was for a dry cleaner in New Orleans. I drove there. Six hours across some of the most boring stretches of road. When I got there the clerk told me Durst brought in a comforter. It had blood on it. Why drive three hundred and fifty miles to clean a bloody comforter?"

Becerra didn't reply. He was thinking back to the NYPD file, to Mike Struk's report, about Bobby visiting a Laundromat in New Jersey, supposedly to wash a coat.

Cazalas continued on about how last April Bobby had told his sister, Wendy, the only family member he was communicating with, that he would be away for a while. That he'd drop out of sight.

"I think he's very calculating, meticulous," said Cazalas, who added that Bobby had been sighted throughout Galveston, walking around in an ill-fitting dress, using the computers at the local library. He appeared to act like a man who needed immediate psychiatric help, but Cazalas thought differently.

"I don't buy into this psycho stuff," he said. "Durst was acting like a fugitive long before Black was killed, like he was setting things up. What for, I don't know. And when it all comes down to it, I don't have a motive."

Cazalas leaned forward, not wanting anyone other than those in his group to hear what he had to say next.

"I'll tell you this," he said. "I saw how Black was cut up. This guy Durst, he's done this before."

———

JEANINE Pirro stood outside the Galveston Courthouse, surrounded by reporters and television cameras and answering questions about Robert Durst and her investigation.

It was Tuesday, October 16, and Pirro was here for Bobby's hearing.

Election Day was three weeks away, and the polls were not looking good. Pirro was up by only a few percentage points. What should have been a cakewalk victory over her opponent was now a nail-biter. Even without a debate, her challenger had made an issue out of Pirro's husband's legal problems, and she couldn't get away from it.

September, of course, had been marked by the attack on the World Trade Center, and this had given Pirro some breathing room.

But one month later Pirro's campaign needed a shot in the arm, so she decided to travel to Galveston for Robert Durst's hearing, not that she had any real business there. District attorneys don't usually show up in court for simple hearings. And Bobby Durst wasn't facing any charges in Westchester County, which made her presence in Texas even more questionable.

But there she was, surrounded by the media and standing next to Galveston district attorney Mike Guarino, waiting along with a host of other people to see if Bobby would actually appear. No one had heard from him or seen him since his arrest. His local attorney, Mark Kelly, told the court that Bobby would be present for the hearing. But Kelly had been appointed by the court, and he really didn't have a clue about whether or not Durst would show.

The assembled media asked Pirro about her investigation, and she said she traveled to Galveston to speak with Guarino and the Los Angeles police, to see if the three cases were connected. The L.A. police wouldn't even confirm publicly that Bobby was a suspect in Susan Berman's murder, but that didn't stop Pirro from mentioning her intention to speak with them.

"California authorities will be joining us. We will sit down together and see if any of the pieces of the puzzle fit together," she said.

It was a Broadway show in the heart of Galveston, the other actors unaware of their supporting roles.

But in reality, Pirro was just the opening act. The real star was Bobby Durst, and Pirro stood there, along with Guarino, Becerra, Cazalas, and others, waiting for him to arrive.

As the minutes turned to hours, it became apparent that Bobby was not going to attend the hearing and had no intention of appearing in any court.

Nor did he have any intention of remaining in Texas.

23

BOBBI Sue Bacha was a purebred, full-figured Texas gal with jet-black hair, matching black clothes, and the voice of a ten-year-old.

When she answered the phone at Blue Moon Investigations, Galveston County *Daily News* reporter Ted Streuli didn't know if he was talking to a seasoned private investigator or a child who had accompanied a parent to work and mistakenly picked up the phone.

Or maybe he'd just dialed a wrong number.

"Hi, this is Bobbi," came the sweet, innocent voice.

Streuli had been working the Sunday night when Morris Black's body parts washed up in the bay. After Black was positively identified, Streuli began the task of putting the dead man's history together. The only problem was that it appeared that Black had no history.

Aside from a previous address in Galena Park, Texas, and one in South Carolina in the late 1990s, Black was an enigma. No wife, no kids, no car. Nothing.

So Streuli turned to Bobbi Sue.

Bobbi Sue was born and raised in Galveston and just happened to have grown up in the neighborhood where

Black's remains had been found. She knew those waters well, having gone fishing and swimming there daily.

She was now forty-two years old, on her third marriage, and so full of sweetness she still called her father Daddy. To everyone else he was Robert Trapani, a retired Galveston police officer who'd served on the force for thirty-seven years.

When Bobbi Sue's first marriage, to her high school sweetheart, ended after several years and one child, she needed a job—so she decided to become a private eye. Considering her father's background, the career choice wasn't far out of line. Investigative work was in Bobbi Sue's blood.

She caught on quickly, and by the mid-1990s was running a growing private investigative firm.

Her life seemed to settle down after she married her third husband, Lucas Bacha, a soft-spoken NASA engineer whose résumé included work on the space shuttle. He even took in Bobbi Sue's three children, one of whom, a fourteen-year-old daughter, was a budding model. They all lived in a large, neatly maintained white Colonial home on a corner lot in nearby League City.

Blue Moon's offices were on the second floor of a sleek, glass-enclosed office building in Webster, a town off I-45 between Houston and Galveston that was peppered with restaurants that catered to NASA employees who worked nearby. Bobbi Sue had thirty-seven employees of her own, and over the years had carved an impressive reputation for herself as a relentless investigator. Along with catching cheating spouses, her firm specialized in research, insurance fraud, and criminal investigations.

Lucas Bacha served as the CEO of Blue Moon, handling the finances and business affairs, and had been blessed with the kind of office a CEO deserved. The furniture was cherry wood, and included a seven-foot-tall bookcase that covered an entire wall, a big desk, sofa, two upholstered leather chairs, assorted photos, and a marble chess set.

Bobbi Sue's office was across from Lucas's and

much smaller, but she didn't care. She had her computer and access to every searchable database imaginable. If you wanted to find someone, or information about someone, Bobbi Sue was the person to turn to. She was, at her core, a bloodhound. Private investigation wasn't just a job for her. She thirsted for every opportunity that came her way.

So when Ted Streuli called, asking Bobbi Sue to look into the history of one Morris Black, she didn't hesitate.

It took her but two weeks to organize a preliminary file on the man, but it wasn't the kind of thorough information Bobbi Sue expected she'd obtain.

Morris had been born in 1929. Originally from Massachusetts, he had several brothers and sisters, some of whom hadn't spoken to him in more than fifty years.

One sister, Gladys, still lived outside Boston and was the only sibling Morris maintained any contact with. He would call her on occasion, becoming infuriated if she wasn't home to take his call. She never had any idea where he was, and when they did talk, he wouldn't say where he was calling from.

He had a brother Harry, who lived in Florida, but Morris spoke on occasion only with Harry's ex-wife, Trudy.

After joining the Merchant Marines and traveling the world, where he developed a preference for coastal towns, Morris had returned to Boston. Bobbi Sue couldn't tell what he did there. There was no information on him. Morris's life didn't pick up again until he turned up in Galena Park, Texas, in the mid-1990s, and North Charleston, South Carolina, in 1998, where he had apparently been arrested for threatening to blow up a utility company over a disputed bill.

Somehow, he ended up in Galveston, living next door to Robert Durst.

As Bobbi Sue studied Morris's past, she could tell that something was amiss. Whole chunks—decades of time—were blank. No previous addresses. No cars. No credit cards. It was as if he appeared for a little while, then disappeared, showing up in the oddest of places. It would take more time, she figured, to get a read on Morris Black. But she was curious. It was her experience that people with no history planned it that way, that they purposely lived in the shadows of society. Thoughts of Morris once serving as a hired assassin or mob soldier crossed her mind.

Frustrated over her inability to learn more about Morris, Bobbi Sue decided to turn her attention to Bobby Durst.

She ran him on Auto Track, a pay service used by police, private investigators, and the media that provides current and previous addresses along with possible phone numbers and information on relatives. Bobbi's Auto Track revealed a host of addresses across the country, including Manhattan, Ridgefield (Connecticut), San Marino (California), Miami, Los Angeles, and Dallas.

As Bobbi Sue studied the report, she noticed something odd. Durst had an address in Belmont, New York, under a different Social Security number. She ran the number through Auto Track, and came up with a name, James S. Fleischman. He was fifty-four, married, and lived in Belmont, which was a suburb of Buffalo.

According to the records, Bobby had obtained a New York State driver's license using Fleischman's Social Security number and home address. The license had expired in April 1998.

Believing she'd stumbled onto something, she turned each of the nineteen pages of the Auto Track, her curiosity fully piqued. She stopped halfway through. Bobby, it seemed, had assumed the identity of yet another man, Robert Jezowski, of New York City. Bobby had used Jezowski's Social Security number and name, but it wasn't clear why.

Bobbi Sue was sitting in her office, trying to make sense out of the different addresses, when Lucas walked by, noticing the quizzical look on her face. He knew that look all too well. His spouse was in full detective mode. She had found something she couldn't quite understand.

"Look at this," she said, waving him into the office. "This man lives near Buffalo, New York. This other one lives in New York City. Durst used both their names and Social Security numbers. I don't get it. What's he doing? And why is he taking people's identities?"

Lucas said nothing. He knew Bobbi Sue was onto something. He also knew she wouldn't stop until she found the answers.

———

MANNING Ogden was on a plane en route to Mexico from his home in New Orleans when he read the *People* magazine story about the heir to a New York real estate fortune who was wanted for murder in Galveston, Texas. When Manning read that the accused murderer had been masquerading as a cross-dressing mute, he nearly jumped from his seat and out of the airplane.

Upon landing, Manning rushed to a phone and called his brother Robert in Philadelphia.

"You're not going to believe this," said Manning. "Do you remember me joking about the weird transvestite in one of my buildings? The deaf-mute? I'm reading this *People* magazine story on the plane about this guy who dressed like a woman in Galveston who's wanted for murder. He's some millionaire from New York. It's the same guy. He rented an apartment in Galveston dressed as a woman who was a deaf-mute. What are the chances there are two of these guys running around like this?"

Manning had received a call in March from a smooth-talking man who claimed to be an assistant of a woman named Diane Winne, who, said the assistant, was a deaf-mute in her fifties interested in renting one of Manning's apartments in New Orleans. She was financially stable, said the assistant, and would pay the $650 rent three months in advance, using money orders, if that was acceptable.

When Winne appeared, Manning immediately knew she was a he. The disguise was awful, and he would joke with his brother about the weird transvestite living in his building. But this was New Orleans, after all, and weird transvestites were the norm, so Manning didn't pay much attention. He didn't really notice that Diane Winne rarely spent any time in her apartment.

When he returned to New Orleans from Mexico, Manning rushed home and was surprised to see that the apartment he'd rented to the cross-dresser had been cleaned out. Winne had left a scribbled note, apologizing for the abrupt departure, but said her plans had changed suddenly, she was leaving New Orleans, and would not be back.

Inside the apartment, Manning found a wig, a CD burner, computer mouse and mouse pad, and a medallion and key chain, both inscribed with the name Davie Berman.

There was also a VHS videocassette, a copy of the ABC special on Kathie Durst, *Vanished,* which had aired during the summer.

Manning found an old telephone bill, all local calls. The phone was still turned on, so he picked it up and pressed Redial. It connected to an answering machine in California. The recorded voice on the other end, the one Manning immediately recognized as belonging to the "assistant" who had called him about Diane Winne, said it was Robert Durst, please leave a message.

Manning told his brother Robert, who in turn called several news organizations in New York, looking to sell photos of some of the items left behind as well as to obtain a phone number for Cody Cazalas in Galveston.

When he got the number, Robert called Cazalas, who immediately drove to New Orleans.

———

JIM McCORMACK didn't know what to say or even what to think when he heard that Bobby was a fugitive. His mind was a bowl of mush, his hopes and dreams of finding closure for his family now all but gone. This whole experience, from the day he received the call from Joe Becerra nearly two years earlier to the call he re-

ceived from Gilberte Najamy just days before telling
him that Bobby had fled, only served to reinforce a
growing feeling that Bobby would never be brought to
justice. Not for the murder of Morris Black, and certainly not for the murder of his sister Kathie. It was a
game, a game the McCormacks were losing once again.

Even the plea that Michael Kennedy, the soft-spoken
and well-respected New York attorney hired by the
Durst family trust, had made for Bobby to "come home"
was met with skepticism by Jim and his family. Kennedy
held a news conference in New York after Bobby's
flight, fearful that his client was desperate, carrying a
gun, and in imminent danger of meeting a violent end
from trigger-happy cops. Kennedy described Bobby as
a "fragile human being."

Jim didn't think much of that description. Bobby was
a lot of things, he thought, but he wasn't fragile.

Despite the disappointing turn of events, Jim and his
wife, Sharon, persevered. When a reporter would call
requesting an interview, Jim would oblige. If it was a
national magazine, he'd invite the reporter to his comfortable home. Jim had never heard of Morris Black, and
the only information he could offer about a possible relationship between Bobby and Morris was that Bobby
had often traveled to New England—Morris was from
Boston—driving up alone or with Kathie.

Sharon even sat in on several interviews, recalling her
fond memories of her long-lost sister-in-law, how beautiful and kind she was, and how during the last years of
her life, she seemed to fall into a vacuum that sucked
her into a lost world of drugs and alcohol.

Sharon remembered the long discussions she and Kathie had had. Once Kathie started drinking wine, she
couldn't stop talking. And her conversations always centered on her husband and his family.

Kathie even told one story about a fire in a Manhattan
building that killed a man. She claimed it had been a
case of arson, that it was part of the never-ending power

grab for real estate in New York, though, of course, there was never any proof.

"You don't know these people, Sharon. You really don't know what they're like," she said to Sharon between long gulps of red wine.

While Jim continued to speak with the media, his sister Mary shut herself off completely. Aside from their mother, the loss of Kathie had affected Mary the most. She was emotionally fried, unable and unwilling to discuss Kathie's disappearance with anyone, especially reporters. She had even found it difficult to talk to Joe Becerra during her four-hour interview.

If a reporter wanted to speak to Mary, they had to go through Jim, ask him the question, and he'd call his sister. If a question was posed to Jim that he couldn't answer, he called Mary.

With Bobby now on the run, Mary refused to answer any questions directed her way. For Mary, the entire episode was a nightmare, a bad dream with no ending.

AS the Thanksgiving holiday came and went and Christmas approached, Bobby Durst was still a fugitive. He had the money and the resources to hide just about anywhere, from an island in the Caribbean to the wilderness in South America. Heightened security, a result of the attacks on the World Trade Center and Pentagon, had made it that much more difficult to sneak out of the United States, so law enforcement, including the FBI in Houston, figured that Bobby was probably still in the country. Just where was the big question. There had been several sightings, including one in San Marino, California, which was about three hundred miles north of San Francisco. Bobby owned property there, in a remote area, but neither that sighting, nor any others, panned out.

America's Most Wanted, a weekly program on the FOX Network, was preparing to air a segment on Durst, having interviewed Jim McCormack, Gilberte Najamy, and Jeanine Pirro. The show was slated to air December 1, 2001.

Police did find and freeze one of Bobby's bank accounts, containing about $2 million, and were keeping an eye on one Debrah Lee Charaton, a real estate broker from New York who, surprisingly, happened to be Bobby's wife.

They had met in the late 1980s, at a Christmas party. Charaton was the successful owner of Bach Realty, a commercial real estate firm with more than $100 million in sales. They married a year earlier, on December 11, 2000, little more than three weeks after Bobby arrived in Galveston. It was a simple ceremony, witnessed only by a rabbi. Bobby flew to New York, where he and his new bride exchanged vows, then he was off again, to destinations unknown.

When news filtered through to the McCormack family that Bobby had remarried, they couldn't figure out how it could be. He was still technically married to Kathie, or so they thought. They would soon learn through news reports that Bobby had divorced Kathie in 1990, placing a single ad in a New York law magazine to fulfill a requirement to publicize the action.

It was another blow, an unexpected hit, but one that Jim took in stride. Following Morris Black's murder, Jim wasn't shy about expressing his theories to reporters, saying that Black's murder only confirmed what the McCormack family had been saying for years—that Bobby had a propensity for violence.

Jim didn't mind saying that.

He had lost patience with Jeanine Pirro, who had won her bid for reelection by only six percentage points.

Pirro spent $1.4 million on her campaign against Tony Castro, who spent little more than $100,000. Included among Pirro's campaign contributions was $24,500 from Hushang Ansary. A former Iranian ambassador, Ansary was now a U.S. citizen and oil-field-equipment-company owner who was worth millions. A major contributor to Republican Party candidates, he was a longtime supporter of President George W. Bush. Ansary contributed $100,000 to the Bush presidential campaign in 2000.

Pirro, with her deep Republican ties, parlayed the visit to Texas for the Durst hearing into a visit with Ansary, who lived in Houston, only forty-five minutes from Galveston.

Ansary's $24,500 check was the largest single contribution to Pirro's campaign, making the trip to Texas a successful campaign stop, but adding nothing to the Kathie Durst investigation.

24

A security camera hanging on a ceiling inside the Wegman's supermarket was pointed at the strange little bald man, who had taken a Band-Aid from a box and placed it over his upper lip.

The man looked over his shoulder, then down the aisle. Convinced that no one was watching, he took a few more Band-Aids, slipped them into his coat pocket, and moved on. Another camera in the large, upscale supermarket near Bethlehem, Pennsylvania, followed the man as he walked to the front of the store, looked at a cart filled with sandwiches, reached down, and took one, placing it inside his jacket.

A security guard followed the man as he walked outside and brought him to the second-floor security office.

Officer Dean Benner of the Colonial Regional Police was in his patrol car when he received the call at 12:36 P.M. on Friday, November 30, that a shoplifter had been detained at the Wegman's. Benner drove down Route 512, parked in front of the store, and walked up to the security office. He entered the room and quietly listened as Wegman's security questioned the man, who said his name was Robert Durst.

Benner, who at six-feet two-inches was built like a linebacker, was caught off guard by Durst's appearance. His head was shaved, as were his eyebrows. He looked to be in his fifties. As Wegman's security continued their questioning, Bobby replied that he hadn't stolen anything in more than ten years.

"I'm just an asshole for doing this," he said, shaking his head.

Benner interrupted the interview, asking Bobby if he had a shoplifting problem.

"Yeah, I did, until about ten years ago," said Bobby. "I've always had problems stealing. I once saw a psychiatrist for help. I thought I beat it. I don't know what made me do it."

Bobby spoke slowly, deliberately. There was a slightly shrill quality to his voice, which seemed to proceed from somewhere other than deep inside his mouth. It sounded otherworldly. Bobby said he had been to this particular store three days in a row.

"It's a very fine establishment," he said. "I really don't know what possessed me to steal this stuff."

Wegman's security asked Bobby for his Social Security number, which he was reluctant to give them. He had no physical identification, no driver's license or credit cards.

"They're in my car," he said. "It's a red Corsica. It's in the parking lot."

He finally gave them a Social Security number. Benner then pulled out his handcuffs and told Bobby to stand up.

"You mean I have to get arrested?" asked Bobby.

"Sorry, pal, but I have to take you in," said Benner, who escorted Bobby out of the store and placed him in the back of the cruiser for the ten-minute ride to the police station in Bath.

Bobby sat there with his hands cuffed behind his back and mumbled to himself.

Benner couldn't make out what he was saying, so he reached over and slowly turned down his police radio, wanting to hear every word.

Bobby was looking out the car window, talking about his age, and saying how stupid he was.

"I can't believe this. I'm fifty-eight years old and I get caught for theft! What an asshole! What an asshole!"

Benner couldn't escape that voice, that shrill. And Bobby's strange physical appearance didn't help either. Benner was spooked.

Once they were inside the cramped police station, Benner sat Bobby down, cuffing his hands to a chair, and repeated some of the questions Wegman's security had asked, including his name, address, and Social Security number.

Bobby gave a New York home address and said he was here in eastern Pennsylvania visiting his daughter, who was a student at Lehigh University, which was only twenty minutes away in Bethlehem.

"I graduated from Lehigh in 1965. My daughter knows about my shoplifting problem. She's the one who sent me into therapy. She's really going to be disappointed with me today," he said.

Benner explained that since Bobby was not a resident of Pennsylvania, he would have to be brought in front of a magistrate and pay a fine, probably around $300 plus court costs.

"What happens after that?"

"I let you go."

Bobby seemed relieved and told Benner he had $500 in his pocket.

Benner would have just written Bobby up and taken him immediately to the district justice if not for Bobby's strange ways, with his continuing rant about his shoplifting problems. And aside from the lack of hair on his head, and eyebrows, which was disconcerting, there was something about his facial expressions that kept Benner on edge. Bobby's eyes were beady and he looked distant, vacant. His face twitched. He was beyond weird. Benner wasn't getting a good feel from him.

Benner looked at the paperwork from Wegman's and noticed that Bobby had given him a different Social Security number from the one he gave the store.

Benner looked over to Bobby.

"Okay, what are we doing here?"

Bobby just stared at him.

"You gave Wegman's one Social Security number, and you just gave me a different number. Don't play with me. Which number is it?"

"It's the second number, the one I just gave you," said Bobby, his face tightening.

Benner paused for a moment. He wanted to know more about this little man with the shaved head, so he called the Northampton County dispatch, giving both Social Security numbers.

Dispatch called back within seconds. Benner listened intently, quickly jotting down some notes, answering questions "yes . . . yes . . . yes," his eyes growing wide by the end of the conversation. Benner hung up the phone and spun around toward Bobby, looking straight into his small, beady eyes.

"So, when was the last time you were in Texas?"

Bobby froze. His eyes slid back into his head and his jaw dropped to the floor.

"You going to answer me?" said Benner.

Bobby said nothing. He knew the charade was over.

Benner called out for Detective Gary Hammer, who was sitting nearby, and told him this supermarket shoplifter was wanted for murder in Texas.

Hammer walked over and looked at Benner's notes.

"You want to tell us what's happening here?" he said.

Bobby remained quiet. He had managed to compose himself and decided to frustrate the Pennsylvania police the same way he'd infuriated Cody Cazalas in Texas, refusing to answer even the simplest of questions.

He was placed inside a locked and secure room while Benner and Hammer called the FBI and the Galveston police, informing them that the Colonial Regional Police had just captured one of the most wanted men in America.

THE call to the Somers barracks from Galveston was brief and to the point: Robert Durst had been captured in Pennsylvania.

The details were sketchy, but he had apparently been arrested for shoplifting, and the cop in Pennsylvania had been smart enough to run Bobby's Social Security number.

"Bingo!" said Joe Becerra, who called Jeanine Pirro to give her the good news.

Pirro didn't waste any time. The election was over, but the DA wasn't finished politicking, and as the news quickly spread and the calls came in from the media, she painted a scenario that Bobby's capture was the result of a relentless pursuit mounted by the combined forces of the Galveston police, the New York State Police, her office, and the Los Angeles police.

"There was no question in my mind that sooner or later, with the coordinated law enforcement effort, that he would be apprehended. We've been following a money and paper trail," Pirro told the media.

Money and paper trail? Bobby was gone, off the radar screen, the last sighting coming from a car rental in Biloxi, Mississippi, weeks earlier.

No one had had a clue as to where he was. These were the weeks after September 11, and the FBI and every available law enforcement officer in the New York area was either working the World Trade Center probe or on the lookout for terrorists. Pirro's comments, as usual, made good copy. But if Bobby hadn't stolen seven dollars' worth of goods from a supermarket, he'd have still been free.

Becerra paid little attention to what Pirro was saying, as did Cody Cazalas in Galveston, who was preparing to hop on a plane for a flight to Pennsylvania. Cazalas and the rest of the Galveston police had grown tired of Pirro's public posturing. They wished she'd just shut up. If only she was more like the authorities in Los Angeles, who remained so tight-lipped about the Susan Berman investigation.

Pirro, on the other hand, was saying too much, but doing little. She had become a gadfly, a nuisance in their investigation.

Put up or shut up was their philosophy.

Pirro did neither.

———

AFTER informing the district attorney, Becerra also made calls to Jim McCormack and Gilberte Najamy. Both responded with utter relief.

Najamy, the always-quotable best friend, again told every reporter who called her for comment that it was she who had applied the pressure that made Bobby fall apart. His eventual capture was the direct result of her hard work, she said.

"I made a promise to Kathie, and I kept that promise," said Gilberte.

Jim McCormack was just happy and relieved that Bobby was finally behind bars.

Maybe now, after all this time, he'd tell the Mc-Cormacks, and the world, what had happened to his sister Kathie.

And Jim now looked to Jeanine Pirro to finally bring him and his family justice.

———

AS the stunning news that one of America's most wanted fugitives had been arrested spread throughout the country, Officer Dean Benner and Detective Gary Hammer were working the phones quarterbacking calls from police in Texas, Los Angeles, and New York when they heard a loud *boom* noise coming from the direction of the room that held Bobby Durst.

"What the hell was that!" Benner said as he ran to open the door, looked inside, and saw Bobby standing, but slumped, having slammed his head against the wall.

"Pissed off at yourself, aren't ya?" said Benner, who

sat Bobby down, warned him to stay put, and locked the door.

"What he do?" asked Hammer.

"Dumb bastard slammed his head against the wall. I'd say he's pissed off big time that he just got busted over a chicken-salad sandwich," said Benner. "I mean, how stupid can you be? What did he have, five hundred dollars in his pocket?"

Benner walked back into the room to check on Bobby while Hammer answered a call from the FBI.

Bobby sat there, emotionless, his eyes vacant.

Benner was alone with a man who was wanted for one murder and a suspect in two others, and he decided he'd try to pick his brain.

"So, you want to tell me what a millionaire is doing stealing a Band-Aid and a sandwich?" Benner said.

Bobby said nothing. He sat there, his face twitching, eyes focused on the wall.

Benner moved closer.

"You want to tell me why you did that guy in Texas?" said Benner. "C'mon. You were talking to me just a few minutes ago, telling me what an asshole you are. I'd say I'd have to agree."

Bobby wasn't going to say a word. Earlier, after he'd been brought up into the security office at the Wegman's, he made one phone call, to Michael Kennedy's law office in Manhattan. An hour after arriving at the Bath police station, he received a call from that office, telling him to say nothing.

By 5 P.M., Bobby was taken to the local district magistrate, Barbara Schlegel, for arraignment. Schlegel asked him his name, but Bobby refused to answer.

"All I'm asking is for your name," said Schlegel.

"I'm not answering any questions," said Bobby.

Schlegel denied bail and remanded Bobby to the Northampton County prison in Easton, Pennsylvania, where he was placed in a solitary cell and declared a stage-one suicide watch.

———

THREE days later, Cody Cazalas arrived in Pennsylvania, and was taken to the Colonial Regional police station. Waiting for him was Jeanine Pirro, who had driven two and a half hours from New York and surprised everyone by appearing.

Pirro needed to get out of town and was hoping to draw more publicity from the Durst case, especially after a weekend during which her husband, Al, had returned home from prison. The *New York Times* ran a lengthy story, rehashing Al's trial and subsequent imprisonment. He had served eleven months of a twenty-nine-month sentence, his time reduced by twelve months for good behavior. He would serve only six more months in a halfway house. His law license was suspended for seven years, but there were no restrictions on rejoining his lobbying firm, Buley Public Affairs.

Pirro's only comment to the media when asked about her husband was that she was happy her family would be together for Christmas.

Privately she lashed out at reporters who dared ask her about her husband. After the *Times* piece was published, Pirro was asked during a phone interview with a reporter if her husband had ever been employed by the Durst Organization. It seemed a logical question, given that her husband was a major lobbying force in Westchester real estate, having represented, among others, Donald Trump.

Pirro became enraged and screamed at the reporter. "How dare you ask that question! I can't believe you would ask me such a question! This is an independent office!"

She then hung up without answering the question. Ten minutes later one of her assistants called the reporter, sheepishly asking if there were any other questions for Ms. Pirro. When the reporter said no, the assistant asked about that last question, the one about Al Pirro and the Durst Organization.

"Is that going to appear in print?" said the assistant.

"No," said the reporter. "The story is about the Durst case, not Al Pirro."

The assistant seemed relieved.

Two days later Pirro looked on as the red Chevy Corsica was searched, explaining that her presence in Pennsylvania was warranted since there was a possibility that evidence could be found that would be germane to the Kathie Durst case.

Joe Becerra remained behind in Westchester, scratching his head and wondering why he wasn't in Bath, Pennsylvania, at this moment.

The search of the car produced two .38 handguns, $38,500 in cash, marijuana, a driver's license, and Medicaid card, both in the name of Morris Black.

Bobby had rented the Corsica at a Rent-A-Wreck in Mobile, Alabama, on October 17, using Black's name but paying in cash. He drove east to Baltimore, then up to the Atlantic City, New Jersey, area before stopping in Bethlehem, which was less than eighty miles west of New York City.

He arrived in the Lehigh Valley on November 18, checking into the Staybridge Suites. He was familiar with the area, having attended Lehigh University in the 1960s. During his twelve days there he had been seen, sometimes dressed in drag, talking to himself, even scaring customers at C. L. Checkers Pub, where he cleared his side of the bar with his unintelligible ramblings. There was a similar reaction from customers at the Golden View Diner, where he wore a brown wig and white mustache.

Bobby showed all the signs of a seriously disturbed individual.

The Galveston police weren't buying it. They traced two guns—the .22 with the missing shell casing that had been found in the garbage pail behind the house on Avenue K and the nine-millimeter found in the car when he was arrested in Galveston—to Bobby.

He had purchased the nine-millimeter in 1993 in Tyler, Texas, a small town about an hour's drive east of Dallas, where he owned a condominium. He purchased the .22 in August, a month before Black's murder, at Carter's Country, a gun store near Houston.

Galveston district attorney Mike Guarino made it clear that he planned to extradite Bobby to Texas, where he would be tried for the murder of Morris Black.

Following Bobby's capture, his old friends in New York rushed to his defense. Doug Oliver told reporters that Bobby was a "great guy" and that he didn't believe the charges against him.

"The Bob Durst I know could never do anything like that," said Oliver.

Julie Baumgold, the writer who was Bobby's childhood friend from Scarsdale, went one better. Baumgold's husband, Ed Kosner, was the editor of the *New York Daily News*. On December 5, the *News* printed a front-page "exclusive" entitled "My Friend Bobby Durst," written by Baumgold.

Two full pages long, Baumgold's story was part love letter, part defense. He couldn't have killed Susan Berman, she wrote, because Bobby had told her so. Following Susan's death, Bobby told Baumgold that Susan would have supported his theory concerning his wife's disappearance, that Kathie died at the hands of drug dealers.

How could Bobby commit such heinous acts? asked Baumgold. He was a gentle soul who chose to buy old cars and wear old clothes. His disturbing physical appearance upon his capture was the result of his being hounded for weeks and his having stopped taking his medications.

Baumgold also dismissed theories that Bobby's $50,000 gift to Susan Berman prior to her death was hush money. Baumgold claimed she was the one who had asked Bobby to help Susan out, since Susan was broke and desperate.

Baumgold also slam-dunked John O'Donnell, the senior investigator in Jeanine Pirro's office, describing a conversation she had with him in November, when O'Donnell called to ask if she had heard from her old friend.

She said no. O'Donnell told her he believed Bobby had killed Morris Black. Baumgold printed O'Donnell's comments.

As kids, Baumgold said, they shared birthday parties and days on the Jersey shore. Bobby's father, Seymour, had always worried about him, though Baumgold didn't say why.

The story enraged the *Daily News* beat writers who were covering the Durst case. A good friend of Bobby Durst, the wife of the editor, was allowed to write a front-page story trying to explain her friend's behavior? It was journalism in its lowest form.

When Jim McCormack read the story, he was filled with rage and frustration. Here we go again, he thought. Bobby's friends and family were coming to his defense. They had the influence to soften his image, to explain away his actions. Off his medication—are you kidding me? He's charged with dismembering a human being, and this woman is remembering days at the beach and mocking an investigator with the Westchester District Attorney's Office?

If there was a silver lining to the story, Jim decided, it was that Bobby stood charged with murder in Texas, where Galveston judge Susan Criss had had enough of the publicity surrounding the case and imposed a gag order on all involved.

25

THE *Talk* magazine story on Bobby and Kathie Durst
was published in early January, and when Janet Finke
read it, she wanted to open a window and scream from
her Connecticut home.

Talk was a New York magazine edited and published
by Tina Brown, formerly of the *New Yorker,* and the
Durst story was written by Lisa DePaulo, the veteran
journalist who had been on the same October 15, 2001,
flight to Galveston as Jeanine Pirro, and who just a year
earlier had written a piece about the death of Susan Berman for *New York* magazine.

DePaulo's *New York* piece had pointed the finger for
Susan's death squarely at her manager, Nyles Brenner,
who, it turned out, had had a love/hate relationship with
Susan—with the hate decidedly in the ascendant.

For *Talk,* DePaulo wrote a somewhat different version, now pointing the finger at Bobby and offering
gushing praise for Jeanine Pirro, describing how she was
"fixated" on solving the Durst case.

It was Pirro, wrote DePaulo, whose investigation had
forced Bobby to act irrationally over the past year and
a half.

But it wasn't the praise for Pirro that had so riled up Janet Finke.

It was the story of Kathie's last night alive as told by Gilberte Najamy.

Again, Gilberte had found her way into a magazine article, telling the world that she had relentlessly pursued Bobby for nineteen years, all to keep a promise she made to her friend Kathie Durst. Gilberte again told how Kathie had arrived at her house, how Bobby called several times demanding that she return home, and how Kathie was at her wit's end.

Janet was furious after reading Gilberte's comments about Bobby's insistent calls.

Following her conversation with Bobby in August, just weeks before Morris Black was killed, Janet had hoped that she'd never speak to him again. She realized that Bobby was living a strange, vagabond life using false identities for reasons unknown to anybody. Whatever he was doing, Janet concluded it was something he had been working at for a long time. Though Bobby spooked her, Janet nevertheless thought that Gilberte's story of that last Sunday when Kathie was seen alive should be told truthfully, at least from Bobby's point of view.

Janet remembered that day. She and her then boyfriend, Alan Martin, were scheduled to have dinner with Bobby and Kathie, but Janet called Bobby around 5:30 P.M. to cancel, saying she didn't feel like driving in the bad weather. Janet remembered Bobby being calm during that call, saying not to worry about it, that Kathie was at Gilberte's house and probably wouldn't be back until later anyway.

Bobby wasn't angry, thought Janet. So what's Gilberte talking about?

———

IN mid-January, two weeks after the *Talk* piece was published, another lengthy story on the Durst case appeared, this time in *Vanity Fair*.

And when Jeanine Pirro opened the magazine, she was irate.

Unlike the *Talk* piece, which credited Pirro in glowing terms as Bobby Durst's main antagonist, the *Vanity Fair* piece fawned over Joe Becerra. Even worse, there was a photo of Becerra accompanying the story, in which he looked dapper in a tie and suit.

It didn't matter that the story's real focus was Gilberte Najamy, again relaying her story about how she suffered through extreme personal anguish to continue on a now twenty-year crusade to bring Bobby to justice.

Gilberte's story was so good, *Variety* reported, that the author of the piece, Ned Zeman, had sold it to a production company owned by Bruce Willis for close to $1 million. Zeman would write the screen play, and Gilberte would not only be paid a handsome sum for telling her story but would also be a consultant on the film.

Gilberte was ecstatic when she received the contract in the mail with an initial check for $5,000. It was a small deposit. Once the film went into production, a bigger payday would come.

Joe Becerra was also asked if he'd be willing to participate in the movie. He declined, telling the producer he was still involved in an active investigation.

The producer told him not to worry about it, that it was Gilberte they really wanted.

It was, after all, her story.

As soon as Becerra hung up the phone with the producer, he called Gilberte and told her in no uncertain terms that if she signed that contract she could forget about testifying at Bobby's trial, whenever that would occur.

"What are you talking about, I'm not signing anything!" said Gilberte.

"You better not," said Becerra. "If you take any money or sign any contract, you're done. Understand?"

Gilberte seethed after hanging up with Becerra, angered at the stupidity of the producer to have told Becerra about her involvement. It was supposed to be a secret. She knew if word leaked that she accepted money for a film, she'd never testify. She'd be useless to the prosecution. She was even more enraged with Becerra, who had the audacity to think he could tell her what to do and try to blow her deal. After all, Ned Zeman had told Gilberte that hers was by far the most interesting story relating to the disappearance of her friend Kathie.

Gilberte was bitter, and the focus of that bitterness was Joe Becerra.

———

ON January 25, more than a dozen television cameras lined the hall on the second floor of the Northampton County Courthouse in Easton, Pennsylvania, waiting for Bobby Durst to emerge from an underground waiting area to stand before commonwealth judge James Hogan and waive his extradition to Texas.

Minutes earlier, Gilberte Najamy was outside the courthouse, having made the three-hour drive from central Connecticut. The cameras and reporters swarmed around her, and for each interview there was no shortage of tears.

"I was Kathie's best friend, and I'm here to see Bobby. I want him to tell me what he did with Kathie," said Gilberte.

Inside, Jeanine Pirro stood on the marble floor in front of the courtroom, looking as beautiful as ever in a sharp business suit cut to the knee, her heavy lipstick reflecting the ceiling lights. She unintentionally brushed her shoulder against Cody Cazalas, who had flown up from Texas that same day just in case Bobby was released to Galveston authorities. Cazalas would say nothing to the reporters mulling around, saying he was under a gag order. He could only offer a "no-comment" and a big, wide smile.

When Gilberte was finished with the television crews outside, she took the elevator up to the second floor and walked over to the courtroom, where she saw Pirro standing in front. The two had never met before. Gilberte, wearing a worn, gray sport coat and black pants, walked over to the DA, put her arm around her neck, and introduced herself. The two women huddled for ten minutes. When it was over, Gilberte was beaming, and hurriedly walked over to a reporter she knew and proclaimed, loudly, that Joe Becerra was off the case.

"What?" said the reporter, with other members of the media looking on.

"Joey B, he's off. Gone. Pirro's going to take him off the case. She's pissed that Joe never introduced me to her. She's very upset. And I'm going to visit her on Monday. She wants *me* to come in and personally tell *her* everything I know."

With one fatal slice, a quick conversation with Pirro, Gilberte got her revenge on Joe Becerra.

She then turned around and headed toward the courtroom while, on the other side of the long hall, television cameramen positioned themselves to get clear shots of Bobby, who was being led upstairs.

When he came into view, handcuffed and led by two sheriff's deputies, it was the first time most reporters covering the case had ever seen him in person. He was a runt of a man, his once-bald head and shaved eyebrows now sporting gray hair. Wearing gray-rimmed eyeglasses, a dark blue sport jacket, and blue shirt, he walked calmly past the media and into the courtroom, taking a seat next to his attorney, Michael Kennedy, who had driven in from New York.

Pirro took a seat directly behind Bobby, though she had no role to play in the proceedings.

Bobby sat passively, his face twitching violently as Northampton County district attorney John Morganelli told the court he wanted Bobby out of his jurisdiction.

Bobby glanced around the courtroom and noticed Cazalas off to the side. He leaned over to one of Kennedy's assistants and asked if the big man was from Texas.

Judge Hogan told Bobby to stand, then began to ask a series of questions. Bobby's answers, though only yes and no, were drawn-out responses, "yessssss" and "noooooo." His drawl was disconcerting to some in attendance, who were spooked by his shrill voice.

The hearing was brief. Judge Hogan approved the extradition. Everyone stood as he left the bench. Sheriff's deputies stepped in front of Bobby and led him out of the courtroom. Gilberte watched from the back, where she stood in the last row, next to the aisle. It was the first time in twenty years that she was only a breath away from Bobby, and as he approached her, Gilberte reached out.

"Tell me what you did to Kathie," she said.

Bobby didn't recognize her at first, but he knew that voice, and for a split second after he realized it was Gilberte, he stared at her intensely, then he walked on by and out of the courtroom.

It was a dramatic moment. Right out of a Hollywood script.

Gilberte put her hands to her face and began sobbing, again.

———

MINUTES later Morganelli and Pirro stood downstairs in front of Morganelli's office for a press conference. The questions came in rapid fire and all centered on the extradition. Morganelli did all the talking as Pirro stood by, impatiently waiting for a question, any question, about her investigation. But none came, and as Morganelli finished answering yet another question about the extradition, the Westchester DA moved in.

"And as far as the New York case is concerned . . ." she began, making sure she got her sound bite for the local news that night.

Off in the corner, behind the cameras, Gilberte Najamy was giving yet another interview, this time to a print reporter. As she expressed her feelings about her dramatic confrontation with Bobby, the reporter asked her who she was.

"I was Kathie's best friend," she replied as the tears flowed once again.

BOBBY arrived in Galveston around 3 P.M. on Sunday,
January 27, 2002, taking a flight from Philadelphia to
Houston, escorted by Cody Cazalas and two sheriff's
deputies. They sat at the back of the plane, Bobby taking
a window seat. His hands were cuffed, and he remained
quiet throughout the flight—so quiet the other passen-
gers had no idea he was on board.

He was taken to the Galveston County jail, processed,
and placed in a cell.

He appeared in court three days later and entered his
plea before state district judge Susan Criss.

"I am not guilty, your honor."

His trial was set for June 3.

Bobby's attorney, Dick DeGuerin, a Houston-based
criminal lawyer who was considered one of the best in
the state, had been handpicked by Michael Kennedy.

Over the last few months, as many as nine investigators working for DeGuerin had traveled the country,
tracking down and interviewing every friend and ac-
quaintance of Bobby, and nearly all the witnesses in the
Morris Black murder case, feeling them out for incon-
sistencies in their stories.

After Bobby delivered his plea, DeGuerin made a
motion to suppress any testimony or mention of Kathie
Durst or Susan Berman during the murder trial.

DeGuerin also asked the court to order Jeanine Pirro
and Gilberte Najamy to appear at an upcoming hearing,
claiming their public statements could impair Bobby's
right to a fair trial.

"Every day Jeanine Pirro is out there grandstanding,
holding press conferences," said DeGuerin.

Judge Criss ruled that neither Kathie Durst nor Susan
Berman could be mentioned during the trial.

She declined to order Pirro or Najamy to Galveston.

26

GILBERTE Najamy canceled her planned meeting with Jeanine Pirro the Monday after Bobby's extradition hearing, explaining she had more important work to do. Instead she drove from her home in Connecticut to the Garden State Parkway and on to Long Beach Island, New Jersey, to meet with Tom Brown Jr.

Brown is a world-famous survivalist and tracker who had grown up in south Jersey. Gilberte heard about him from a reporter. It was explained that Brown, the subject of several books, could be tossed into the middle of a thick forest, buck naked, and come out a week later dressed in leaves and vine and ten pounds heavier.

His specialty was the Pine Barrens.

When he was just a child, as the story of Tom Brown Jr. goes, he was taught the art of tracking and surviving in the harshest of elements by an old Apache Indian, and in his lifetime he has covered large parts of the 1.1-million-acre natural wonder, part sand dune and part forest, filled with exotic trees, plants, and animal life. Brown lived there, alone, often for weeks. And he taught there, taking students deep inside to ready-made huts to teach them the basics about living and surviving outdoors.

Over the years Brown developed a number of talents in the Pine Barrens, including the recovery of long-buried bodies.

During his long stays there, Brown sometimes came across a depression in the ground, which signaled the sandy earth had once been disturbed, probably with a shovel.

His fame, and ability to detect gravesites, went far beyond New Jersey. Police departments throughout the country would call, asking for his help in finding missing bodies.

So it made sense to Gilberte to call Brown following a conversation with her old friend Eleanor Schwank.

Eleanor was working as a nurse in Matagorda, Texas, a one-restaurant town on the Texas coast southwest of Galveston. A Texas secret, Matagorda was known by only a few for its great fishing and beautiful beaches.

Schwank put up with the burning-hot weather and never-ending mosquito onslaught for the peace and quiet of Matagorda. She had a small cabin next to a winding river that filtered into the ocean. It was a great fishing spot and a place she hoped to one day rent out to earn a few extra dollars.

After hearing about Tom Brown, Gilberte called Eleanor to see if perhaps she would agree to chip in to pay Brown to search for Kathie's remains.

It was a long shot, but Eleanor agreed, as did Ellen Strauss. But after Gilberte met with Brown in his house and he agreed to undertake the search, telling him the story of her lost friend who everyone believed was buried somewhere in the Pine Barrens, she didn't call Eleanor or Ellen to let them know.

Instead she made another call.

Brown had explained that given the fact that Bobby had been in Ship Bottom and across the bridge in Manahawkin, there were a few old, long-forgotten trails nearby that Bobby might have been able to drive through. And it was possible that if Kathie's remains were buried there, they could be found. Brown said he would put together a group of his students to help in the search, and they could do it sometime in April, after he returned from a training session in Florida.

Gilberte was absolutely delighted, and instead of calling her friends to share the news, she promptly called Jeanine Pirro.

After explaining where she had been and who she had talked to, Gilberte handed the phone to Brown, who said that yes, he could possibly find someone who had been buried twenty years earlier.

"I doubt he'd go far into the Pine Barrens," said Brown.

Pirro told Brown that Bobby was probably driving a maroon Mercedes at the time. Considering its low clearance from the ground, the burial possibilities were narrowed even more.

Pirro agreed to an April search, but asked Brown not to tell the press or the Ocean County police. Confidentiality was a top priority.

Brown gave the phone back to Gilberte, who said her good-byes to Pirro. The two women agreed to meet the next week, when Gilberte would finally tell Pirro her story.

Since the start of his investigation two years earlier, Joe Becerra had collected written depositions from nearly all of Kathie's old friends, except for Gilberte. She always had excuses, even for people like Ellen Strauss, who asked why it was taking so long. Gilberte said she didn't like what she had written, it was far too long, or that there were things she had forgotten about but needed to include. With Becerra now out of the picture, Gilberte felt comfortable that her deposition wouldn't be needed. Instead, she'd tell her story directly to Pirro.

After leaving Brown, Gilberte floated back to Connecticut, convinced that she would be the heroine of the story if Brown could find Kathie's remains. It would make her version of things complete. Best friend keeps long-held promise.

Pirro hung up with Gilberte convinced that she would raise her stock immeasurably if Brown was somehow able to locate the last resting place of Kathie Durst.

It would be the press conference of all press conferences.

Joe Becerra knew nothing about Tom Brown or the planned search. Pirro stopped talking to him after the *Vanity Fair* story was published. He was still working on the Durst case, but any relevant information was written up and sent to Pirro's office.

There were no face-to-face meetings, no phone calls. Becerra was cut off.

———

THE constant hum from the traffic crossing the causeway in the distance sounded like a large beehive from the concrete pier where Bobbi Sue Bacha stood looking down into the waters of Galveston Bay.

It was 7 A.M. on Friday, February 7, and Bobbi Sue was scoping the pier and inlet where Morris Black's remains had been found bobbing in the water. The tide on this morning and the next was expected to be the lowest of the month, so low you could see the rocks and boulders on the bottom of the bay. It was the perfect time to search for and possibly locate Morris Black's head.

Bobbi Sue was investigating the Black case on her own time, helping his family back in Boston. One of the sisters, Gladys, had even filed a wrongful-death suit against Bobby.

Bobbi Sue was fascinated by the case. Although she was initially frustrated with her inability to find out more about Morris and Bobby Durst, the frustration spurred her to work even harder.

It took several months, including interviews with Morris's siblings, but Bobbi Sue eventually learned more about Morris Black.

And what she discovered was both frightening and sickening.

His parents had suffered from apparent mental problems, forcing them to place their six children in foster homes. One of his brothers was later placed in a mental institution in Boston. Some of the children, including Morris, eventually returned home. But home was hell, with charges against the father of sexual abuse, abuse in which Morris had participated. Some of the siblings hadn't spoken to Morris in decades and were not the least bit disappointed upon hearing the news that he was dead.

Morris left home for the Merchant Marines when he was eighteen, following his older brother Harry. He returned in the early 1950s, but there was no trace of him until 1972, when he bought a building near Boston Harbor with a woman named Lorraine Black, who was apparently his wife. They had no children anyone could remember, and no one knew what became of Lorraine.

His sisters Gladys and Beatrice never heard of her.

The building was taken by the city of Boston in 1976 after a bank foreclosed on Morris. In 1980 he scraped up enough money, $6,500, to buy another building in the Boston area, a three-story tenement at 10 Hannon Street.

Bobbi Sue tracked down an old tenant, Carrie Williams, who was now living in South Carolina. An elderly woman, Williams described Black as the landlord from hell.

He refused to pay for any repairs, opting to do them all himself to save money. He once sued the TV cable company because a technician put a small hole in a wall while wiring an apartment. He personally picked up the rent every month, money orders or cash, and spent his time limping along the streets wearing a red knit hat, even during the summer. The limp was the result of an injury suffered when he was a child.

Morris had no phone, no car, and never any visitors, said Williams. He was a testy, mean, nasty, and difficult man who would argue with anyone and everyone. He often expressed a profound hatred for women.

He had one quality, though, that Bobbi Sue found interesting: he was fearless.

A shopkeeper around the corner from 10 Hannon Street described an occasion when Morris learned that one of his tenants was dealing drugs. When the shopkeeper suggested that he call the police, Morris said no, he'd handle it himself. He went into the building, grabbed the suspected dealer by the neck, and tossed him out onto the street, along with his clothes and personal items, screaming and yelling throughout the "eviction."

The dealer was never seen again.

There were times during the early 1980s when Black would disappear. He landed in New York in late 1981, renting space in a barbershop in the lobby of a midtown office building and working as a watch repairman. Bobbi Sue thought it was odd that Morris would be in New York around the time that Kathie Durst disappeared.

Morris returned to Boston in late 1982 and tried working as a watch repairman in that city, along with other assorted jobs. Bobbi Sue wondered if he had traveled to Boston every month to collect the rent checks during his stay in New York.

By 1987, his $6,500 investment on Hannon Street was worth $137,500, and Morris decided to sell the building and take off for warmer climates in the South. He bounced around a variety of harbor towns, including Charleston (South Carolina), Long Beach (Mississippi), and Galena Park (Texas).

He arrived in Galveston shortly before Bobby Durst.

The profile Bobbi Sue created contained much more information on Morris, and gave her a clear indication he had been a troubled, and dangerous, individual. But she knew the file was far from complete, and she tested every search engine she knew of to find more information, but there was none. He was still an enigma, a man who, for some still-unknown reason, hung around the homeless and down-and-out of society during the last year of his life.

Something was missing, and it grated on Bobbi Sue

to no end. Durst wouldn't have killed Morris just because he was an annoying old man, would he? She was aware of the story that came out of the Jesse Tree, that Ted Hanley believed Durst was the wealthy man Morris knew who could provide a loan for a new building.

Another thought occurred to Bobbi Sue. She learned from New York reporters about the itinerary Bobby allegedly wrote in 1982. There was a name, Marshall Bradde, that Bobby wrote down and supposedly met on Monday, February 1, the day after his wife disappeared.

The reporters were familiar with the names of most of Bobby's friends, but none had ever heard of a Marshall Bradde. Bobbi Sue searched for the name but came up empty. She wondered, could Bobby have possibly written "Marshall Bradde" as a pseudonym for Morris Black? They had the same initials, M.B. If so, did Morris help Bobby dispose of Kathie's body? It was just a theory, a wild shot in the dark. But this was a case full of theories, since there was little history on the mysterious Morris.

Even more grating to Bobbi Sue was that Morris's head was still missing, believed to be at the bottom of Galveston Bay.

The Galveston district attorney, Mike Guarino, appeared to be confident that the evidence in hand would be more than enough to convict Bobby of murder, even without the head.

Bobbi Sue wasn't so sure.

To make it a slam dunk, Bobbi Sue decided that prosecutors needed the head, and if they weren't going to search for it, she would.

Along with her husband, Lucas, and Jeff Moore, Blue Moon's chief investigator, she walked the pier in the morning sun preparing for their search the next day.

Even "Daddy"—Bobbi Sue's ex-cop father—came along for the ride, and as soon as he got out of Lucas's Dodge Durango, he walked out toward the water and then headed back inland, following the coastline.

"Daddy, where you going?" said Bobbi Sue.

Her father didn't reply.

"I can't stop that man," she mumbled.

As they looked out over the water, they knew that the police had theorized that Black's torso had washed up between the pier and a rock jetty, the garbage bags filled with body parts on the other side of the pier. The police said Bobby had probably come by late at night, probably around 2 A.M., and dumped everything somewhere near the rock jetty. They arrived at that theory after discovering through interviews with neighbors that Bobby was in the neighborhood earlier that day, asking people if anyone fished these waters at night, or if the police were ever in the area.

This theory may have worked for the police, but it didn't wash with Bobbi Sue. Dropping Morris's body near the rock jetty made little sense. Bobbi Sue wondered out loud how anyone could walk along the jagged rocks carrying such heavy weights. She believed it was far more feasible for someone to toss the torso and garbage bags off the end of the flat concrete pier, expecting everything to float out toward the shipping lanes, where it would sink and never be found.

Instead, the tide pushed it all back to shore.

But as she gazed out over the water, Bobbi Sue wondered why the torso would have floated one way, toward the jetty, which was over to the right, and the garbage bags the other way, to the left, on the other side of the pier. Bobbi Sue knew how unpredictable these waters were. She'd practically lived in them as a child. But it didn't seem possible that the currents had been going in separate directions.

Unable to solve the question about where the remains were tossed into the water, Bobbi Sue walked up and down the concrete pier, dressed to her ankles in black, bending over to look into the murky water, which was only a few feet deep. Dark objects of various sizes, which appeared to be rocks, could be seen. One particular object was small, about the size and shape of a human head. It appeared to be covered with green algae and had two white, stringy objects floating upward. They looked like they were coming from where the eyes would be.

"Think that's a head?" said Jeff.

"I don't know. It sure looks like something," said Bobbi Sue, who sat down on the pier to take her shoes off and walk into the water to retrieve the object. She was stopped by Lucas, who reminded his wife that they had a planned search for the next day at a considerable cost.

"It's right there. I can go in and get it," she said.

The water was cold, and the object was in water that was four feet deep.

"No, let's wait until tomorrow. Everything is planned for tomorrow," said Lucas.

Bobbi Sue put her shoes on, and spent the next half hour studying the waters around the pier when she suddenly realized that her father was gone.

"Where's Daddy?" she said, looking around the shoreline.

The last she'd seen of him he was walking down toward an electrical station about a quarter of a mile away, then continued along the shore, heading for the causeway.

Bobbi Sue, Lucas, and Jeff finished their presearch preparations and drove back to Harborside Drive, making a right and looking for a road or driveway to take them back toward the water. They found one, the old causeway that ran alongside the railroad tracks. Jeff jumped out and ran down the road while Bobbi Sue and Lucas waited in the Durango. Fifteen minutes later Lucas's cell phone rang. It was Jeff saying he found Daddy.

Another ten minutes passed before everyone was back in the car, and Jeff had some news. He and Daddy had found a couple of old wigs, clothing, and makeup lying off the side of the road.

"Could be hookers," said Lucas.

"Probably is. They go back there. But then again, I

don't know. Maybe worth checking out tomorrow," said Jeff.

They returned to Blue Moon's offices by 1 P.M. with Bobbi Sue still thinking about that "rock" in the water. Her thoughts were interrupted by a letter on her desk. It had a Connecticut postmark, and inside were Gilberte Najamy's criminal records.

Of all the people Bobbi Sue had read about who were related to the Durst case, the one person who seemed to agitate her the most was Gilberte. During her numerous discussions with New York reporters, who called Bobbi Sue to pick her brain about the Morris Black murder, they all told her about Gilberte's theatrics during the extradition hearing in Pennsylvania, how it was so painfully obvious that her tears were for the TV cameras, and how she would immediately say "I was Kathie's best friend" when a reporter fresh to the case would ask who she was.

Bobbi Sue's curiosity about Gilberte only grew stronger when she read about Gilberte's pending film deal, which was reported in the New York papers. Gilberte had denied there was any deal, telling reporters she would never accept any money. But Bobbi Sue's instincts took over after hearing from a reporter that Gilberte might have a criminal history. The New York State Police apparently knew about it but had remained mum. Bobbi Sue decided to look into Gilberte's past, checking criminal records in New York and Connecticut.

She almost fell to the floor when she opened the letter and read that Gilberte had been arrested six times.

The first arrest had ocurred on St. Patrick's Day, March, 17, 1987, in Danbury, Connecticut, for possession of cocaine, possession of drug paraphernalia, and the issuing of two bad checks.

The cocaine charge was a felony, and she was sentenced to eighteen months to three years in jail.

The records didn't indicate how much actual time she spent in jail, though it appeared Gilberte was on the streets again by March 1988 when she was arrested again, this time for violating her probation. In November 1988 she was arrested yet again, this time in Waterbury, Connecticut, for possession of narcotics, a felony.

In May 1990 Gilberte was again arrested for possession of narcotics in Danbury, her third felony arrest. There was another arrest in January 1991 for stealing a car in Danbury. She was fined seventy-five dollars. The final arrest came in March 1991, when she was picked up again for possession of narcotics, her fourth felony drug conviction.

Gilberte was sent to prison, though it was unclear just how much time she served. By 1995, she had ended up in a halfway house.

"I knew it!" screamed Bobbi Sue. "I knew this woman wasn't telling the truth. Her story was all bull. She's capitalizing on the death of her supposed best friend. She has to go down!"

Bobbi Sue didn't waste any time, calling in an assistant and giving her the rap sheet with instructions to call the Associated Press and *New York Daily News* with the information.

The story broke the next day in the New York papers, and Gilberte, the always-quotable source, first denied that she'd ever been arrested. When told her criminal record was now circulating around the country, she stopped talking to reporters. Calls to her home were met by an answering machine. Even reporters whom she had developed working relationships with, such as Andy Geller from the *New York Post* and Kevin Flynn from the *New York Times,* were ignored.

For their part, those in the media who had dealt with Gilberte were enraged. Many were seasoned journalists, but Gilberte had flown under their radar. They had trusted her, but now they felt manipulated, used.

For all they knew, Gilberte's entire story wasn't true, and nothing she said could be believed.

THE morning after she received the letter about the arrests, with the New York papers revealing Gilberte's history, Bobbi Sue was back at the pier, accompanied by a dozen investigators, mostly kids out of college or high school, several reporters, and a single Galveston police officer, Gary Jones, who looked on as an observer.

A dive team was also in place, and they focused on the end of the pier, which stretched out into the bay. The young investigators donned waterproof pants and jumped into the cold water. They began their search, walking in grids marked off around the pier, along the shoreline, and the rock jetty.

The search took about two hours. A production team from Court TV was there, filming the search for a special program they planned to air on the Durst case.

The search was thorough, but after three hours they had failed to find the head. Bobbi Sue reasoned that if it was here, then either it had been tossed farther out into the water or some large fish had gotten hold of it.

Officer Jones waited patiently for the search to end, and frowned when told about the wigs that had been sighted the day before on the path by the old causeway.

"Can't be anything," he huffed. "You know hookers go back there."

But Bobbi Sue was going back anyway. She was in her zone, and no one was going to stop her.

Jeff led the three-car caravan to the wigs. One was red and lying on the road. It appeared to be short in length. The other one, dirty blond and shoulder length, was in the grass. Both were faded, like they had been there for a while, at least several months. Some ladies' clothing was also found in the brush. It was nondescript, a pink dress and button-down shirt. They also found mascara, eyeliner, and red lipstick, all new and unused.

Jones shrugged his shoulders and called in the crime scene investigators. The wigs, clothing, and mascara were now evidence to be tested.

A patrol car arrived with two uniformed officers. They slipped on rubber gloves, then photographed and tagged the items. Bobbi Sue looked around the high grass and weeds that grew alongside the road and railroad tracks as she slowly made her way along the old causeway, ending up over the bay. She looked down at the water, studying the current. She then looked out toward the pier and rock jetty in the distance to her right.

Lucas saw her standing there, alone, deep in thought, and walked up to her.

"He was here," said Bobbi Sue.

"Who was here?" said Lucas.

"Durst. He was here. This is where he dumped the body. Not over there on the pier, but over here, off the causeway."

Lucas listened as his wife explained her theory.

"See, he didn't dump the body over there. He came by that afternoon asking the neighbors if anyone was out at night, but he thought it was too dangerous, that he'd get caught. So he found this place and threw the bags over the bridge into the channel. The current goes toward the pier, and the body and bags went in different directions. See, the bags filled with the body parts turned immediately toward the shoreline, as they should have," said Bobbi Sue. "The torso was heavier, so it took longer to turn to shore. I'm telling you. This is the spot. This is where the body was thrown in the water."

To Lucas, this theory sounded more than plausible. How else to explain how the torso ended up near the rock jetty and the garbage bags on the other side of the concrete pier and down the shoreline?

The police had it all wrong, Bobbi Sue said. This had to be the spot.

"What do we do next?" said Lucas.

Bobbi Sue didn't hesitate.

"We come back. We schedule another hunt. The head is down there," she said, pointing beneath the old causeway. "I know it's down there."

After the police tagged their new evidence, placing each item in a brown paper bag, Bobbi Sue returned to her office in Webster. Lucas tried to dissuade her from moving forward with another hunt, saying it would cost $1,000 and reminding Bobbi Sue that the Galveston police, not a private investigation firm, should be out there combing the waters.

But Bobbi Sue didn't want to hear it. Something was bothering her. Not finding Morris Black's head was a disappointment, to be sure. But she now realized she had spent the entire morning looking in the wrong place.

Something else was bothering Bobbi Sue, too, a feeling that came over her as she stood on the old causeway looking out over the water.

Someone doesn't just kill, coolly dismember a body, then casually search for a place to dispose of the remains she thought. Especially not someone with Bobby Durst's pedigree.

So she closed her office door, turned on her computer, settled into her chair, and began searching various databases, typing in the name Robert Durst and all the other names associated with it, along with the different Social Security numbers.

For Bobbi Sue, it was time to get to the bottom of it all.

27

THE early-morning sun bounced off the dark glass covering the six-story building that housed Blue Moon's offices in Webster. Bobbi Sue knew it was morning only because Lucas came in with a cup of tea and bag of doughnuts.

She had worked through the weekend, alternating between several different search databases on her computer and cross-referencing the name Robert Durst.

By the time Lucas walked into the offices that morning, Bobbi Sue was exhausted, and excited.

Laid out on her large, cherry-wood desk was the evidence of a trail of stolen identities, some going back at least twenty years. They crossed through a host of states, including Massachusetts, New York, New Jersey, South Carolina, Florida, Texas, Mississippi, Virginia, and California.

There were dozens of names, identities Bobby used to rent or buy late-model cars, or obtain credit cards, or use as aliases in paying utility bills or for rental properties.

There was Robert Jezowski of New York, whose name Bobbi Sue found in October and determined that

Bobby had been using since the early 1980s. There was another name, James Fleischman of Belmont, New York, a suburb of Buffalo. Fleischman was married and had several grown children. He worked for a company that made large generators, had never lived anywhere but the Buffalo area, and said he never heard of a man named Robert Durst. Yet there it was, Fleischman's name and Social Security number underneath Bobby's Auto Track. Bobby had used Fleischman's Social Security number to obtain a New York driver's license, which expired in April 1998.

As Bobbi Sue went down the list, she read off the other names to Lucas.

"Look at all these names and identities. He took James Klosty, someone he went to high school with in the 1950s, and used his name to get an American Express card. There's a James Cordes, an old photographer he knew," said Bobbi Sue. "Douglas Duncan, Robert Kitts, Lance Davis, Susan Bert, Jim Turss, Robert Klein, Martin Ryan. He even used the Social Security number of his dead wife, Kathie Durst, in 2000 to rent an apartment in California. And look at these addresses. South Carolina, Florida, Virginia, Massachusetts. They're all over the place."

Bobbi Sue reached down to the papers on her desk and pulled up the file for the name Martin Ryan.

"This guy was from Albany and once worked pumping gas. I called up there and found out that Ryan bounced around from minimum-wage job to minimum-wage job. He was always scrounging for money and lived in some hotel. The address was 18 North Allen Street. I read through Ryan's report, and here, I found somebody else who lived at the same address. A guy named Robert Ryan. They're not related. Robert Ryan now lives in Pennsylvania," said Bobbi Sue. "That address, 18 North Allen Street, was some old house. A mansion with fifteen separate rooms the owner rented to transients, people with nowhere else to go."

Bobbi Sue reached over her desk and picked up another file.

"Martin Ryan also had a girlfriend. Her name was Diane. So I took a shot and pulled up an Auto Track for Diane Winne, the name Durst used when he posed as a woman in New Orleans. Look at this," she said, pointing to the list of addresses in Winne's file. They were all in Albany. One of them, 99 South Pearl Street, was also listed on Martin Ryan's Auto Track.

"They lived there before moving to the Allen Street address. The gas-station guy said they lived together. That's where they met Durst, at Allen Street, at this hotel, this mansion, this place for people who are one paycheck removed from being out on the street."

"Okay, so what are you saying, that Durst killed these people and took their names?" said Lucas.

Bobbi Sue paused for a moment. She was a veritable volcano of information, spewing out everything she'd learned over the long weekend. She knew it was difficult to comprehend, to understand in one shot.

"No. I think they're still alive, but he took their identities. He used Winne in New Orleans. Martin Ryan has another address listing, in South Carolina. Durst was in different cities, staying in places where he knew he could find people no one cared about. He was here, in Galveston, over at the Jesse Tree, a place that serves who? The down-and-out, right? And he's up in Albany, staying in some house with people who come and go all the time. Don't you see how perfect this is? If he was a killer, someone with a thirst for blood, what better way to do it than riding around in old cars, using other people's identities, and preying on transients and the homeless? These are people no one would give a damn about if they disappeared. And if the police were on his trail, what trail are they on, a man named Martin Ryan or a woman named Diane Winne?"

Lucas nodded in agreement. It was a good plan. A devious plan. It still didn't make much sense, a man of Durst's wealth and means spending his time driving throughout the country, assuming other peoples' identities, and living among the poor and homeless.

"And there's no doubt he carved up Morris Black, right?" said Lucas.

"Durst killed him, but he screwed up. He thought the body parts would sink into the ocean. Imagine if he'd been successful? We wouldn't be sitting here talking about this. No one cared about Black. Who's gonna call the cops and report him missing, the landlord? No. It would be logical to think that Black just took off. That's the beauty of this whole scheme."

Lucas was taken back by the simplicity of it all. But as he looked at Bobbi Sue's desk, and all the paperwork, it was clear that she had just scraped the surface. They needed help, and they needed it in a big way.

"Are you going to tell the Galveston police or the district attorney?" he said.

Bobbi Sue leaned back into her chair. The urgency in her voice dissipated to a level tone.

"No, they won't be able to track this down. I don't even think they're interested. They have a murder and they think they have enough to convict. But this is bigger than one murder. I think we have something here that is too big for any of us to understand," said Bobbi Sue. "Morris Black was dismembered by someone who knew what he was doing. You can't cut somebody up like that without having done it before. Cody Cazalas said that, didn't he? Now go back twenty years. They never found his wife, Kathie Durst. The district attorney there, the one who can't stop talking, she said publicly she believed his wife was dismembered. Think about it. There's no telling how long Durst could have been doing this."

Bobbi Sue pushed herself up from the chair and looked out the window. The morning rush to the NASA buildings just a few miles away was filling the local roads.

She took a sip of tea, which was now cold.

"Let's go back to his wife, Kathie. Do you really believe she was his first? He was beating her, right? And he even sent her to the hospital. When she went home that last night, from that party at her friend Gilberte's house . . . something set him off, and she was gone," said Bobbi Sue, who directed her attention to the papers piled on her desk.

"Look at all that. Do you think she knew she was married to a monster?"

The enormity of what Bobbi Sue was saying struck Lucas in the gut.

"So what's next?" he said. "If he's running around the country killing people like you say, there's no way the Galveston police, or New York police, or anyone else can solve this. They need the FBI. Look at all this stuff on your desk. I bet there's even more here that we can't figure out."

"There is more, and there's no way you or I or anyone else other than the feds can track all his movements," said Bobbi Sue. "But we can't bring this to the FBI. The Galveston police have the case and they're the ones who would have to bring in the feds. What we need is Morris Black's head. If we can find that, I believe we'll find he was shot to death, right in the head. The same way Susan Berman died. It was premeditated. And it was done for a reason."

———

ON February 25, 2002, three divers plunged into the choppy waters of Galveston Bay underneath the old causeway, searching for Morris Black's head.

The waters weren't as shallow as they were supposed to be, and the strong currents pulled the divers out toward the shipping lanes.

Bobbi Sue was going to call off the hunt when she saw some of her young investigators pull an object from the water. It was a piece of carpeting, about twelve feet long and two feet wide. It had been rolled up and placed in a clear plastic wrapping. They brought it to the shore and delicately rolled it out.

To their surprise, inside was blood and some kind of tissue embedded in the carpet.

"Look at that," said Bobbi Sue, staring at the blood stains on one end of the carpet and the tissue that had meshed into the fabric.

"Is that brains?" she said, staring at the substance.

Bobbi Sue pulled out a kit and tested the carpet for human blood.

The test was positive.

Lucas suggested that the tissue or whatever it was on the carpet had remained intact because the carpet was rolled up, making it impossible for fish and other marine life to get to it.

"Okay, let's tag this stuff and give it to the police," said Bobbi Sue.

By the end of the morning her investigators had tagged and bagged more than one hundred pieces of evidence, which included still more clothing found down along the shoreline. She gave it all to the Galveston police.

On the drive back to Webster, Lucas was still perplexed as to why Blue Moon Investigations had to spend the resources and money to search the waters for Morris Black's head, rather than the Galveston police.

But he said nothing. He knew his wife. She was working on instinct. And that meant it was time to get out of her way.

28

WHEN the story about Gilberte's film deal was reported in the pages of the *New York Post*, Eleanor Schwank and Ellen Strauss had let out a cry in unison: "Gilberte, how could you?"

Like Gilberte, the two women had given countless interviews, hoping any new story would lead to some new information on the case. They had never asked for any money, or sought to profit from the loss of their friend, knowing their position would be compromised in the event that Bobby was ever indicted. They knew Gilberte had taken the lead when it came to telling the Kathie Durst story to the world, and they didn't mind when she appeared on numerous television programs, including *The View* on ABC, in which Gilberte told her story, at length, to Barbara Walters. Gilberte was even flown out to Seattle to appear on an afternoon talk show.

Gilberte had often said things that Ellen and Eleanor privately questioned, like the often-repeated statement that she was Kathie's best friend.

Eleanor knew that wasn't the case. Kathie had had a wide circle of friends. But Eleanor had said nothing, not wanting to deter Gilberte from pressing ahead.

Following the revelation of the film deal, Gilberte had called both Eleanor and Ellen. She knew they'd be upset. She denied that she had signed a deal, saying she was offered the opportunity to sell her story but turned it down and never accepted any money.

"Do you think I would ever do that?" was her reply.

But soon after, confident she had soothed the ruffled feathers of her two friends, Gilberte had agreed to another television interview, this one with Brian Conybeare, a reporter for Channel 12 News in Westchester. When asked about the film deal, she had given an answer that was far more cryptic than the one she told her friends.

"Once the trial is over, you can never tell what could happen," she said.

Gilberte had thought she managed to control any damage to her credibility, and had been confident Eleanor and Ellen would believe her story.

She thought otherwise when her criminal history was made public soon after. She shut down, refusing to take calls from reporters and didn't answer her phone, at home or at work, from which she took a two-week leave of absence.

She spoke only to Eleanor, who was less inclined to dismiss Gilberte completely. She'd had no idea her longtime friend had been arrested six times, but Gilberte explained that she had fallen apart after Kathie died and never recovered.

Eleanor didn't necessarily buy this explanation.

"We were all her friends, Gilberte. Her loss affected us all, but life goes on."

"But you know how close I was to Kathie. You know what I went through," said Gilberte.

"We were all close to Kathie," said Eleanor. "That's no excuse to lie to your friends."

Gilberte said she hadn't lied. Her past was her business, and the revelations about her criminal record were part of a conspiracy on the part of the Durst family to discredit her.

"You should have been up-front from the beginning,"

said Eleanor. "Now it looks like you were hiding something. You really pissed a lot of people off, not just with that, but with that film deal."

"They came to me," Gilberte said. "They came to me, but I told them no."

Others who had dealings with Gilberte, including Jim McCormack, were stunned by the news of the felony arrests.

McCormack had trusted her, even breaking his promise to Becerra to withhold important information about the investigation and sharing it with Gilberte, who promptly, and behind his back, went to the press.

Joe Becerra just shook his head when he heard the news, though one could detect a slight measure of satisfaction. He knew that Gilberte was badmouthing him, and he knew about her duplicity at the courthouse in Pennsylvania. He heard the news from a reporter who witnessed the contact between Gilberte and Pirro, and Gilberte's subsequently loud and unabashed claims that Becerra was off the case.

If anything, Becerra knew that Gilberte had poisoned his case. Bobby Durst's chief accuser, the last woman to see Kathie Durst alive, was a convicted felon. The investigator realized that if Bobby was ever brought to trial in New York, his attorneys would have a field day with Gilberte.

For her part, Gilberte tried to call Ellen, but Ellen wasn't home. When Ellen saw Gilberte's number on her caller ID later that day, she decided she wouldn't call back. She was thoroughly disappointed in Gilberte and didn't know what she'd say if she spoke to her.

Ellen knew Gilberte had once had legal problems, that she'd been arrested for drug possession. Gilberte's sister, Fadwa, had even called Ellen to ask for her help. Ellen obliged, with the understanding that Gilberte would seek counseling. But Ellen was surprised and shocked to learn that Gilberte had been arrested five other times, and angered that Gilberte never told her.

Ellen thought the friends were all on a unified mission, to bring Bobby to justice. Or so she had thought. Now she began to rethink her friendship with Gilberte, reevaluating everything Gilberte had told her over the last twenty years. If she could lie about her past, Ellen figured Gilberte could lie about everything else.

THE People's Bank was on Post Road in Westport, Connecticut, and Ellen Strauss hurried there from her home, down Route 53, to Route 57 past the Merritt Parkway. Once she arrived, she rushed inside the bank, her fur coat flying behind her. She said a quick hello to the bank manager, then asked him to retrieve her safe-deposit box.

As she stood waiting on the bank floor, a thousand thoughts filled her head. Ellen had wanted to come here first thing in the morning, but she couldn't cancel what turned out to be a long day in court. So she raced to the bank afterward.

Ellen had spent the last couple of days thinking about Gilberte. Prior to Kathie's disappearance, they had met only once. Gilberte belonged to another part of Kathie's life, to a lifestyle Ellen had no idea Kathie was involved in.

Between Ellen and Gilberte, the only mutual connection was Eleanor Schwank. After Kathie disappeared Gilberte and Ellen became closer as they tried in vain to search for their friend. They had been drawn together by tragedy, and Ellen's emotions had sometimes wedged themselves between her and common sense. Ellen wasn't the suspicious type, and she'd had no reason to doubt anything that Gilberte ever said to her.

Years later, when Gilberte called her to help her out of a drug arrest, Ellen thought it was a simple, onetime event. A character flaw. She was an attorney and she obliged, figuring she was helping a friend. She even put aside stories she'd heard about Gilberte's visits to several crack houses in the Danbury area.

When Joe Becerra began investigating Kathie's disappearance, Ellen saw it as a last great chance for justice.

Like most of Kathie's friends, including Eleanor and Kathy Traystman, Ellen offered to help in any way she could. She even set time aside to search for Susan Berman, finding her address in Los Angeles and forwarding it to Becerra.

Ellen thought all the friends were working toward one goal, to find out what had happened to their friend Kathie Durst. So it came as a great shock when she read about Gilberte's film deal. She was confused by the story and didn't know what to make of it.

This can't be true, she thought.

Then came the crushing blow—Gilberte's criminal past, all of it.

Ellen had always considered herself smart, a good judge of people. She'd believed Gilberte all these years, even Gilberte's claim that Kathie's loss was the reason why she fell as hard as she did. But now Ellen felt used, manipulated, deceived. She realized that Gilberte had never been straight with her. The more she thought about it, the angrier she became. She began to dissect everything Gilberte had ever told her, particularly over the last year. The more she remembered, the more she saw through Gilberte's duplicity.

Ellen decided to reach out to a friend named Tom Egan* who had at one time dated one of Gilberte's sisters. She hadn't spoken to him in years, yet when she called him at home he was pleased to hear from her. They chatted like old chums, talking about the old days and what had become of each of them. As the conversation continued, it shifted to Bobby Durst and all that had happened over the last two years.

Tom asked Ellen what she thought of Bobby dressing as a woman and the news reports that he had used several different identities, even those of old high school classmates.

"He's obviously had some kind of breakdown. I mean, who would act like that?" said Ellen.

*Name has been changed to protect identity.

Tom had a different theory. He'd never met Bobby, but he read most of the newspaper and magazine stories and concluded there was more to Bobby Durst, more than anyone could imagine.

"Serial killer?" said Ellen. "That's pretty frightening stuff."

"I would suggest that he's a pretty frightening guy. At least that was what Kathie was saying at Gilberte's party."

"Which party?"

"The one where Kathie disappeared," said Tom.

Ellen was floored. "You were there? Do you remember it?"

Tom had been there, a guest of Gilberte's sister, and he said he remembered the event clearly, even now, twenty years later.

"I've read in the papers and seen on television how Gilberte described it as a simple, catered, low-key family affair. I can tell you, that was no family party," said Tom.

Ellen listened intently as he described the throbbing music, the catered food, and the cocaine and booze, which was flowing.

"You have to remember, this was 1982. Cocaine was *the* drug in those days. And we had never heard of AIDS. Coke, sex, booze. It was part of the times," said Tom.

"I know, it was just never anything I got involved in," said Ellen. "Did you see Kathie?"

Tom remembered Kathie, his heart dropping the moment she walked in the door. She was dressed in sweats and wore little makeup. But Tom was struck hard by her natural beauty. He said she arrived late in the afternoon and headed straight for the wine, downing several large glasses in succession. She then began snorting excessive amounts of cocaine. One line, two lines, three lines. When that wasn't enough, Gilberte would be there at her side with a coke spoon. Kathie would dip it, then bring it up to her nose.

The more Kathie drank and snorted, the more she ranted about her problems with Bobby. She was wild, talking incessantly and loudly, telling anyone who would listen about the papers she had and how Bobby was beating her. And Gilberte was no help, said Tom, standing there egging her on, telling her again and again that it was finally time to get her divorce and her settlement and leave his sorry ass once and for all.

Between the ranting and the drinking and the drugs, Tom found a chance to walk by and say hello.

"I introduced myself, and she just smiled at me, drinking away. You could tell she was in pain. All that drinking and snorting, it was to hide the pain," said Tom.

And there was something else, he said. It had to do with Gilberte, how she had reacted when Kathie finally arrived.

"Gilberte had a look in her eye. You could tell just by the way she gazed at Kathie, how she hovered over her, how she touched her, that she had a thing for her. It was more than a thing. She was in love with Kathie. Someone actually said it at the party, that Gilberte was in love with Kathie. Jesus, if I had the chance, I would have been in love with Kathie. She was that beautiful."

Ellen was shaken. This wasn't what she had been told. This wasn't what she was led to believe all these years. Gilberte had said the party was a quiet affair, that Kathie had perhaps a glass or two of wine. Cocaine? Gilberte never said anything about that. She always denied stories that Kathie was doing drugs.

As Ellen listened, it was apparent that Gilberte had hid a lot of things.

Tom said he remembered a phone call, that Kathie spoke to a man who he later learned had filed suit against Bobby. But the man told Kathie that the suit had been dropped, and she was infuriated, screaming between snorts of cocaine how she couldn't believe how Bobby had gotten away with it.

"She was livid. Absolutely livid. And her anger was heightened by the drugs," said Tom.

"That had to be Peter, Peter Schwartz," said Ellen. "That's the guy Bobby kicked in the face."

Tom didn't remember the name, but he did remember Gilberte telling Kathie that there was no way Bobby should be allowed to get away with this.

"Gilberte kept pushing and pushing," said Tom.

By 7 P.M. Gilberte didn't have to push anymore. Kathie had had enough and called Bobby, telling him she was coming home. It was time to settle this.

"She was going to go home and confront him. She was telling everyone that he was hitting her, but the way she was talking, she didn't seem to be concerned. And neither was Gilberte."

After Kathie said her good-byes to everyone, Gilberte walked her outside.

"I don't know what they said, but I've heard Gilberte tell that story, about Kathie warning her that Bobby might do something," said Tom.

"Gilberte's told that story a thousand times, how they were outside and Kathie told her if anything happened to her, it was Bobby," said Ellen, who was near tears. "Now I don't believe it happened that way."

"I never did," said Tom. "And I never understood how Gilberte let Kathie drive home that night in her condition. And that's not all highway. There were some dark mountain roads to go over on a rainy, snowy night. Gilberte must have thought that Kathie was serious, that she was going to finally end it with Bobby, and didn't want to stop her. She was in love with her."

"Why didn't you ever say anything?" said Ellen, her voiced filled with a sadness that reached deep inside her soul.

"No one ever asked me," said Tom.

The two old friends promised to stay in touch, and maybe even go out for dinner sometime. After hanging up the phone, Ellen wiped her eyes and blew her nose. She was numb. This was not what she had expected to hear when she called Tom. She needed a drink, and was walking over to her bar when she was jolted by a thought.

"Oh, my God!" she said.

———

THE next afternoon she was at the People's Bank, sitting inside a small room and frantically searching through her safe-deposit box. She was looking for the letter. It was here, in a book, tucked away in a cellophane covering. Ellen found it, pulled it out, and held it up to the window, the light illuminating the typeface. It was dated October 28, 1953, and it was addressed to a Dr. Ralph B. Jacoby of Park Avenue, New York. Ellen slowly read each line.

> Dear Dr. Jacoby:
>
> I am writing to you at the request of Mr. Seymour Durst with reference to Robert Durst. I have known Robert for the past three years. Physically the only abnormalities have been seasonal pollenoses. Robert tends to be somewhat smaller than the average child of his age, but this is not due to any endocrine disorder. Because of concern on the part of Robert's grandfather, there was a complete checkup by Dr. Samuel Z. Levine in May 1952. Dr. Levine's conclusions were that Robert was normal in all respects, that he had allergic rhinitis, and that most of his symptoms were on an emotional basis.
>
> In last April I sent Robert to Dr. William Schonfeld for assistance. Dr. Schonfeld saw Robert only twice, further sessions being impossible because of marked resistance on the part of the patient. It was Dr. Schonfeld's opinion that Robert's hostility toward his father and his younger brother was of such intensity that it might constitute a destructive psychodynamic force sufficient

*to produce a personality decomposition and pos-
sibly even schizophrenia.*

*I might add that a glucose tolerance test was
done with determination of the blood sugar approximately five hours after a meal. This was
found to be quite normal.*

*Sincerely yours,
Alexander G. Silberstein, M.D.*

Ellen read the letter over and over again, focusing on
the paragraph that ended with the words "personality
decomposition and possibly even schizophrenia."

She'd read the letter before, back in 1982 and again
that day more than a year ago when she and Gilberte
went through her file, which she had kept in her home.

All the letter had ever meant to Ellen was that Bobby
had once had some psychological problems as a child.
He was only ten years old when this letter was written
and the grim psychological diagnosis was delivered to
the Durst family.

It was clear that the Dursts knew Bobby had psychological problems, and apparently severe problems at that.
With Susan Berman and Morris Black dead, and news
stories suggesting that perhaps there were still others,
the letter now meant so much more.

Ellen now saw it as a clue into Bobby's past, and to
his future. Kathie had once told her that the death of
Bobby's mother caused him great anguish. Just how
much no one really knew.

Ellen put the letter aside and reached back into the
box, searching through the remaining documents and papers, looking for that other piece of paper that Gilberte
demanded be hidden, kept out of view from the police
and reporters and never revealed.

Ellen found it, in the corner of the box, and held it
up to the window. She studied it, then began to cry.

It was a time line she and Gilberte had written in
1982 several weeks after Kathie's disappearance. It was

an attempt by the two women to reconstruct Kathie's last day in South Salem and at Gilberte's house.

Gilberte had recalled the day's events, and Ellen, the budding attorney, wrote it down.

The time line began at noon, with a phone call to Gilberte from Kathie, who was with Bobby in South Salem for the weekend. Gilberte told Kathie to come to her house for the party. Kathie had other plans. She and Bobby had dinner reservations with Janet Finke and her boyfriend, Alan Martin. Kathie said she needed to think about Gilberte's invitation. Gilberte reminded Kathie that she needed to get away from Bobby. They hung up, with Kathie promising to call back, which she did an hour later. Again Gilberte tried to convince her to come to her house. Kathie said she'd let her know.

At 2 P.M. Kathie called Larry Cohen, her medical-student friend from Einstein. At 3 P.M. she called Gilberte again, telling her she'd decided to make the forty-five-minute drive from South Salem to Newtown, Connecticut, and would probably arrive in an hour.

Kathie arrived at Gilberte's at 4 P.M. and stayed until 7 P.M.

Written on the side of the time line were two short sentences.

"Two grams of coke. Two bottles of wine."

That's how much cocaine and alcohol, Gilberte told Ellen, Kathy ingested during her three-hour stay at the party.

"Oh, Gilberte! Gilberte! Gilberte!" screamed Ellen. "How could you have done this? You lied all these years."

Ellen remembered what Tom had said the night before, that Gilberte had been prodding Kathie to finally end it all with Bobby. Don't just ask for a divorce, demand it. And don't just ask for a settlement, demand it. And if he doesn't give in, then tell him you'll release all those documents, the bogus tax returns and stock statements. And you'll tell about the mysterious fires, and Bobby's embezzling from the company. Make him understand that he'll be fired from the family business, and the Durst Organization will suffer great embarrassment. Make him understand that you finally mean business.

When Kathie left the house that night, her five-foot-five-inch body filled with enough cocaine and wine to floor an elephant, she was ready to explode at Bobby.

Only Kathie hadn't known that her husband was a time bomb.

And she hadn't known that she was the fuse.

And she'd had no idea that Gilberte was the match.

Ellen closed her eyes, imagining the crazed state of mind Kathie must have been in when she arrived home that night in South Salem, the cocaine and wine fueling a torrent of anger that rained on Bobby.

He didn't plan to kill her, Ellen figured. It just happened. She didn't just get into his face, she stomped all over it, and he struck back.

He even said so, in the newspapers in 1982. He said she came home in a foul mood, angry over their personal situation.

"Oh, Gilberte, how could you, how could you?" said Ellen, mumbling loud enough her voice escaped the small room she was in and could be heard outside. She put her hand over her mouth but couldn't stop talking.

"How could you let Kathie leave your house and drive home that night in that condition? You were supposed to be her friend! And how could you even think she'd leave her husband for you? And how could you hide all of this for so long? You knew what really happened that day, yet you told no one. You didn't tell the police when Kathie disappeared and you didn't tell them now. You manipulated everyone. How could you!"

Ellen was venting, her emotions spilling all over the bank floor. She knew Gilberte's secrets. It finally all made sense. Gilberte had been obsessed all these years, but not because of some self-proclaimed mission to bring Bobby to justice because of a promise she made to Kathie. There had been no promise. Only guilt. The kind of guilt that consumes a person and twists their soul. Gilberte didn't just lie to her friends, the police, and the media. She misled Kathie's family—Kathie's mother and brother and sisters.

All they'd ever wanted was the truth. They wanted closure. All Gilberte did through her distortions was add to their great pain and anguish.

Ellen looked to blame herself. How could she not have seen this? She'd seen these papers before, the letter and the time line. But Gilberte told her they meant nothing. Just put them away and never let anyone see them, she said.

Am I really that stupid? thought Ellen. That naive?

She'd believed Gilberte was her friend. She'd believed Gilberte was Kathie's friend.

In the end, Ellen realized Gilberte was a friend to no one.

Ellen slowly put the papers back into the box, closed it, wiped her eyes, and opened the door.

She gave the box to the bank manager and walked out to her car. She wanted to drive straight to Hamden, to Gilberte's home, and confront her. But when she reached the Merritt Parkway, Ellen decided to stay on Route 57 and drive home.

She wouldn't confront Gilberte. What for? Ellen realized it wouldn't make any difference. Gilberte would deny it, just like she denied everything else.

When Ellen arrived home she went to her bedroom, pulled the covers over her head, and cried.

29

IT had been at least a year since Joe Becerra last spoke with Mike Struk. The two detectives, one retired, had spent a combined three and a half years investigating the Kathie Durst case.

Both men were haunted by Bobby Durst, both believed that Bobby should have been indicted and tried for the alleged murder of Kathie Durst long ago. Both were frustrated that their hard work had yet to pay off.

Becerra had Struk's old log book, which he'd borrowed when he and Struk first spoke sixteen months earlier. Struk wanted it back, and sent word through a reporter.

Their phone conversation lasted roughly twenty minutes, Becerra telling Struk what he could about the progress of the case, the frustrations he'd encountered, and the upcoming trial of Bobby Durst in Texas.

Both men took a measure of satisfaction from the recent news about Gilberte Najamy.

Struk had remained silent and out of sight after the ABC *Vanished* program aired during the summer, denying all requests for interviews. He knew Gilberte had poisoned him; the reputation of the onetime tough detective who had his picture in the *New York Times* for solving the Murder at the Met case, had been sullied by a woman with a gift for gab and an ability to manipulate people. She was a one-woman cult of personality who'd received her comeuppance, thought Struk.

But, as was his way, he didn't waste any time, or conversation, on Gilberte. Struk wanted to know about the case, where it was going, if anywhere.

"Any clue who that guy Black was?" said Struk.

"No. It's still a mystery," said Becerra. "But it seems Bob Durst's life was a mystery. Maybe their true relationship will come out in court. I don't know. I can tell you this: I doubt that I'll be there to see it."

Becerra hadn't spoken with Jeanine Pirro since January, and he didn't expect to be sent to the trial, which was set for June. The Westchester DA was still apparently upset over the *Vanity Fair* story.

Struk joked that Becerra should expect a transfer to Buffalo in the coming weeks.

"Don't even say that in jest," said Becerra, who'd incurred Pirro's wrath yet again in April when he was interviewed for a five-part series on the Durst case aired by Channel 12.

When reporter Brian Conybeare interviewed Pirro for his series, she casually asked who else he had spoken with. Conybeare mentioned Becerra's name, and Pirro's eyes turned red with anger. She immediately instructed one of her subordinates to call Becerra's boss, and demanded that he discipline Becerra.

Becerra's comments, included in the series when it was aired in April, were simple, to the point, and offered little insight into the case.

His bosses listened to Pirro but denied her request.

Becerra was watching his back. There were too many instances of Westchester County–based police officers who'd been forced to find new addresses because they crossed Jeanine Pirro.

Becerra didn't want to become one of them.

"I'm just doing my thing," he said. "If we get any new information, I'll write it up and send it to her office."

Becerra said he was hopeful that a break would come during the summer, when Gabrielle Colquitt planned a major renovation of the South Salem house.

Construction crews were going to open the walls and Becerra had been invited to come and watch; he was particularly eager to see behind the wall that held the cupboard with the dried mud on it.

"Maybe we'll find something. It's worth a shot," he said.

But he realized it could be a last shot, and the only hope after that was that Bobby Durst himself would tell the world what had happened to his long-lost wife.

"We worked this case, and worked it hard, you and I. Given all of the identities Bobby was using, I'd love to see Pirro refer this to the FBI," said Becerra. "But that won't happen. She hates the feds for what they did to her husband."

"So around and around we go. Nothing but a complete waste of time," said Struk.

There was one bit of information Struk had heard and asked Becerra to confirm.

The 1982 phone records from the house in South Salem had been retrieved by the state police and revealed that Bobby made a phone call after returning from south Jersey on Tuesday, February 2, 1982.

The call was to Susan Berman.

"And she's dead, so anything she had to offer is dead with her, which is real convenient for him," said Struk.

Becerra could hear a tint of sarcasm in Struk's voice. Struk's guard was back up.

"So you think we're done?" said Becerra.

"Remember what I asked you when you first came to my house? I said, 'Whaddaya got?' "

"And I laid it out," said Becerra.

"And you may have enough, like I thought I did twenty years ago, to bring him to trial. But this Pirro, she's interested in other things, like being governor. And she's not going to piss off the Dursts. They're worth what? A billion or two? So I'm going to tell you again what I told you when we first met," said Struk. "You have what I had, and right now that's nothing."

———

INSIDE the Galveston County prison, behind a double-paned Plexiglas window, Robert Durst was leaning forward, trying to talk into and hear from a small hole. It was early March, and he had a visitor, Sareb Kaufman, the son of the man Susan Berman had dated in the late 1980s. He'd flown in from Los Angeles to talk about Bobby's best friend, Susan.

Sareb had considered Susan his mother, and was still grieving over her death. With Bobby locked away behind bars awaiting trial, he'd decided to pay him a visit . . . just to clear the air.

Sareb knew Susan had considered Bobby one of her closest friends and that Bobby felt likewise. Sareb had always liked Bobby, who he considered kind and sensitive. It was Bobby whom Susan had trusted more than anyone else in her life, and Sareb found the stories linking Bobby to Susan's death disturbing.

As Sareb settled in across the window, he saw that Bobby wore a powder-blue prison outfit—pants and smock—and had grown a full head of hair. Gone was that bald, bizarre image seen on TV and in newspapers across the country when Bobby was captured in Pennsylvania.

During his five weeks in custody in Galveston, Bobby had been considered an ideal inmate. He was respectful of the guards, and spent most of his time in the prison library, preparing for his defense.

Until this day, aside from his attorneys, he'd accepted few visitors.

As Bobby and Sareb talked over the conversations coming from other parts of the room, Bobby repeated over and over that he did not, and could not, kill his oldest, dearest friend.

"How could I kill Susan, you know I could never do anything like that," said Bobby. "How could I kill anyone?"

EPILOGUE

THE short man in the green, county-jail jumpsuit and sandals looked rather harmless as he stood before state district judge Susan Criss. The sheriff's deputies on hand were of the opinion that Bobby, judging by his small size, would be hard-pressed to kill much of anything.

Needless to say, they became more attentive to their prisoner when he changed his plea from not guilty to not guilty by reason of self-defense and accident.

He now admitted he killed Morris Black, but wouldn't say why. His attorney, Dick DeGuerin, of Houston, promised a full explanation at the trial.

While now admitting that his client killed Morris Black, DeGuerin said Bobby could not help locate the missing head.

"Everyone is looking for the head, Your Honor. The police are looking, we are looking, and I believe a third party is looking," said DeGuerin.

The third party was Bobbi Sue Bacha.

Prior to the late March hearing, another magazine story, this one in *GQ*, produced yet another bizarre wrinkle: that Bobby had not only been cross-dressing but had taken to frequenting gay clubs. The *GQ* story produced a source for the information, a black dancer named

"Frankie" who said he met Bobby Durst at the Kon Tiki, a Galveston gay bar.

The story suggested that Bobby was picking up men and taking them back to his apartment at 2213 Avenue K for sex, and he enlisted Frankie to help him.

Bobby was using another name, Roberta Klein, and, according to the story, allegedly admitted to Frankie that he had "blown away folks."

Bobbi Sue Bacha didn't waste any time searching for Frankie. Instead she found another man, a cross-dresser who claimed to be the only black drag queen at the Kon Tiki. He'd been dancing at the club for fifteen years and never heard of or saw anyone resembling Bobby there. He was also incensed that someone might have been passing himself along as the black drag queen from the Kon Tiki.

Bobbi Sue determined that the story was a hoax.

After Durst changed his plea, DeGuerin made a point of criticizing Westchester County district attorney Jeanine Pirro, whose never-ending statements concerning the Durst case, said DeGuerin, had pushed Bobby to the brink, forcing him into the drastic actions he'd taken.

Pirro offered little comment. After learning about Gilberte Najamy's criminal record, she canceled their face-to-face meeting, though she still maintained contact with the survivalist Tom Brown. They canceled the April search of the Pine Barrens, with Pirro saying she'd get back to him over the summer.

Before the hearing ended, Bobby was taken into the judge's chambers and allowed to change into a business suit.

When he came out, a motion was made for Criss to extend the gag order. It already included the Galveston police, attorneys, and local media, and DeGuerin wanted other names added to the list: Bobbi Sue Bacha and Jeanine Pirro.

Criss agreed, and included Pirro and Bobbi Sue, who happened to be the judge's cousin.

Several days after the hearing, the report from the

autopsy performed by Dr. Charles Harvey on Morris Black on October 2, 2001, was finally released.

According to the report, the amputated areas around the torso, including the arms, legs, and head, were all "sharply incised skin edges with occasional short, sharply incised, parallel satellite incisions. The muscle tissue also appear to be sharply incised and are without significant fragmentation."

The report revealed other new, startling information.

Black's lungs were filled with blood and his torso was heavily bruised. He had been severely beaten before he died. As he sucked in his last breaths, he drew the blood into his lungs and suffered a heart attack.

The cause of death: homicide by unknown means.

When Cody Cazalas read the report, especially the part about the "sharply incised skin edges," he realized that his initial instincts after seeing Black's remains had been correct, that whoever dismembered Black had known what he was doing.

And now that Bobby admitted he killed and dismembered Black, Cazalas could only sit back and wonder how the man had learned such a delicate craft.

THE hope that had filled the McCormack family when they first heard from Joe Becerra two years earlier was now replaced by a bitter and overwhelming frustration.

Bobby was in jail in Galveston, Texas, but he wasn't there for their little sister Kathie.

He finally admitted to killing and dismembering someone, but not the person the McCormacks cared about.

Despite that admission, and the death of Susan Berman, it appeared that Westchester County authorities were no closer to bringing closure to the McCormack family than the New York City police had been twenty years earlier.

And that was odd in itself, thought Jim McCormack, since Kathie Durst was still listed as a missing person with the NYPD, and the investigation was still, technically, an NYPD case.

Since first receiving the call from Becerra, Jim had done what he didn't want to do: he became so overwhelmed and obsessed with the case that his home-based sports merchandising business began to suffer. Even worse, right before Christmas, 2001, his sister Mary stopped talking to him and his wife, Sharon, following a bitter argument.

Mary became enraged when it was suggested that she and her husband were living in a Durst-owned building. Jim had no idea that it was Gilberte Najamy who was privately telling the media that Mary had long ago made some kind of deal with Bobby. So when Jim received a call from a reporter with the information about Mary's apartment, he asked her about it. She exploded, cutting ties with her brother and his family.

This wasn't the outcome Jim expected.

He believed after all this time that Joe Becerra meant business. He believed Becerra was close to solving his sister's case, so close that he would finally bring closure for the McCormack family.

But it was not to be.

Becerra, like Mike Struk before him, had done all he could.

But in the case of Kathie Durst, that wasn't enough.

AFTERWORD

I first met New York State Police Investigator Joe Becerra in November 2001 at a diner in Katonah, New York, just a few miles from the South Salem home once owned by Robert and Kathie Durst.

Becerra and I had spoken before, on the phone a year earlier, during my initial reporting on the Durst case for *People* magazine.

But now I was preparing a Durst story for *Reader's Digest* and in the formative stages of preparing this book, and I needed to see Becerra up close. I had heard a lot about the veteran detective from those familiar with the Durst case. He was well liked, said to be extremely competent, and had spent two years directing the Durst investigation and gathering evidence.

Before meeting with me, Becerra needed to gain permission from Westchester County District Attorney Jeanine Pirro, which he did. He also made it clear that he couldn't, and wouldn't, talk about the specifics of the case.

Since this was my first book, and my goal was to tell a *story* in these pages, I wanted to meet him anyway.

After ordering breakfast and talking a bit (and determining he was, in fact, a likable guy) I decided to try anyway and pressed for specifics about the Durst case, only to meet with gentle reminders to back off.

I then turned the conversation to questions about his career and his personal life. Again he hesitated, wondering out loud why I needed to know small details such as where he went to high school, his hobbies, and his family. I told him I was trying to get an idea of what he was really like, and what molded him into becoming a detective.

Unbeknownst to Becerra, I was searching for a central character, a protagonist, to guide the narrative of the book.

Becerra was hesitant to divulge any family information, but I would soon learn enough through others who knew him well to get a good feel for his character. One thing I did notice as we ate our eggs and drank our coffee was that Becerra was frustrated. It wasn't anything he said—more his body language. It's hard to hide your feelings after spending two years of your life on a case.

Unfortunately for Joe Becerra, the Durst case would bring him even more disappointments.

———

TWO weeks after the publication of the hardcover edition of *A Deadly Secret* in September 2002, the New York State police began an internal investigation of Joe Becerra, based on a complaint from Westchester District Attorney Jeanine Pirro.

Pirro was unhappy with the book for any number of reasons—most of all she was angered that her actions were now bared to all.

According to union officials representing Becerra, he initially fought the complaint, maintaining, quite accurately, that he did nothing wrong. But with less than three years until retirement, and realizing he was but a foot soldier up against not just a political figure, but a political machine, Becerra grudgingly agreed to a deal that would see him transferred out of the Somers barracks, his home for fifteen years. He also agreed to give up any role in the Durst investigation, which he nurtured and worked for two years.

Mike Struk, as he predicted months before, was right—only Becerra didn't go to Buffalo. He was transferred to another barracks in Westchester County to serve as an instructor.

———

AS events further unfolded in Westchester County during the fall of 2002, it was clear that the book had struck a nerve. The Kathie Durst investigation, and the unsettling politics that went along with it, had been revealed.

The Galveston police, who were helpful and cooperative during interviews in November 2001, subsequently denied making negative comments directed toward Jeanine Pirro's actions during the investigation.

My lengthy interview with the Galveston police was taped, and their comments reported accurately.

For her part, Jeanine Pirro denied ever talking to me. I interviewed her by phone on three occasions. Twice she was quoted in Durst stories I reported, for *People* magazine and *Reader's Digest*. My final interview with Pirro was in December 2001, where she reacted angrily to questions concerning her husband, Al Pirro.

A month later we met in person in Pennsylvania before Robert Durst's extradition hearing. We spoke for a few minutes and she was warm and cordial. She said she wanted to talk to me after the hearing. I told her I was busy with interviews and asked if she could give me a call later in the week. She said fine. She never called.

———

THE extradition hearing was the last time I would see or talk to Jeanine Pirro. It was also the last time she really had anything to say publicly about the Durst case. Pirro spent nearly a year talking about the Durst case in a very public way (so public she earned inclusion in the gag order handed down by Texas judge Susan Criss, a rare feat for a district attorney sitting in another jurisdiction, and something Pirro said she would ignore).

As it was, Pirro stopped talking anyway and the case itself seemed to go away.

It wasn't until November 2002 when the investigation picked up again.

It was an election year in New York, with Governor George Pataki seeking a third term. Supporting him were his very good friends Al and Jeanine Pirro as well as the Durst family. The Dursts provided contributions to ·Pataki from various Durst-owned companies totaling roughly $500,000, which made the Dursts one of the single largest contributors to Pataki's campaign.

Perhaps it was purely coincidental, but it wasn't until mid-November, after the election, that Pirro renewed her investigation into the disappearance of Kathie Durst.

Given the new information concerning the Durst case revealed in *A Deadly Secret*, particularly Kathie Durst's agitated state of mind the last day she was seen alive, Pirro's investigators began re-interviewing all the old witnesses, including the McCormack family, Eleanor Schwank, Ellen Strauss and, yes, Gilberte Najamy.

Jim and Sharon McCormack met with Pirro and Galveston police sergeant Cody Cazalez at a Westchester hotel in November. Schwank repeated to investigators during a trip to visit family in New Jersey what she already had told Joe Becerra and was disturbed that Pirro's people were even bothering with the exercise, believing it to be yet another ruse.

Ellen Strauss met with investigators in December who were eager to see the documents held in her safe deposit box, most importantly the time line written twenty years earlier. The time line now provided Pirro with a motive: a distraught and angry woman who returned home to confront a mentally unstable husband.

The McCormacks, Schwank and Strauss asked why Joe Becerra was not involved in the interviews. They were told that Becerra was "overseeing" the investigation.

They had no idea he had been officially removed from the probe.

As for Gilberte Najamy, given the truth about her duplicity, investigators wanted to speak to her, but knew they had to tread lightly.

———

INTERVIEWS continued through January 2003 with talk that Pirro was preparing to go to a grand jury seeking an indictment of Robert Durst for the murder of his wife, Kathie.

By the spring there was still no indictment, but events took another strange, and sad, turn.

In late April I received a call from a New York State police investigator. He also served as a police union official and was representing Joe Becerra, who now faced formal departmental charges based on yet another complaint filed by Jeanine Pirro.

According to the investigator, Pirro became enraged when Becerra was again credited for his work on the Durst case during a local New York radio program aired in early April.

Pirro was in the midst of a return to the limelight, even appearing as a frequent guest on CNN's *Larry King Live*, but now using her maiden name and identified as "Jeanine Ferris Pirro."

Part of the makeover apparently did not include any mention of Joe Becerra or his role in the Durst case, even if it was on a radio program.

In early May, Becerra, who believed his agreement to a transfer six months earlier put a stop to any harassment, was grilled for five hours by internal affairs detectives who focused their questions not on any of the important case evidence revealed in *A Deadly Secret*, but on the negative portrayal of Jeanine Pirro. Present with Becerra was a union official.

A week later I learned that my publisher, The Berkley Publishing Group, received a subpoena demanding they turn over any official New York State police documents on the Durst case as well as photo releases. Of major

concern to the investigators was who supplied a photo
of Joe Becerra for inclusion in the book. (There's no
secret here. It was his brother, who happens to be a
photographer.)

My publisher transferred no documents to the New
York State police or investigators from the Westchester
County district attorney's office.

———

AS for this book, it was my decision to feature Joe Becerra in *A Deadly Secret*, a sound decision, I believe,
given his important role and efforts to bring closure to
the family of Kathie Durst. It did occur to me prior to
publication that Becerra's role and limited participation
(during interviews approved by Ms. Pirro and the New
York State police) could be misconstrued given the information I was privy to from countless other sources.

Still, I thought it the best way to tell this story then,
and I remain confident I made the correct decision, a
decision that took into consideration the fact that Becerra
had already been unofficially removed from the Durst
case by Jeanine Pirro months before the publication of
A Deadly Secret. His sin? Having his photo published
in *Vanity Fair* magazine.

———

AS of this writing Robert Durst is still being held in a
jail cell in Galveston, Texas, awaiting trial for the murder of Morris Black. That trial, which has already been
postponed four times, is scheduled for the latter part of
2003.

The Los Angeles police remain tight-lipped concerning their investigation into the murder of Susan Berman.
No charges have been filed to date.

As for the New York probe, investigators from Jeanine Pirro's office and the New York State police continue to re-interview old witnesses, covering the same
ground as Becerra did before. Interestingly, the FBI has
not been contacted or asked to join the investigation, a
strange fact given that Robert Durst has used dozens of

different identities in small- and medium-sized towns throughout the United States over the course of the last two decades.

It appears that no one was interested in why a man of Durst's wealth and influence would travel the country for more than twenty years assuming numerous identities.

That changed in June 2003.

Police in Oakland, California, investigating the 1997 disappearance of a college student from North Carolina began probing Durst's activity in northern California.

Acting on a tip, investigators learned that Durst had had eight different addresses from 1994 to 2002, stretching from the Bay Area up north to remote Trinidad, California.

One of those addresses, 1220 Jones Street in San Francisco, was just blocks away from the St. Anthony's Foundation, a homeless center.

Durst's presence in the San Francisco area, the eight addresses, and other compelling evidence already in their posession prompted the investigators to call their FBI contacts to help dig deeper in Robert Durst's activity in northern California, and beyond.

Lost in the politics and pettiness of the Kathie Durst investigation is the McCormack family. Jim and Sharon McCormack are two of the nicest people I've ever met. They opened their home to me, answered all my questions, and helped me find the road to telling a tragic, twenty-year-old story. I was pleased to hear that Jim and his sister, Mary, have since overcome their problems and are close again, but I know this has not been easy on them or the rest of the McCormack family as old wounds are opened once again.

The loss of Kathie and the twenty-one years that have passed since she disappeared have taken a toll on the McCormacks.

One can only hope that one day they will find their peace.

Matt Birkbeck
May 2003